THE WORKS OF SHAKESPEARE

EDITED FOR THE SYNDICS OF THE
CAMBRIDGE UNIVERSITY PRESS
BY
JOHN DOVER WILSON

CORIOLANUS

EDITED BY
JOHN DOVER WILSON

THE TRAGEDY OF
CORIOLANUS

CAMBRIDGE UNIVERSITY PRESS

CAMBRIDGE
LONDON · NEW YORK · MELBOURNE

Published by the Syndics of the Cambridge University Press
The Pitt Building, Trumpington Street, Cambridge CB2 1RP
Bentley House, 200 Euston Road, London NW1 2DB
32 East 57th Street, New York, NY 10022, USA
296 Beaconsfield Parade, Middle Park, Melbourne 3206, Australia

Hard covers ISBN: 0 521 07529 7
Paperback ISBN: 0 521 09472 0

First published 1960
Reprinted 1964
First paperback edition 1969
Reprinted 1972, 1975

This text and glossary were first made available
in The Cambridge Pocket Shakespeare in 1958.

This edition, the New Shakespeare, incorporating
a revised text and glossary, and with the other
editorial matter added, was first published in 1960.

First printed in Great Britain at the University Press, Cambridge
Reprinted in Great Britain by Hazell Watson & Viney Ltd,
Aylesbury, Bucks

CONTENTS

PREFATORY NOTE

The text and glossary below are reprinted in a slightly revised form from those which appeared in the 1958 edition of the play for *The Cambridge Pocket Shakespeare*. And in all I have had the benefit of his advice and criticism from Mr. J. C. Maxwell.

Furthermore I cannot allow this play, which is the last in the canon I am solely responsible for in the present edition, to go out into the world without recording the great debt I owe to Mr C. B. Young. After the death of Harold Child in 1945 he took over all the stage-histories and from 1947 onwards has been always at my side drafting the glossaries, for me and others to work upon, checking the multifarious references and cross-references, reading through each volume, often more than once and never without cleansing it of error and inconsistency, and above all giving to everyone concerned the benefit of his wisdom and learning.

J.D.W.

March 1960

INTRODUCTION

I. Date

The only substantive text we possess of *Coriolanus* is the one printed in the First Folio of 1623, and since the entry of that volume in the Stationers' Register names the play as one of sixteen 'not formerly entred to other men' we may probably assume that no quarto of it, good or bad, had appeared previously. Nor is there any trace of it among the rather scanty references to theatrical performances before the Restoration. Indeed that of an adaptation by Tate referred to on the title-page of that version published in 1682 is the first record we have of stage production in any form.[1]

Its early theatrical history being thus blank we must turn to the play itself for possible clues to the date of composition. First then it was written after the beginning of 1605, which saw the publication of Camden's *Remaines concerning Britaine*,[2] since, as Malone observed, Menenius's tale of the Belly and the Members, although in the main derived from Plutarch, owes a phrase or two to Camden.[3] And second, it was written before the beginning of 1610 when *The Silent Woman* appeared, because in that play Jonson pokes fun at 'He lurched all swords of the garland' which Cominius says in praise of Coriolanus at 2. 2. 99, and Jonson would hardly have applied this description of the superlative prowess of the hero of an epical tragedy to the super-

[1] Cf. 'Stage-history', p. xli below.
[2] As it was entered in the Stationers' Register on 10 November 1604 it may actually have appeared in the booksellers' shops before 1605, the date which the title-page bears.
[3] See below § II.

lative intrigue of the hero in his comedy, had he not expected the audience to recognize the parallel.[1] And this suggests that *Coriolanus* had held the stage many months after its first production. For by then it was probably two years old, since most critics are agreed that in style and metre it follows close upon *Antony and Cleopatra*, which belongs to 1607. Moreover, as Professor Harrison has pointed out, the perennial theme of *Coriolanus*, the struggle between the rich and the poor, would have had considerable significance for the first audiences of the play since

in May and June 1607 the grievances of the poor and the greediness of the rich were being hotly debated in England during a series of insurrections in the counties of Northampton, Warwick and Leicester where the rioters destroyed the hedges and ditches made to enclose common lands. These disturbances were the most violent for many years and lasted for several weeks.[2]

And if the reference to 'the coal of fire upon the ice' (1. 1. 172) was suggested to Shakespeare by the great frost of 1607–8, when in January 'pans of coals' are recorded to have been burning upon the frozen Thames, we may perhaps date the composition of the play early in 1608, which is where Chambers puts it.[3] Certainly there is nothing about coals on ice in North and the phenomenon was so unusual—the Thames had last been frozen over in the year of Shakespeare's birth—that the simile must have seemed odd, even puzzling, unless it called to mind something within recent experience.

Other supposed allusions can, I think, be dismissed as far-fetched. It is idle, for example, to explain the mention of 'the ripest mulberry' as prompted by the

[1] See note 2. 2. 99.
[2] G. B. Harrison, 'A note on *Coriolanus* (*Adams Memorial Studies*, 1948), p. 239.
[3] *William Shakespeare*, I, 480.

encouragement given by King James in 1609 to the planting of mulberry trees for the breeding of silkworms, when the fruit is twice mentioned in *A Midsummer Night's Dream*[1] and may well have come into Shakespeare's head as he sat beneath his own mulberry tree at New Place; or to associate references to the dearth in Rome with the famine in England, 1608–9, when North's *Plutarch* speaks of 'sedition at Rome, by reason of famine'.[2]

II. The Fable of the Belly and the Members

Except at one point the sole source of *Coriolanus* is what Shakespeare found in the seventh of Plutarch's *Lives*, as translated by Sir Thomas North from the French version by Jaques Amyot. The exception as already noted is the 'pretty tale' that Menenius tells the riotous citizens, which in Shakespeare's blank verse is patently a blend of the story as told by Menenius in North and an expanded version of Plutarch's story told by Pope Adrian IV to John of Salisbury given in Camden's *Remaines*, while it may owe something to the version in Livy also. And as the three versions are short they may be quoted here as an illustration of how Shakespeare often makes use of the actual words of his sources.

'*An excellent tale tolde by Menenius Agrippa to pacifie the people*' (North's *Plutarch*, II, 149)

The Senate...dyd send unto them certaine of the pleasantest olde men, and the most acceptable to the people among them. Of those, Menenius Agrippa was he who was sent for chief man of the message from the Senate. He, after

---

[1] 3. 1. 158; 5. 1. 147. Cf. *Venus and Adonis*, 1103.
[2] *North's Plutarch*, vol. II (Tudor Translations, vol. VIII), p. 156.

mainy good persuasions and gentle requestes made to the
people, on the behalfe of the Senate: knit up his oration
in the ende with a notable tale, in this manner. That on a
time all the members of mans bodie, dyd rebell against the
bellie, complaining of it, that it only remained in the middest
of the bodie, without doing any thing, neither dyd beare
any labour to the maintenaunce of the rest: whereas all
other partes and members dyd labour paynefully, and was
very carefull to satisfie the appetites and desires of the bodie.
And so the bellie, all this notwithstanding, laughed at their
follie, and sayed: It is true, I first receyve all meates that
norishe mans bodie: but afterwardes I send it againe to the
norishment of other partes of the same. Even so (quoth he)
O you, my masters, and cittizens of Rome: the reason is
alike betweene the Senate, and you. For matters being well
digested, and their counsells throughly examined, touching
the benefit of the common wealth: the Senatours are cause
of the common commoditie that commeth unto every one
of you.

Extract from Camden's 'Remaines of a greater worke concerning Britaine' (edition 1605, pp. 198–9)

All the members of the body conspired against the stomacke,
as against the swallowing gulfe of all their labors; for whereas the eies beheld, the eares heard, the handes labored, the
feete traveled, the tongue spake, and all partes performed
their functions, onely the stomacke lay idle and consumed
all. Here uppon they ioyntly agreed al to forbeare their
labors, and to pine away their lasie and publike enemy.
One day passed over, the second followed very tedious, but
the third day was so grievous to them all, that they called
a common Counsel; the eyes waxed dimme, the feete could
not support the bodie, the armes waxed lasie, the tongue
faltered, and could not lay open the matter; therefore they
all with one accord desired the advise of the Heart. Then
Reason layd open before them that hee against whome they
had proclaimed warres, was the cause of all this their misery:
For he as their common steward, when his allowances were
withdrawne of necessitie withdrew theirs fro them, as not

receiving that he might allow. Therefore it were a farre
better course to supply him, than that the limbs should
faint with hunger. So by the perswasion of Reason, the
stomacke was served, the limbes comforted, and peace re-
established. Even so it fareth with the bodies of Common-
weale; for albeit the Princes gather much, yet not so much
for themselves, as for others: So that if they want, they
cannot supply the want of others; therefore do not repine
at Princes heerein, but respect the common good of the whole
publike estate.

*Extract from 'The Romane Historie written by Titus
Livius of Padua'* [Livy Bk. ii, xxxii], (translated
by Philemon Holland, 1600)

Whilome (quoth he) when as in mans bodie, all the parts
thereof agreed not, as now they do in one, but each member
had a several interest and meaning, yea, and a speech by it
selfe; so it befel, that all other parts besides the belly, thought
much and repined that by their carefulness, labor, and
ministerie, all was gotten, and yet all little enough to serve it:
and the bellie it selfe lying still in the mids of them, did
nothing else but enjoy the delightsome pleasures brought
unto her. Wherupon they mutinied and conspired altogether in this wise, That neither the hands should reach
and convey food to the mouth, nor the mouth receive it as it
came, ne yet the teeth grind and chew the same. In this
mood and fit, whiles they were minded to famish the poore
bellie, behold the other lims, yea and the whole bodie
besides, pined, wasted, and fel into an extreme consumption.
Then was it wel seen, that even the very belly also did no
smal service, but fed the other parts, as it received food it
selfe: seeing that by working and concocting the meat
throughlie, it digesteth, and distributeth by the veines into
all parts, that fresh and perfect blood whereby we live, we
like, and have our full strength. Comparing herewith, and
making his application, to wit, how like this intestine, and
inward sedition of the bodie, was to the full stomacke of the
Commons, which they had taken and borne against the
Senatours, he turned quite the peoples hearts.

Aldis Wright doubted whether Shakespeare made
any use of Camden's version, asserting that its 'slight
variations' from the language of North might be
accidental, and that 'to account for them as Malone has
done is to attribute to Shakespeare "a plentiful lack"
of invention and little command of language'.[1] This
ignores Shakespeare's unconscious habit of picking up
from his sources and retaining in memory words that later
came in useful. Evidence of this may be found in all
the history plays, whether English or Roman, to say
nothing of a play like *Romeo and Juliet* in which he can
be shown to have remembered to a surprising degree
the actual words and phrases of Brooke's rather wooden
poem, or again of play after play in which Golding's
vocabulary keeps cropping up. Moreover the publication of the *Remaines* by Ben Jonson's old schoolmaster
was a literary event of which Shakespeare could not
have been unaware and the probability is that he read it
at once and quite independently of *Coriolanus*, which
by that date must have been already partly in draft and
North's version of Menenius's fable in his mind. Thus
the discovery of a second version among Camden's
'Grave speeches and wittie apothegmes of woorthie
personages of this realme in former times' may well
have come as a pleasant surprise for him who always
welcomed new light upon the material he was working
up. In any case Aldis Wright is quite wrong in
describing the difference between Camden and North
as 'slight'. The framework of the story in *Coriolanus* is
North's; it begins and ends as North does and like
North Shakespeare makes the Belly 'laugh' and address
the other members. But it is Camden who calls the
'stomacke' a 'swallowing gulfe' that lies 'ydle' while
the rest labour; it is he who refers to the several mem-

[1] *Coriolanus* (Clarendon edition), p. vii.

bers and their functions; and, most striking of all, it is only by reading him that we can solve the puzzle of

Even to the court, the heart, to th' seat o' th' brain.[1]

Further, in reporting Pope Adrian's tale Camden remarks that it 'is not unlike that of Menenius Agrippa in Livie'. And it was perhaps in response to this clue that Shakespeare turned to the third version either in the original Livy or more probably, I think, in Philemon Holland's translation of 1600. For Livy he certainly consulted also, though MacCallum[2] appears the only critic seriously to have entertained the possibility, noting that Livy alone has a passage corresponding with the following words spoken by the Belly in Shakespeare:

> True is it...
> That I receive the general food at first,
> Which you do live upon....
>   But if you do remember,
> I send it through the rivers of your blood,...
> And, through the cranks and offices of man,
> The strongest nerves and small inferior veins
> From me receive that natural competency
> Whereby they live. (1. 1. 129–39)

Set beside this Livy's close-wrought Latin:

Inde apparuisse ventris quoque haud segne ministerium esse, nec magis ali quam alere eum, reddentem in omnis corporis partes hunc quo vivimus vigemusque, divisum pariter in venas, maturum confecto cibo sanguinem.

and Holland's expanded translation:

Then was it wel seen, that even the very belly also did no smal service, but fed the other parts, as it received food it selfe: seeing that by working and concocting the meat

[1] See note 1. 1. 135.
[2] See footnote 2 on pp. 456–57 of his *Shakespeare's Roman Plays* (1910).

throughlie, it digesteth and distributeth by the veines into all parts, that fresh and perfect blood whereby we live, we like, and have our full strength.

Is not Shakespeare's debt clear and is it not likely also that the debt was to the English and not the Latin text? The passage must have struck him rather forcibly for he recurs in mind to it in a later speech by Menenius (5. 1. 50–5) which suggests that Coriolanus's rude reception of Cominius was due to the fact that he had not dined.

> The veins unfilled, our blood is cold, and then
> We pout upon the morning, are unapt
> To give or to forgive; but when we have stuffed
> These pipes and these conveyances of our blood
> With wine and feeding, we have suppler souls.

Can we not hear in these lines an echo of Holland's words 'that fresh and perfect blood whereby we live, *we like, and have our full strength*'? Moreover the physiological notion of 'concocting' (not present in Livy) which was 'part of the very marrow of contemporary medical teaching'[1] can, I think, be felt behind both passages in Shakespeare.

III. SHAKESPEARE'S ANGRY YOUNG MAN AND PLUTARCH'S[2]

Coriolanus, as we saw, almost certainly followed close upon *Antony and Cleopatra*. Why did Shakespeare turn from one to the other in North? Partly, I suggest,

---

[1] C. Sherrington, *Jean Fernel* (1906), p. 69.
[2] The argument of this section, already drafted in July 1957, but laid aside because I had then to turn to *King Lear*, has points resembling, I find, that of an interesting article by Professor S. K. Sen in *Shakespeare Quarterly* (summer 1958), pp. 331–45.

because the two heroes were at once like and unlike. Both were soldiers, both cast in the heroic mould, both subject to fits of vehement passion which in the end brought them to disaster. But their passions were of a very different nature and their general characters even more so. One a courteous middle-aged sensualist who, though lacking no courage in the field, a skilful swordsman, the idol of his men, and the most magnanimous of leaders, could yet desert his army in the middle of a battle and throw away an empire owing to his infatuation for a woman he did not even trust. The other dour and violent-tempered, little more than a boy in years, but a giant in strength, who had eyes for two women alone, his mother and his wife; who was incapable of action that sank him below his ideal of honour or integrity; who was unconscious of fear, insensitive to wounds, and contemptuous of any life but that of the field or of any occupation but that of fighting; who understood neither himself nor anyone else so that both leadership and compromise were beyond him. Shakespeare was always trying something new and the character of Coriolanus presented problems unlike those he had ever tackled before; for if that of Henry V had some similarity it was very slight.

A second reason for his choosing yet another soldier play was, I suspect, a theatrical one. It provided more exciting battle scenes than *Antony and Cleopatra* and a tumultuous riot as well. Battle scenes, nearly always including a hand-to-hand bout between two expert fencers, which are troublesome to modern producers and often boring to modern audiences, were so constant a feature of Shakespeare's English and Roman history-plays, and at times of his tragedies also, that they must have been very popular with the audience of his day, though I think more so at the Globe, which lent itself to the movement of crowds upon its large forestage and where noise would appeal to the groundlings, than at Blackfriars for which most of what he wrote in his final period was presumably chiefly intended. *Coriolanus* is indeed the last of his plays to contain them, for the little skirmish in *Cymbeline* 5. 2 looks like an exception that proves the rule.

Yet if Plutarch's life of Coriolanus attracted Shakespeare as a sequel to Antony for these reasons, we know little of his spirit if we fail to see that what chiefly fascinated him as a dramatist, and moved him as a man, was the encounter between son and mother when she pleads for Rome. Here it is in North's lovely direct prose:

Now was Martius set then in his chayer of state, with all the honours of a generall, and when he had spied the women comming a farre of, he marveled what the matter ment: but afterwardes knowing his wife which came formest, he determined at the first to persist in his obstinate and inflexible rancker. But overcomen in the ende with naturall affection, and being altogether altered to see them: his harte would not serve him to tarie their comming to his chayer, but comming downe in hast, he went to meete them, and first he kissed his mother, and imbraced her a pretie while, then his wife and little children. And nature so wrought with him, that the teares fell from his eyes, and he coulde not keepe him selfe from making much of them, but yeelded to the affection of his bloode, as if he had bene violently caried with the furie of a most swift running streame.

There was a situation after his own heart and almost ready-made to his hand. And phrase after phrase of Volumnia's speeches that follow are taken over from North with scarcely any alteration.

With Plutarch, however, Volumnia is a majestic lay-figure who first appears in this scene, before which she is only referred to incidentally, while with Shakespeare of course she has been a leading and very living character from the beginning. But we can hardly doubt that it was at this point of the story Shakespeare discovered her and realized her dramatic possibilities. In other words, I suggest it was probably Plutarch's account of the interview between mother and son that originally fired his imagination to compose yet another Roman play, the central theme of which should be not politics or fighting, but Nature, or if you will human-kindness, a leit-motif of all his last plays. It was this interview too that taught him, I think, how to shape his plot.

Coriolanus falls into two distinct movements, the dividing line being the hero's departure from Rome. In the first Shakespeare takes over the principal ingredients of Plutarch: patricians and plebs at loggerheads, the former incited to unwise harshness by Caius Marcius and the latter to violent action by the tribunes. But, while the dramatist makes use of most of the chief events the historian offers, he suppresses much detail and rearranges considerably. Plutarch, for example, speaks of two economic crises at Rome, which North calls 'seditions', one due to the people being oppressed by usurers before the Volscian war and the capture of Corioli, and the other due to a famine afterwards. In Shakespeare both are combined and in operation when the play opens (the citizens in the first scene complaining of starvation and of the exactions of usurers), and are dealt with allusively rather than as occasions for dramatic action. There is in fact not even a riot on the stage. In the first scene the citizens, as has been said, seem riotous in intention; Menenius declares that 'Rome and her rats are at the point of battle'; we hear of a rising on 'the other side of the city'; and we are told immediately after that the Senate has granted the tribunes. That is all. According to Plutarch, to take another instance, as the Senate are debating a proposal to make a free grant of corn to the starving people Marcius delivers a long speech in which, as his habit is, he accuses them of seditious designs, a speech which Shakespeare throws into blank verse with not a great deal of change in substance, and uses as part of Coriolanus's invective in the 'mutiny' concerning the consulship. Moreover Plutarch makes Menenius relate the fable of the Belly in reply to the complaints about usury, whereas Shakespeare saw that it was far more apt to those about famine, and borrowed from Camden the word 'gulf' for the belly to make it more so. Plutarch again, though aristocratic in sympathy, cannot conceal his feeling that the plebs had much justification for their complaints, and attributes their seditious tendencies to the demagogues Sicinius and Brutus who flatter them to gain power for themselves. Shakespeare takes over the character of the tribunes and their motives practically unchanged, shows the people 'fickle' as Plutarch does, but uses their economic grievances mainly as debating points in the dialogue. On the other hand his own general standpoint is rendered sufficiently clear by the conspicuous position he gives to Menenius's 'pretty tale'. Whereas Plutarch introduces it incidentally and as one of the 'persuasions' that 'pacified the people', implying at the same time that the permission to elect tribunes weighed much more with them, Shakespeare places it at the very forefront of his play, since it expressed the point of view of all right-minded persons in his audience about the issue between populace and nobility in general, a point of view in fact that held the field in political economy down to the nineteenth century.

In the scenes at Rome in which the citizens play a prominent part (1. 1 and 2. 3) Shakespeare depicts them as he does his citizens in other plays, as muddle-headed, but kind-hearted folk; and I do not find anything in Plutarch which might have suggested Menenius's tribute:

> For they have pardons, being asked, as free
> As words to little purpose.[1]

On the other hand Plutarch gave him even less authority for representing them as cowards and shirkers on the field of battle. They refuse more than once to enlist at the consuls' order, but that is for political reasons. When in the ranks they generally fight most valiantly;[2] and Menenius actually urges his fellow patricians to prove themselves as valiant as the common soldiers. And though Plutarch, however, gave Shakespeare the point about the greed of the rank and file for booty, he makes the most of it. Why does Shakespeare blacken their character in this way? Partly, I suggest, to heighten the glory of Coriolanus by contrast: 'Alone I did it!' is no empty boast; partly perhaps to supply him with more matter for invective. Certainly not because he was animated by a party-political antipathy to the common people. Inasmuch as its main theme or rather its political shell or envelope bears an accidental resemblance to the political controversies that dominate the modern world, the play is often read, and sometimes produced, as if it were a political pamphlet. The fact that some interpret in fascist and others in communist terms should be enough to prove the fallacy of such anachronism. In *Coriolanus*, as in his other plays, Shakespeare is interested in dramatic art and nothing else, and particularly here in giving effective artistic form to a type of tragic hero he has not previously attempted to create. If, therefore, in reshaping his source material, he seems to tilt the balance here in favour of the patri-

---

[1] 3. 2. 88–9.
[2] The one exception is a portion of the army which is beaten back to the trenches before Corioli. See 1. 4. 30 n.

cians or there in favour of the plebs, he does so for no
other purpose than to keep his tragedy moving upon
an even keel or to give a character an opportunity for
an interesting speech.

So much, in general terms, regarding Shakespeare's
treatment of Plutarch's political and military data up
to the beginning of the section embracing the business
of the consulship and the banishment. But throughout
the whole of the first movement of the play there runs
a female and domestic thread binding it together,
though completely lacking in the biography; and to
understand this addition to the source we must first
examine how Shakespeare plotted his second movement, covering the career of his hero after banishment.

Plutarch, with much else beside Shakespeare's
purpose, gave him all the events and facts he needed for
this in approximately the right order, so that there was
little to do by way of plot construction. Shakespeare
made, however, additions which went some way towards determining the shape of the play as a whole,
apart from their effect upon its spirit which was considerable. In the course of Volumnia's speech referred
to above may be found, for example, the following
passage:

> There's no man in the world
> More bound to 's mother, *yet here he lets me prate*
> *Like one i' th' stocks*. Thou hast never in thy life
> Showed thy dear mother any courtesy,
> *When she, poor hen, fond of no second brood,*
> *Has clucked thee to the wars, and safely home*
> *Loaden with honour.* (5. 3. 158–64)

The lines I have italicized are pure Shakespeare—
may we not say, Shakespeare of Stratford?—the rest is
derived, slightly reworded, from North. It is by such
touches that the dramatist transforms Plutarch's
stately lay-figure into a woman. And there is a more

life-giving additional touch in the last half-dozen lines
of her speech, which are once again pure Shakespeare:

> Come, let us go:
> This fellow had a Volscian to his mother;
> His wife is in Corioli, and his child
> Like him by chance. Yet give us our dispatch.
> I am hushed until our city be a-fire,
> And then I'll speak a little. (5. 3. 177–182)

It is these words, as many critics have observed, that
finally win him over. To quote Bradley:

Her son's resolution has long been tottering, and now it
falls at once. Throughout, it is not the substance of her
appeals that moves him, but the bare fact that she appeals.
And the culmination is that she ceases to appeal, and
defies him.

and Bradley notes further, as MacCallum also does,[1]
that

on a lower level exactly the same thing happens where she
tries to persuade him to go and deceive the people. The
moment she stops, and says, in effect, 'Well, then, follow
your own will', his will gives way. Deliberately to set it
against hers is beyond his power.[2]

That last sentence, as we shall find, does not cover the
whole facts. But the two quotations taken together reveal the dramatic pattern Shakespeare had in mind, or
unconsciously followed, as he plotted the play. For it is
the clash of wills between mother and son that marks
the culmination of both movements. It should be
observed in passing that Aufidius, another leading figure
in the first movement is, like Volumnia, borrowed from
the last section of Plutarch's story.

Aufidius is needed early as both military and moral

---

[1] MacCallum, *Shakespeare's Roman Plays*, p. 554.
[2] A. C. Bradley, *Miscellany*, (1929), p. 100.

foil to Marcius as also for the fencing bout before
Corioli. But Volumnia serves not only to infuse a
lively human interest into what would else consist almost
wholly of politics and fighting, but as an additional
character that enables Shakespeare to impose dramatic
shape and unity upon the rather disparate elements of
Plutarch's history.

We are told in the first scene that the valorous deeds
for which Marcius is famous he performed 'partly to
please his mother' And though Shakespeare actually
takes this point from Plutarch, he immediately enlarges upon it in the third scene after a fashion all his
own, giving us the entry to the home of Marcius and
introducing us to Volumnia in person. We hear her
rejoicing in the blood Marcius sheds, glorying in having
given birth to so fierce an offspring, and when told that
her little grandson in a rage tears a butterfly to pieces
with his teeth, remarking in delight 'One on's father's
moods!' And all her dreams are evidently of him in
battle. 'Methinks', she cries to her gentle daughter-
in-law,

> I hear hither your husband's drum;
> See him pluck Aufidius down by th' hair;
> As children from a bear, the Volsces shunning him.
> Methinks I see him stamp thus, and call thus:
> 'Come on, you cowards! you were got in fear,
> Though you were born in Rome.' His bloody brow
> With his mailed hand then wiping, forth he goes,
> Like to a harvest-man that's tasked to mow
> Or all or lose his hire. (1. 3. 30–8)

A veritable tigress purring over her cub!

Gentle as she is, however, the daughter-in-law
neither echoes the purr nor applauds the 'mammocking'
of butterflies by her little son. And she quite firmly
refuses to go out visiting with Volumnia, while her
husband is in constant and deadly peril. Here is a

second woman in the hero's life, another addition to Plutarch, introduced to show us a side of Coriolanus's character that will not be fully revealed until the reconciliation scene before the walls of Rome.[1]

Plutarch, I say, has nothing of all this. Nor, as will be presently noted, does he say anything of the mother that might give occasion for proud boasts like

> Thou art my warrior;
> I holp to frame thee[2]

or the earlier

> Thy valiantness was mine, thou suck'dst it from me.[3]

And from the point of view of plot, making an even more vital addition to Plutarch's outline is her ambition. This comes out in a passage generally I believe over-looked by critics.[4] Just before Coriolanus, now returned crowned with victory from Corioli, passes into the Senate house to be nominated consul as both he and she know, she exclaims

> I have lived
> To see inherited my very wishes
> And the buildings of my fancy: only
> There's one thing wanting, which I doubt not but
> Our Rome will cast upon thee.

and he replies

> Know, good mother,
> I had rather be their servant in my way
> Than sway with them in theirs.[5]

[1] Middleton Murry's charming essay on 'A neglected Heroine of Shakespeare' (*Countries of the Mind*, pp. 18–32) makes somewhat more of Virgilia than I feel the text warrants. Indeed he has to emend the text a little to fill out the portrait of his vision.

[2] 5. 3. 62–3.   [3] 3. 2. 129.

[4] See, however, S. K. Sen in *Shakespeare Quarterly* (summer, 1958), p. 333.   [5] 2. 1. 195–201.

She tells him, in other words, that her greatest ambition
is to see him consul and he in turn tells her that he has
no ambition of the kind at all. Shakespeare's Marcius in
fact is not an ambitious man in any sense, least of all in
the ordinary sense of aspiring to political power.[1] He is
a soldier man with almost superhuman bravery, though
with but slight gifts of leadership; one only has to
compare the abuse and threats he heaps upon his troops
when they retire in battle with the encouragement
Cominius gives to his in the same situation.[2] He therefore stands for the consulship with reluctance, goes
through the repulsive business of begging for votes,
from people he despises as cowards and hucksters, with
irony and ill-concealed contempt, and gives his fiery
temper rein when the tribunes tell him the votes have
been revoked. After that it remains to discover whether
his mother can persuade him to do something far more
difficult than standing in the market-place, dressed as
a citizen and exposing his wounds, which last by the bye
he manages to avoid. For he must now ask pardon for
the violence of his language when the tribunes and their
aediles had attempted to arrest him, and humbly to
promise amendment; to act a lie in fact. She argues
with him for 120 lines[3] and he replies she is asking him
to be false to his nature,[4] to behave like a harlot;[5] and
finally he gives her this complete answer:

> I will not do't;
> Lest I surcease to honour mine own truth,
> And by my body's action teach my mind
> A most inherent baseness.[6]

[1] Cf. Alexander, *Shakespeare's Life and Art*, p. 179.
[2] Cf. 1. 4. 30–42 with 1. 6. 1–9.
[3] 3. 2. 13–137.   [4] 3. 2. 15.
[5] 3. 2. 112.
[6] 3. 2. 120–3. Overlook this crucial passage and one
may misinterpret Coriolanus's character entirely, as Palmer

Volumnia does not understand—perhaps no woman of Shakespeare's time could have understood—such an appeal to conscience; and she interprets it as pride. Yet, as Professor Alexander alone among critics seems to have realised,[1] it is not pride but his spiritual integrity, his sense of honour, his truth to himself—'mine own truth' as he calls it—that makes her counsel so abhorrent in his eyes. Pride, indeed, though commonly laid to his charge by the critics, as it constantly is by his enemies in the play, does not really hit the mark at all. True, he entertains the greatest contempt for the populace, a contempt Shakespeare often shows to be unjust, but he is like the other patricians in that, and like, one may guess, many a young nobleman of Shakespeare's acquaintance. True also, he expresses his contempt more openly than his fellows, but that merely shows him too honest to conceal his sentiments as they do from motives of political expediency. And if he expresses it in violent terms, that is because he is Shakespeare's study of the choleric man. His choler is several times insisted upon by Plutarch, but he links it with self-will and obstinacy, whereas in Shakespeare it is always found in company with indignation or contempt. And Shakespeare keeps us constantly aware of it, or looking for outbursts of it. Marcius is in a fury at his first entry, enters Corioli single-handed in a fury, twice ruins his chance of the consulship by his fury, lays siege to Rome in a fury, and in the end perishes in a fury, at the hands of Aufidius and his myrmidons. Clearly the impression we are intended to receive is that of a young Hector with an ungovernable temper. Both Plutarch and

does, who actually writes: 'There is no hint anywhere of a protest against the political dishonesty of the course to which he is invited' (*Political Characters of Shakespeare,* p. 279).

[1] *Op. cit.* p. 181. But see also S. K. Sen, *op. cit.* pp. 335–6.

Shakespeare trace this lack of self-control to education.
But while Plutarch attributes it to lack of a father who
might have taught him that 'churlishe and uncivill'
manners render a man 'unfit' to associate with others,[1]
Shakespeare puts it down to the influence of the mother
from whom he acquired it, partly by inheritance, partly
by catching her habit of despising the common people,[2]
but chiefly because she had deliberately encouraged
him to give way to his tantrums as a child. For this,
I take it, is the point of the account we are given of
little Marcius running amok, and in his rage tearing a
'gilded butterfly' to pieces with his teeth, an account
listened to by the grandmother with approval, and
followed by the remark of the sycophantic dame who
tells the story, 'Indeed, la, 'tis a *noble* child'.[3] To Shakespeare himself, we can be sure, the action was anything
but 'noble'. And so when Volumnia tells Coriolanus

Thy valiantness was mine, thou suck'st it from me[4]

she is speaking within the limits of the truth inasmuch
as the violence of his temper which renders him impossible as a politician, is the secret, or in part the secret,
of his success in battle. Had Shakespeare known the
word 'berserk' he might have used it for this hero, who
cannot fight unless he hates and who whips himself up
into a passion as he hurls himself against the enemy.

Yet of pride, as the Oxford Dictionary defines it,
'a high and overweening opinion of one's own qualities
or attainments...which gives rise to a feeling or attitude
of superiority and contempt for others', if by 'others'
we mean members of his own class, he shows not the
slightest trace. On the contrary, as if to counter-
balance the accusation of pride which the citizens, the
tribunes, and even his own mother level against him,

[1] P. 144. [2] 3. 2. 7–13. [3] 1. 3. 60–8. [4] 3. 2. 129.

his creator gives him a number of opportunities of displaying a sincere humility.

Granville-Barker, I feel, sadly misrepresents Shakespeare on this point. He speaks of Marcius's 'obsessing self-consciousness'; finds that 'his repeated protests against the praises lavished on him become somewhat less than genuine'; and exclaims 'Neglect to praise him; he will be the first to resent that!'—though what passage in the text he might quote to support this last astonishing judgement I am at a loss to discover.[1] Bradley is much fairer, but still I think wide of the mark, when he writes:

Though he is the proudest man in Shakespeare he seems to be unaware of his pride, and is hurt when his mother mentions it. It does not prevent him from being genuinely modest, for he never dreams that he has attained the ideal he worships; yet the sense of his own greatness is twisted round every strand of this worship. In almost all his words and deeds we are conscious of the tangle. I take a single illustration. He cannot endure to be praised. Even his mother, who has a charter to extol her blood, grieves him when she praises him. As for others:

> I had rather have one scratch my head i' the sun
> When the alarum were struck, than idly sit
> To hear my nothings monster'd.

His answer to the roar of the army hailing him 'Coriolanus' is, 'I will go wash'. His wounds are 'scratches with briars'. In Plutarch he shows them to the people without demur: in Shakespeare he would rather lose the consulship. There is a greatness in all this that makes us exult. But who can

[1] Granville-Barker, *Prefaces to Shakespeare* (Fifth Series) pp. 17–18. Even Alexander, who seems to me to see Coriolanus more clearly than most who have written about him, though perhaps in seeking to redress the critical balance, he tilts Shakespeare's balance a little too far in his hero's favour, likens his 'pride' to 'such as destroyed the great archangel' (*op. cit.* p. 180).

assign the proportions of the elements that compose this impatience of praise: the feeling (which we are surprised to hear him express) that he, like hundreds more, has simply done what he could; the sense that it is nothing to what might be done; the want of human sympathy (for has not Shelley truly said that fame is love disguised?); the pride which makes him feel that he needs no recognition, that after all he himself could do ten times as much, and that to praise his achievement implies a limit to his power?[1]

All this is too over-subtle by far. Why does Shakespeare make him say that praise, even from his mother, renders him uncomfortable, except in order to assure us that the discomfort springs from a feeling that he has only done what any other gentleman might have done in the same circumstances? It is certainly not due to irritation, to a pride 'which makes him feel he needs no recognition'. For to gain her recognition, and give her pleasure, we are told, is in part the object he sets before him when he goes to battle.[2] And why should it surprise Bradley that, after confessing that it makes him shy to hear his mother praise him, he goes on

> I have done
> As you have done—that's what I can: induced
> As you have been—that's for my country:
> He that has but effected his good will
> Hath overta'en mine act. (1. 9. 15–19)

Bradley forgets that these words are addressed, not to the common soldiers who

> prize their honours
> At a cracked drachma,[3]

but to Lartius, Cominius and the officers about him, men Marcius well knows to be no less brave than himself. His attitude may be a little boyish; Coriolanus *is* boyish. But it is the attitude we should find adopted to-

[1] Bradley, *op. cit.* pp. 88-9.
[2] 1. 1. 38.   [3] 1. 5. 4-5.

day by any English gentleman who has learnt at a 'public school' to despise the boaster, the fellow who 'swanks' or 'puts on side', and neither to give nor to expect any praise for conduct which merely conforms to the code that all gentlemen are supposed to observe as a matter of course. And this code which is to a large extent simply the code of medieval chivalry still in vogue among Elizabethan and Jacobean gentlemen[1] involves of necessity a rigid adherence to one's pledged word. Thus 'I do hate thee' Marcius cries on meeting his bitterest foe in the field 'worse than a promise-breaker'.[2]

But he, again, like many men today, especially if they have lost a father in infancy, men of any class or nation, responds to impulses deeper and more compelling than those due to the code of honour and probity he shares with his fellows, namely reverence for his mother and a 'conditioned' or instinctive habit of obedience to her wishes. Difficulties occur when these impulses pull different ways, as they well may since as just noted women often fail to understand the principles that govern men's behaviour. And the drama of *Coriolanus* is built up around two crises that arise from situations in which the hero finds himself forced to choose between his duty as a man of honour and his duty as a son. It is as simple as that, though few students of the play appear to have realised how simple and common-human it is.

The crises take different courses and come to different ends according to difference in the circumstances

---

[1] In *The Canterbury Tales* Chaucer's 'verray parfit gentil knight' is 'of his port as meeke as is a mayde', while of his son, the Squire, we are told

> Curteis he was, lowely and servysable.

Hardly apt descriptions of Coriolanus, yet not wholly beside the point; e.g. see I. I. 240 and n.

[2] I. 8. I–2.

attending them; but the ends are alike disastrous. In
the first, as we have seen, the mother wishes her son to
act a lie, to go hat in hand to the populace he despises
and the tribunes he loathes, ask their pardon on his
knees, and promise to 'be hereafter theirs' if they will
grant him 'their good loves'. In a word, as he says, she
bids him behave in such a fashion that he will for ever
seem base in his own eyes. Yet she has only to treat him
like a disobedient child, turn coldly away, saying

> At thy choice then.
> To beg of thee, it is my more dishonour
> Than thou of them——[1]

and he gives way at once. He is now ready to eat
humble-pie on the market-place, to 'mountebank their
loves', to submit to insults like any ostler in an inn-yard,
and he goes to it muttering 'Mildly, mildly' like a child,
fearing he may forget. But the new mother-bidden
purpose lasts a few moments only because the tribunes
need not submission but violence if this dangerous
person is to be got rid of. And though blind to so much
else about him, they know how choleric he is and understand, being men, one thing even better than his mother
does, namely that 'honour' is his sensitive spot: touch
that and he will break loose into wild career like the
high-mettled thoroughbred he is. The trick works in-
stantaneously for he is able to endure an enemy's
slander no longer than a mother's chiding. At the word
'Traitor', the most intolerable of all words in the ears
of a man of honour, he cannot, as they had promised
themselves,

> Be reined again to temperance; then he speaks
> What's in his heart. (3. 3. 27–9)[2]

[1] 3. 2. 123–5.
[2] See Palmer, *op. cit.* p. 305.

Whereupon they pronounce sentence; the well-drilled plebeian claque endorse the verdict with acclamation; and

> There's no more to be said, but he is banished
> As enemy to the people and his country.[1]

It is worth noting as an instance of dramatic patterning, whether deliberate on Shakespeare's part or not, that the still more fatal disaster with which the second crisis and the play conclude, is also precipitated by the word 'traitor', this time uttered by Aufidius.[2] Now however, though his mother has asked him once again to act dishonourably by breaking his promise given under oath to the Volsces, the cause she pleads for is no longer his own aggrandisement but the very life of family and country, which can only be purchased, as he realises if she does not, by his own death. Nor, though as before it is she that pleads and, in the end, it is a sharp word from her that brings him to heel, is this the sole or even the main reason for his yielding. For now he is not persuaded against his better judgement. Now his conscience applauds his mother, since she as its chief representative pleads on behalf of Nature, the claims of which are recognised by all, even when it comes to the point by Coriolanus himself, as far outweighing any claim of Honour—by all, I say, for it is surely clear that here Shakespeare expected to carry his audience with him.

Moreover, he is half won over before she begins her pleading. At the sight of the little woe-begone family moving towards him he redoubles his resolution to stand firm—a sure sign of weakening. There follows the lovely encounter with Virgilia, who comes first and speaks before Volumnia and who, we may guess, was

[1] 3. 3. 117–18.
[2] See Palmer, *op. cit.* p. 305.

created by Shakespeare just for this moment in the play,
for the kiss and the words of love that go with it, words
in which he allows us for the first time to see into the
heart of this dour hero and compels us almost to love
him in return. Certainly, we can have nothing but
admiration for the speech in which little Marcius
receives his blessing.

> The god of soldiers,
> With the consent of supreme Jove, inform
> Thy thoughts with nobleness, that thou mayst prove
> To shame unvulnerable, and stick i' th' wars
> Like a great sea-mark, standing every flaw,
> And saving those that eye thee![1]

It expresses his own ideal, the soldier's philosophy that
has informed his whole life. And so the lonely dragon
has been transformed into the tender husband and the
heroic father, even before he is compelled to own himself
the dutiful son.

Admittedly the most eloquent stage-direction in
Shakespeare is that which follows Volumnia's appeal—
Holds her by the hand, silent. During this silence
Coriolanus grows up, comes to know himself and to
understand the meaning of life for the first time; and
his reply when he speaks is his first calm, thoughtful,
adult utterance in the play. Shakespeare never mentions his age. Granville-Barker thinks he may be
'about thirty-two' at the opening. But he is arguing
from hints in Plutarch which are not valid evidence;
and when he recollects that this would make him 'as
mature a man as the maturer Hamlet' he sees that it will
not do, and so admits that 'more than one thing in the
story gives colour to youthfulness of temper'.[2] And
Palmer testifies to the same impression, describing him
as 'essentially the splendid oaf, who has never come to
maturity', and his actions as 'more characteristic of an

---

[1] 5. 3. 70-5.   [2] Barker, *op. cit.* p. 15.

adolescent than of a grown man'.[1] 'Oaf' is too crude
a term, robbing him both of the nobility and of the
'unruly charm'[2] that belong to him from first to last.
In any case, whatever his age in years his conduct is
boyish, and it is his own realisation of this in retrospect
that, we may believe, makes the insult 'thou boy of
tears' so especially enraging in the last scene.

Youthfulness accounts for so much. Above all it
accounts for his simplicity and 'self-ignorance' as
Bradley calls it, adding 'To adapt a phrase in the play,
he has no more introspection in him than a tiger'.[3]
For a man is never more ignorant of self or more tigrish,
if given to outbreaks of fury, than during adolescence.
He understands himself so little that having promised
his mother to abase himself before the tribunes and
people in the forum, he imagines he has sufficient self-
control to play the part when he gets there. And we
can only smile when he protests to himself at 5. 3. 34–7
just before he yields to her a second time

> I'll never
> Be such a gosling to obey instinct, but stand
> As if a man were author of himself
> And knew no other kin.

This reminds us ludicrously of Richard Crookback's
'I am myself alone';[4] and it would be difficult to
find any two Shakespearian characters more unlike
each other. In Shakespeare's universe indeed such an
attitude is untenable: even Richard is unable to sustain
it. Yet we are expected to believe Marcius manages to
do so after banishment. For the words remind us also
of something he himself says as he leaves Rome. They

---

[1] Palmer, *op. cit.* p. 297.
[2] Barker, *op. cit.* p. 15.
[3] Bradley, *op. cit.* p. 89.
[4] *3 Henry VI*, 5. 6. 80–3.

give us the clue in fact to the change that takes place
in him between then and now, the clue to the turning-
point of the play between his departure and 4. 4. when
he enters the house of Aufidius. Shakespeare offers no
explanation to account for the *volte-face* which brings
Marcius to deny everything he has hitherto stood for,
and worst of all which makes him a promise-breaker and
the traitor his soul loathes. Nor can one evade the problem by saying that the dramatist found it all in North
and just took it over. For, as Palmer has shown, North's
account is quite different. The Marcius of Plutarch had
no plan of destroying Rome at all. On the contrary, his
idea obviously was to establish an alliance between the
aristocracies of Antium and Rome, in order to restore
the latter to its former ascendancy over the plebs, while
the terms of peace he offered were comparatively mild.[1]
Such conduct would probably have seemed almost
excusable to the original audience, at any rate to the
young inns-of-court students of noble birth. But there
was one fatal objection to it in Shakespeare's eyes: it
would have ruined the tragedy by draining the scene
between Coriolanus and his mother of more than half
its passion and much of its point. For that scene Shakespeare needed a complete renegade with an 'eye red as
'twould burn Rome' and a Rome cringing for mercy.

No explanation, I said, is provided in the play for the
psychological change involved. And as Shakespeare
loves springing such unexpected changes upon his
audience—he does so at the beginning of the last act of
Othello[2]—it is natural to ask whether in this case he
purchased a fine dramatic climax at the cost of a little
straining in probability. Granville-Barker makes a
persuasive plea for something of the sort. After asserting

[1] Palmer, *op. cit.* pp. 284–5.
[2] See pp. xlvii–xlviii, Introduction to *Othello* in this
edition.

that we are 'never made free' of Coriolanus's 'inward man' he continues

And the juncture which could best bring this into play, the spiritual crisis in which he decides for his renegade revenge on Rome, is boldly and neatly side-stepped. It is strange, says Marcius in that one short soliloquy, how quickly enemies may become friends and friends turn enemies.

> So with me
> My birthplace hate I, and my love's upon
> This enemy town.

We are (this is to tell us) past the play's turning point already. The crucial change in the man has already taken place; and of the process of it we learn nothing. But this is not necessarily a shortcoming on Shakespeare's part—as were Marcius a Hamlet it would be. *Was* there any such explicable process? He is not a man of reason, but of convictions and passionate impulses, which can land him in a sudden decision—and he will not know how he came by it. That may help make him a good fighter, less good, probably, as a general, certainly a poor politician. And it justifies Shakespeare's treatment of him here. By his mere looks, in the bitter humility—the old pride so quickly breaking through, as the unlucky third serving-man discovers— with which he encourages Aufidius' servants to mock him, we are to discern the sufferings of his lonely exile, and surmise the pent-up wrath, vented at last in that blind resolve to be revenged on his own ungrateful people or let the Volsces take revenge on him....But picture and action significantly 'placed' are as legitimate, and often as important, a dramatic resource as the spoken word can be. And what, at this juncture, could be more fittingly eloquent than the simple sight—and the shock it must give us—of this haggard, hardly recognisable figure? It will flash into our imaginations, as words might not, a sense of the suffering that has brought him to such a pass.[1]

All this is admirable and for the most part true. Yet is it sufficient? Not at any rate for the critics, who 'have

[1] Granville-Barker, *op. cit.* pp. 10–12.

combed the text for some sign of the actual moment
of its happening; since surely, they argue, Shakespeare
could not have let such a significant one slip by un-
marked'.[1] Yet if the account of Marcius's character as
we have viewed it so far be a true one, is it not clear
that what brings about the change in him is the solitude
he has to endure after his banishment? As he takes farewell of mother, wife, and friends in 4. 1, he seems to be
cheerfulness itself. He rallies his mother, bidding her
call to her aid the aristocratic stoicism she has so often
bidden him cultivate in himself. He speaks with deep
affection to his 'old and true' friend Menenius and to
his honoured 'sometime general' Cominius. He assures
them that he will 'do well yet', that his banishment can
only be temporary since 'I shall be loved when I am
missed'. And finally he concludes:

> While I remain above the ground you shall
> Hear from me still, and never of me aught
> But what is like me formerly.[2]

The notion, entertained by some critics, that all this is
mere duplicity concealing an intention already formed
of alliance with Aufidius, may be dismissed out of
hand. Shakespeare does not play tricks like that. The
only deception is one the self-confident, self-ignorant
hero practises on himself. In the rosy picture he paints
of his coming exile there is, however, one shadow.
All will be well, he tells them,

> *though* I go alone,
> Like to a lonely dragon that his fen
> Makes feared and talked of more than seen.[3]

Just a passing thought, a warning from the subconscious,
but it gives us, as Shakespeare surely intended it should,

[1] Granville-Barker, *op. cit.* p. 11.
[2] 4. 1. 51–3.   [3] 4. 1. 29–31.

a glimpse of what exile would really mean to one who could never have happily stood for a day

> As if a man were author of himself
> And knew no other kin. (5. 3. 36–7)

How many weeks went by before he found his way to Antium we are not told. But his 'mean apparel' and the hint to Aufidius's servant that he had been sleeping in the open[1] show what his life had been, the life of a beggar and an outcast. And though we are not told anything either about the reasons for or process of the psychological change, there is a passage in Plutarch which explains it, and would have offered an explanation to Shakespeare, if he needed one. In a paragraph headed 'The force of anger' North first notes Coriolanus's apparent 'constancy of mind' after the verdict of banishment had been passed and then continues:

He only of all other gentlemen that were angrie at his fortune, dyd outwardly shewe no manner of passion, nor care at all of him selfe...bicause he was so caried awaye with the vehemencie of anger, and desire of revenge, that he had no sence nor feeling of the hard state he was in....For when sorow (as you would saye) is set a fyre, then it is converted into spite and malice, and driveth awaye for that time all faintnes of harte and naturall feare. And this is the cause why the chollericke man is so altered, and mad in his actions, as a man set a fyre with a burning agewe.[2]

Whether Shakespeare took note of this passage or not, we cannot tell. If he did, he must have quoted the first sentence. But at any rate we can hardly doubt that *his* Coriolanus, once torn from his roots—deep roots—in camp and home, once cut off from the only activity he knew, that of war, once given unlimited opportunity of brooding upon his wrongs with no opportunity of venting his too irritable spleen in the

---

[1] 4. 5. 39–44. [2] North, *op. cit.* pp. 167–8.

torrent of words that came too readily to his lips, would be 'altered and mad in his actions, as a man set afire with a burning ague', or that his noble heart would be so 'converted into spite and malice', so that, hearing nothing from them, he began to think his best friends, perhaps even his own family, had basely deserted him. To such a man in such a mood only one thing remained—revenge; and revenge meant going to Antium and burning Rome.

But this, as we have seen, is not the Marcius Shakespeare wished to leave with us. For as Professor Alexander has well said:

There is at the heart of it all a rare tenderness whose native quality is only enhanced by the rough wars and civil tumults on whose dangerous slopes it so shyly reveals itself.[1]

And the 'heart of it all' is the heart of this great, unself-conscious, and tempestuous soldier to whom Shakespeare has given some of the finest and most violent vituperation in the language, but whose 'native quality' he does not fully reveal until near the end, so that when at last the 'boy' falls basely murdered by traitors in a foreign land, his glory shining all the brighter for their perfidy, we shall contemplate that 'instantaneous cessation of enormous energy'[2], touched not only with awe but with the tenderness of sorrow and even with the pity which Bradley denies him.

J. D. W.

July 1957–*February* 1959

---

[1] Alexander, *op. cit.* p. 179.
[2] Bradley, *op. cit.* p. 95.

THE STAGE-HISTORY OF
CORIOLANUS

No record is known of the earliest performances.
We first hear of the play in the theatre in a bad adaptation by Nahum Tate, *The Ingratitude of a Commonwealth*, or *The Fall of Coriolanus*, published in 1682,
'as it is acted at the Theatre-Royal' (title-page). We
cannot assign any nearer date than this year; Downes in
his *Roscius Anglicanus* (1708) does not mention the
play. The printed edition gives no cast. Tate frequently
murders Shakespeare's poetry by pointless rewording;
but for his first four acts he follows the original plot,
with many cuts and curtailments. He also introduces
one new character, Nigridius, a discharged Roman
officer, who has joined Aufidius and inflames him
against Coriolanus. At the end of Act 4 (=Shake-
speare's 5.3) the hero incredibly supposes the women
have come to join him as 'Spectators of our keen
Revenge'—his burning of Rome. Thereafter Tate
remodels the rest of Act 5, borrowing little from Shakespeare. In this new climax we sup full with horror.
The women and the young boy are imprisoned by
Aufidius, and he and Coriolanus fight and wound each
other. Aufidius, passionately in love with Virgilia, says
he will rape her before her husband's face, but when she
is brought in self-wounded, he expires on seeing 'the
piteous sight'. So, after a love-dialogue of 27 lines,
does Virgilia. Meanwhile Nigridius has tortured the
son and flung him mutilated into the arms of Volumnia;
raving mad, she enters carrying him,[1] snatches a partizan

[1] Whereupon Coriolanus ludicrously exclaims, 'Con-
vultions! Feavours! blewest Pestilence!'

from a guard, kills Nigridius with it and rushes away.
Father and son then die after sixteen more lines which
mingle some pathos with absurdity. Tate cuts down
the part of Menenius, but adds copiously for comic
relief to Valeria's. 'An affected, talkative, fantastical
Lady', she enters followed by six or seven pages, and
babbles endlessly of her flirtations and knowledge of
State affairs through hobnobbing with great ones at
home and abroad. Behind the adaptation lies the idea
of its political significance; the Dedicatory Epistle points
out 'a Resemblance' to 'the busie Faction of our own
time' and gives the 'Moral'—'to Recommend Submission and Adherence to Establisht Lawful Power'.[1]

Though the Prologue[2] expects the version to 'turn
to Money what lay dead before', it was Tate's play that
lay dead without, it seems, a second revival, and
Shakespeare's was put on in its stead at Lincoln's Inn
Fields in 1718 (13–16 December). But the next year
Coriolanus again fell into the hands of an 'improver'.
This was John Dennis, poetaster, critic and enemy of
Pope, who satirized him as 'Appius' in *The Essay on
Criticism*, ll. 585 ff. His version, *The Invader of his
Country* or *The Fatal Resentment* was played at Drury
Lane, 11–13 November 1719. Barton Booth and John
Mills were the hostile generals, W. Wilks and Walker
the two Tribunes; Thurmond took Cominius, and his
wife and Mrs Porter Virgilia and Volumnia. This play
too fell dead almost at birth. Lincoln's Inn Fields put
on a rival piece on 14 November, announced with
Dennis's title, but the play-bill stated 'written by
Shakespeare'. The trick seems to have been repeated on

[1] On Tate's version see John Genest, *Some Account of the
English Stage, 1660–1830* (1832), I, 326–9; G. C. D. Odell,
Shakespeare from Betterton to Irving (1921), I, 59–63;
Hazelton Spencer, *Shakespeare Improved* (1927), pp. 265–72.

[2] Written, not by Tate, but by Sir George Rainsford.

1 January the next year;[1] but in November and
December *Coriolanus* was offered. Quin may have
taken the hero.[2] It was revived on three nights of 1721
and 1722. Dennis's version as clearly had the Jacobite
invasion of 1715 in mind as Tate's the 'Popish plot',
but his main aim was to simplify the action. In his
Prologue he claimed to have 'brought to as much
Order as we can' the 'wild Confusion' of the 'Original'.
He rewrote whole passages of the poetry, and added
scores of lines of his own; but he retained the essential
plot with no new ending. Much of Menenius's
humour was cut out, and Valeria put in only one silent
appearance.[3]

On 13 January 1749 Covent Garden offered another
Coriolanus, a new play rather than an adaptation, though
it was based on Shakespeare's plot. It was a blank verse
drama, written by the poet of *The Seasons*, James
Thomson. It begins with Coriolanus in exile and ends
with his murder, by conspirators, not by Aufidius. The
latter (whose jealousy is fanned by 'Volusius', as by
Nigridius in Tate) is here named 'Attius Tullus', for
Thomson bases his play on Dionysius of Halicarnassus
rather than on Plutarch. Accordingly Volumnia is
here 'Veturia' and Virgilia is 'Volumnia'. The two
only appear in the last Act as suppliants, when the hero
is induced to spare Rome by his mother's threat to kill
herself with a dagger which she has hidden under her
robe. The play ends with a long speech on the Roman's
character. Thomson tones down his pride and he is
described as being 'with every virtue | Of civil life

---

[1] On this point see C. B. Hogan, *Shakespeare in the
Theatre: London, 1701–1750* (1952), p. 101.

[2] So Genest thought; see *op. cit.* III, 55; cf. Hogan,
ibid.

[3] On Dennis's version, see Genest, III, 2–5; Odell, I,
239–41; Hogan, p. 100.

adorn'd'; thus the ingratitude of the plebs is left with-
out excuse.[1] The cast included Quin (Coriolanus),
Ryan (Attius Tullus), Delane (Galesus, a philosophic
Volscian), Peg Woffington (Veturia), and 'Mrs' G. A.
Bellamy (Volumnia). It was acted ten times, says
Genest. At last, in 1754, Garrick restored Shake-
speare in what was his only production of the play (at
Drury Lane, from 11 November), and it was played
eight times. He gave the hero's part to Mossop (who
enhanced his reputation in it), Menenius to Berry,
Cominius to Thomas Davies (whose wife played
Virgilia), and Volumnia to 'Mrs' Pritchard. Though
Thomson's play never had a revival, its influence long
remained. A month after Garrick's *Coriolanus*
(10 December) an amalgam of Thomson and Shakespeare, *Coriolanus, or the Roman Matron*, probably
pieced together by Thomas Sheridan and first staged in
Dublin, 29 February 1752, was offered at the Garden
and performed eight times. Sheridan and Ryan played
the two generals, Mrs Bellamy was Volumnia and Peg
Woffington again Veturia. It was repeated each
season there from 1758 to 1760, in 1765, and finally
in April 1768, Smith acting throughout in Sheridan's
place. In 1759 Mrs Vincent played Volumnia, suc-
ceeded in 1765 and 1768 by Miss Macklin, with Mrs
Bellamy now as Veturia. In 1758 Mrs Hamilton had
had the part, and Miss Cadill was Volumnia. This
hybrid version omitted Shakespeare's Act 1, except for

---

[1] On Thomson's play see Genest, IV, 277–9 (also reproduced in *The New Variorum*, ed. by H. H. Furness Jr, 1928,
p. 720), G. C. Macaulay, *James Thomson* (English Men of
Letters), 1908, pp. 281–3; Odell, I, 354–5 (who gives some
details of its staging on p. 421), and Douglas Grant, *James
Thomson* (1951), pp. 246–7 (who finds it 'the poorest of his
tragedies', though the 'action is an improvement on
Shakespeare').

sc. 3, ll. 1–48 which, followed by the original Acts 2 and 3 (with considerable omissions), formed the first and second Acts. The third Act was unadulterated Thomson, while the fourth conflated him and Shakespeare—in Antium (Thomson), in Rome (Shakespeare)—with some new additions. The final act is pure Thomson except for some sixteen lines from Shakespeare.[1]

The next production, Kemble's, spanned most of his managerial career. He took much trouble over the play, the hero being his favourite and probably his finest part. He first staged it at Drury Lane on 7 February 1789, three months after he became manager. He continued to offer it there in five seasons till 1797. At Covent Garden it figured in seven of his seasons. The first began on 3 November 1806, Cooke having meanwhile played his one and only Coriolanus at Drury Lane on 29 May 1804; the last constituted Kemble's farewell to the London stage, with four performances between 26 April and 23 June 1817. He also mounted it in Edinburgh in 1815, and in Bath in 1812 and 1817. Till 1811 his Volumnia was mostly Mrs Siddons. She acted the Roman mother fifteen times in the first season at Covent Garden, 1806–7; her last appearance in the part was on 23 December 1811; but reduced as it was in Kemble's version it gave inadequate scope for her gifts.[2] Earlier she had acted the Veturia of Thomson in Manchester (10 February 1777). The best of her successors was Miss O'Neill,

[1] See Genest, IV, 417–19; Odell, I, 355; C. B. Hogan, *Shakespeare in the Theatre: London 1751–1800* (1957), pp. 157–8. The order of the triumphal procession in honour of Coriolanus is given from the 1755 prompt-copy by Odell, *op. cit.* I, 422–3.

[2] James Boaden does not seem to think so, however; see his *Memoirs of Mrs Siddons* (1827), II, 271–4.

though Hazlitt felt her 'manner, voice and person' to be unsuited to the part.[1] Mrs Powell, who became Mrs Renaud in 1813 (she had been Virgilia at the Lane in 1796) and Mrs Faucit, Helen's mother, were others. In December 1813 Conway stood in for Kemble at Covent Garden, and again when he was laid up with gout in May 1815. The next year, the bicentenary of Shakespeare's death, was commemorated by the play on 23 April, an imitation of Garrick's 1769 Jubilee pageant at Stratford being appended.[2] Boaden judged the later productions superior to the earlier, as the sister became more versed in ancient history and the brother 'more completely Roman'.[3] In his acting versions he departed from Shakespeare more than in any other play. Up to Act 4 he followed him, but with liberal omissions. Menenius all through was cut down to a minimum, and we lose at the outset the fable of the belly and the other members, and at the end his embassy to Coriolanus. Act 1 was reduced to three scenes (1, 3 and 6), so that no actual fighting took place. In Act 2 an arch had been erected for a great triumphal procession, in which Mrs Siddons as Volumnia, utterly absorbed in her son's glory, 'rolled, almost reeled across the stage and held the audience spellbound'.[4] In Act 3 the riot in which the tribunes and plebeians were driven away was excised and the people's case thereby weakened. From Act 4 Kemble turned to Thomson and drew copiously on him, but the action became huddled up

[1] See *A View of the English Stage* (1818), in Hazlitt's *Works*, ed. Waller and Glover (1903), VIII, 350; this is from his critique in *The Examiner*, 15 December 1816.

[2] For details of this see Genest, VIII, 551–2.

[3] James Boaden, *Memoirs of John Philip Kemble* (1825), I, 425; cf. him on the final production, II, 558.

[4] See J. C. Young, *Memoirs of Charles Mayne Young* (1871), I, 61–2.

and difficult to follow. Volumnia's pleading was mainly
cut out and with it her son's surrender at 5. 3. 182 ff.
Instead, his wife, so nearly dumb in the genuine text,
spoke eleven tearful Thomsonian lines, and he yielded
when his mother was about to kill herself with the
dagger (Thomson again). Kemble throughout was
adapting Shakespeare to notions of 'refined' and shapely
drama which would also allow for changes of localising
scenery.[1]

Edmund Kean in his only *Coriolanus* got rid of
accretions from Thomson, but it was a failure, and he
staged it for four nights at most from 24 or 25 January
1820 at Drury Lane.[2] His small figure was unsuitable
for the hero, and according to Hazlitt he could not
represent his unshaken contempt for the people; when
banished, his 'I banish you' displayed, not scorn but
only 'virulence of execration and rage of impotent
despair'.[3] Macready's fortunes as Coriolanus were at
first the opposite of Kean's. When he first essayed the
part three months before Kean (29 November 1819 at
Covent Garden) it strengthened the reputation he had
only just made as Richard III.[4] The 'applause through-

---

[1] For Kemble's version I draw liberally on Harold Child,
The Shakespearian Productions of John Philip Kemble
(Shakespeare Association Lecture, 1935), pp. 12–16; cf.
also Genest, VI, 531–5; Odell, II, 56–8; Hogan, *op. cit.*
pp. 158–9.

[2] Genest, IX, 32, gives the 24th as the first night; Odell,
II, 150, feels sure it was the 25th, because that was the date
of the first advertisement in *The Times*, and a critique
followed on the 26th.

[3] See his *Dramatic Essays* (*Works*, VIII, 402); this is from
the *London Magazine* (February 1820). Cf. Henry Morley
in his *Journal of a London Playgoer* (1866), pp. 261–2; he
contrasts Phelps's 'sublimity of disdain' here with Kean's
cry of 'ungovernable passion'.

[4] See W. Archer, *William Charles Macready* (1890), p. 51.

out' he recorded, 'exceeded my most ambitious hopes'.[1]
Thereafter he acted it fifteen times in revivals during
five different seasons. Three of these were at Drury
Lane in 1824, 1831, and 1833 (six nights in all);
Miss Huddart (about to be Mrs Warner) and Mrs
Sloman were his Volumnias in the last two. For two
productions he was himself responsible as manager at
Covent Garden: 12 March 1838 (for eight nights);
24 September that year (he himself absent) and 6 May
1839. But in these, instead of great enthusiasm from
a crowded house, we hear of lesser takings and thinner
and less responsive audiences.[2] Yet his cast was good:
J. R. Anderson (Aufidius), Bartley (Menenius), Warde
(Cominius) and Mrs Warner (Volumnia)—except that
on 24 September John Vandenhoff, the Garden
Coriolanus with Mrs Sloman in October 1834, took
Macready's place, and Samuel Phelps was Aufidius,
with Miss Vandenhoff playing Virgilia as she also did
the next May on the final night. Nor could the novel
staging be blamed, for it was praised even by his sworn
foe and rival manager, Alfred Bunn.[3] The background
showed the Capitoline hill crowned with its citadel and
temples; down its sloping side were dense clusters of
thatched huts. A starlight view of the port and mole
of Antium with its lighthouse 'was a lovely effect'. The
rioting plebeians, holding murderous implements,
looked like 'a countless mob of barbarians'. In the
Senate 'between one and two hundred sat in triple rows

[1] See Macready's *Reminiscences and Selections from his
Diaries*, ed. Sir Frederick Pollock (1875), I, 202–3.

[2] See his Diary for 13 March and 20 April 1838 (*op. cit.*
II, 103, 107); J. C. Trewin, *Mr Macready: A Nineteenth-
Century Tragedian and his Theatre* (1955), p. 157.

[3] Macready had assaulted and injured him when under
him at the Lane in 1836; Bunn's praise is cited by Odell, II,
214–15; J. C. Trewin, *op. cit.* p. 143.

round three sides of the stage'. At the siege of Rome the soldiers with battering rams and moving towers 'seemed thousands, not hundreds'.[1]

In 1837 there were two other revivals: at Covent Garden in February, J. S. Hamblin as the hero, Mrs W. West as Volumnia; at Drury Lane with Butler and Mrs Lovett as principals in November. But thereafter for twenty odd years the chief credit of keeping the play on the boards belongs to Phelps and his productions as manager at Sadler's Wells, though Charles Dillon's Coriolanus at the Theatre Royal, Marylebone in 1843, and J. R. Anderson's with Mrs Weston as Volumnia at Drury Lane from 6 January 1851 deserve a mention. Phelps produced the play four separate times, himself now the hero. On the first occasion, the first night of his fifth season, 27 September 1848, he received 'overwhelming applause' from a full house. Charles Kemble was there, and several times exclaimed to the actor's nephew, 'That was very fine'.[2] In the cast were Miss Glyn (Volumnia), G. Bennett (Cominius), Marston (Aufidius), Mrs Marston (Valeria) and Miss Cooper (Virgilia). Phelps offered the play again in the autumn of 1850 and in March 1860. On 15 September 1860 he gave the last of the series. In this Hermann Vezin as Aufidius and Kate Saxon as Virgilia were new to the company; Mrs Marston retained her part; Bennett took over Menenius from a now forgotten actor, A. Younge, and Miss Atkinson Volumnia. In Prof. Morley's judgement she 'was wanting in some of the dignity of the character'; her attempts at scorn were hardly more than 'intensity of

[1] This description is from *John Bull* , 19 March 1838; for fuller details, see Archer, pp. 114–15; Odell, II, 211–14; J. C. Trewin, pp. 143–4.
[2] See W. May Phelps and John Forbes-Robertson, *Life and Life-work of Samuel Phelps*, p. 105, note.

spite'. He admired greatly Phelps's rendering of Coriolanus as a man of 'heroic pride' without vanity—a
'virtue overgrown'. His effort to flatter the mob was
'really intense torture to him'. From the word 'Traitor'
he recoiled as from a blow and 'let his wrath have way'.[1]
In London after Phelps the play was under eclipse till
the new century, when in 1901 two revivals were seen:
Benson's at the Comedy Theatre on 13 February;
Irving's at the Lyceum from 15 April. Stratford, however, had seen Benson already twice, in 1893 and 1898,
as the Roman soldier with Mrs Benson as his 'gracious
silence'; in 1893 Lyall Swete and Otho Stuart were
Menenius and Aufidius. In London he had a very fine
Volumnia in Geneviève Ward. But the news of Queen
Victoria's serious illness circulating among the audience
marred the reception of a notable performance.[2]
Irving's was the latest of his Shakespeare revivals, but
the least successful. Alma Tadema's designs for the
settings—he had designed sets for Benson also—made
it a delight to the eye; but neither he nor Ellen Terry
were well suited for Coriolanus and his mother,[3] and
the popularity of the light musical comedies at Daly's
and the Gaiety also interfered with its success. After
thirty-four nights, the last after an interval of time,[4]
Irving abandoned the play.

[1] See the full critique in Henry Morley, *op. cit.* (1866),
pp. 259–63 (from his article in the *Examiner*, 22 September
1860; cf. p. xlvii, note 3).

[2] See Lady Benson's *My Memoirs: Bensonian Memories*
(1926), pp. 189–90.

[3] From this general verdict Arthur Symons dissented;
he had 'never seen Irving so faithfully interpretative of a
masterpiece'; see his *Plays, Acting and Music* (1903),
pp. 51–2.

[4] So Laurence Irving, *Henry Irving* (1951), p. 639; though
Austin Brereton writes, 'thirty-six consecutive performances' (*Life of Henry Irving* (1908), II, 288).

The last fifty years since Irving's have seen more frequent revivals, though for six years none followed his. Then at the Memorial Theatre in Stratford under Benson Miss Ward repeated her triumph in six different years, 1907–19, and in 1910 his production was also staged at His Majesty's in London (19 April). Mrs Benson played Virgilia throughout. In 1919 a much condensed version was combined one night with a shortened *Merry Wives*. Besides the fuller productions, she and Benson (dubbed 'Sir Frank' in the theatre two nights before by King George V) were in a tableau of one scene in the special Tercentenary *matinée* of scenes from nine of the plays on 5 May 1916. Geneviève Ward continued as Volumnia in London with Charles Warburton as Coriolanus in the first revival by the Old Vic from 12 April 1920 with Robert Atkins as producer. In its second revival four years later (24 March), Atkins again producing, Ion Swinley had Hutin Britton as Volumnia. Under Bridges-Adams Stratford next took a hand, offering it as the Birthday Play in 1926 and again (in the rebuilt Memorial Theatre) in 1933. In the former year George Skillan had the title-part; Randle Ayrton and his wife were Menenius and Virgilia. In 1928 Frank Birch produced the play for the Marlowe Society in Cambridge, with Basil Bartlett in the title part; and Nugent Monck offered it at the Maddermarket Theatre with his Norwich players. Meanwhile William Poel with his Elizabethan Stage Circle had produced his *Coriolanus* in the morning of 11 May 1931 at the Chelsea Palace Theatre. He had built out from the proscenium a stage which would be viewed on three sides. Unfortunately his main purpose, to demonstrate that the plays could be acted under conditions akin to those for which Shakespeare wrote them, was not helped by his ruthless dealings with the text. On his theory, expounded in a

note on his Programme, that Chapman was part-author
and had written 'the greatest lines', he so drastically cut
and altered it that the acting took only an hour and
a half.[1] In 1938, from 19 April, the Old Vic offered
its third revival, produced by Lewis Casson and made
memorable by Laurence Olivier's and Sybil Thorn-
dike's renderings of the Roman soldier and his mother.
The next year B. Iden Payne produced the play at
Stratford—Alec Clunes and Dorothy Green as the
principals with Andrew Leigh as Menenius. More
recent productions have been the Old Vic's from
31 March 1948 (John Clements as Coriolanus,
Rosalind Atkinson as Volumnia); a second Marlowe
Society's production in 1951 by Mr George Rylands,
Fellow of King's College (the 1928 Volumnia); and
Glen Byam Shaw's at Stratford with Anthony Quayle
as the hero in 1952. In 1953 the Old Vic announced
its intention to present all the plays in the Folio during
the next five years, and on 23 February 1954, staged
this Roman play as the fifth of the series, Michael
Benthall producing it. Richard Burton and Paul
Daneman took Coriolanus and Aufidius; William Squire
was Menenius; Fay Compton and Claire Bloom played
Volumnia and Virgilia.[2]

Finally, in 1959 Olivier performed Coriolanus at
Stratford no less brilliantly than he had done over twenty
years before at the Old Vic; this time with Peter
Hall producing, Edith Evans as Volumnia, and
Harry Andrews as Menenius.

Coriolanus has had little vogue in the United States;

[1] For a detailed account of Poel's production, and
version, see Robert Speaight, *William Poel and the Elizabethan Revival* (1954), pp. 252, 255–63; for his 'platform
stage' see pp. 115, 285.
[2] See Roger Wood and Mary Clarke's *Shakespeare at the
Old Vic* (1954), pp. 68–72.

Edwin Booth, who himself never appeared in this play, said it had never been very successful on the stage. It was first shown at the Park Theatre, New York on 3 June 1799 with Cooper and Mrs Barrett. Forrest, probably the best American Coriolanus, first appeared in the part in January 1838.[1] The play was often in his repertory later, and his two last revivals ran to some twenty nights (November 1863, and September–October 1864). McCullough was with him first as Cominius and then as Aufidius. Others who played the title part were Hamblin and Eddy (1849–62), and Salvini once (1885).[2] The Pasadena Playhouse in California put on a *Coriolanus* in July 1936. Recently (January 1954) the play was seen at the Phoenix Theatre, New York (Robert Ryan as Coriolanus, John Emery as Aufidius and Mildred Natwick as Volumnia.)[3]

C. B. YOUNG

1957–59

[1] So G. C. D. Odell, *Annals of the New York Stage* (1931), IV, 197; Furness gives him a first appearance in 1832 (New Variorum ed., 1928, p. 729).

[2] Odell, *op. cit. passim.*

[3] Information from C. B. Hogan.

TO THE READER

The following typographical conventions should be noted:

A single bracket at the beginning of a speech signifies an 'aside'.

An obelisk (†) implies probable corruption, and suggests a reference to the Notes.

Stage-directions taken verbatim from the First Folio are enclosed in single inverted commas.

The reference number for the first line is given at the head of each page. Numerals in square brackets are placed at the beginning of the traditional acts and scenes.

THE TRAGEDY OF
CORIOLANUS

The scene: Rome and the neighbourhood; Corioli and the neighbourhood; Antium

CHARACTERS IN THE PLAY.

CAIUS MARCIUS, *afterwards* CAIUS MARCIUS CORIOLANUS
TITUS LARTIUS,
COMINIUS, } *generals against the Volscians*
MENENIUS AGRIPPA, *friend to Coriolanus*
SICINIUS VELUTUS,
JUNIUS BRUTUS, } *Tribunes of the people*
YOUNG MARCIUS, *son to Coriolanus*
A Roman Herald
NICANOR, *a Roman*
TULLUS AUFIDIUS, *general of the Volscians*
Lieutenant to Aufidius
Conspirators with Aufidius
ADRIAN, *a Volscian*
A Citizen of Antium
Two Volscian Guards

VOLUMNIA, *mother to Coriolanus*
VIRGILIA, *wife to Coriolanus*
VALERIA, *friend to Virgilia*
Gentlewoman attending on Virgilia
Usher attending on Valeria

Roman and Volscian Senators, Patricians, Ædiles, Lictors, Soldiers, Citizens, Messengers, Servants to Aufidius, and other Attendants.

THE TRAGEDY OF
CORIOLANUS

Rome. A street

'*Enter a company of mutinous Citizens, with staves,*
clubs, and other weapons'

1 *Citizen.* Before we proceed any further, hear me
speak.

All. Speak, speak.

1 *Citizen.* You are all resolved rather to die than to
famish?

All. Resolved, resolved.

1 *Citizen.* First, you know Caius Marcius is chief
enemy to the people.

All. We know't, we know't.

1 *Citizen.* Let us kill him, and we'll have corn at our 10
own price. Is't a verdict?

All. No more talking on't; let it be done. Away,
away!

2 *Citizen.* One word, good citizens.

1 *Citizen.* We are accounted poor citizens, the
patricians good. What authority surfeits on would
relieve us. If they would yield us but the superfluity
while it were wholesome, we might guess they relieved
us humanely; but they think we are too dear: the lean-
ness that afflicts us, the object of our misery, is as an 20
inventory to particularize their abundance; our sufferance is a gain to them. Let us revenge this with our
pikes ere we become rakes; for the gods know I speak
this in hunger for bread, not in thirst for revenge.

2 *Citizen.* Would you proceed especially against Caius Marcius?

I *Citizen.* Against him first: he's a very dog to the commonalty.

2 *Citizen.* Consider you what services he has done
30 for his country?

I *Citizen.* Very well, and could be content to give him good report for't, but that he pays himself with being proud.

2 *Citizen.* Nay, but speak not maliciously.

I *Citizen.* I say unto you, what he hath done famously he did it to that end; though soft-conscienced men can be content to say it was for his country, he did it partly to please his mother and to be proud, which he is, even to the altitude of his virtue.

40 2 *Citizen.* What he cannot help in his nature you account a vice in him. You must in no way say he is covetous.

I *Citizen.* If I must not, I need not be barren of accusations; he hath faults (with surplus) to tire in repetition. ['*shouts*']. What shouts are these? The other side o' the city is risen: why stay we prating here? To th' Capitol!

All. Come, come.

I *Citizen.* Soft! who comes here?

'*Enter MENENIUS AGRIPPA*'

50 2 *Citizen.* Worthy Menenius Agrippa, one that hath always loved the people.

I *Citizen.* He's one honest enough; would all the rest were so!

Menenius. What work's, my countrymen, in hand?
     Where go you
With bats and clubs? The matter? Speak, I pray you.

1 *Citizen.* Our business is not unknown to th' Senate; they have had inkling this fortnight what we intend to do, which now we'll show 'em in deeds. They say poor suitors have strong breaths: they shall know we have strong arms too.   60

Menenius. Why, masters, my good friends, mine
    honest neighbours,
Will you undo yourselves?

1 *Citizen.* We cannot, sir; we are undone already.

Menenius. I tell you, friends, most charitable care
Have the patricians of you. For your wants,
Your suffering in this dearth, you may as well
Strike at the heaven with your staves as lift them
Against the Roman state, whose course will on
The way it takes; cracking ten thousand curbs
Of more strong link asunder than can ever   70
Appear in your impediment. For the dearth,
The gods, not the patricians, make it, and
Your knees to them (not arms) must help. Alack,
You are transported by calamity
Thither where more attends you; and you slander
The helms o' th' state, who care for you like fathers,
When you curse them as enemies.

1 *Citizen.* Care for us! True, indeed! They ne'er cared for us yet. Suffer us to famish, and their store-houses crammed with grain; make edicts for usury, to 80 support usurers; repeal daily any wholesome act estab-lished against the rich, and provide more piercing statutes daily to chain up and restrain the poor. If the wars eat us not up, they will; and there's all the love they bear us.

Menenius. Either you must
Confess yourselves wondrous malicious,
Or be accused of folly. I shall tell you

A pretty tale: it may be you have heard it;
90 But, since it serves my purpose, I will venture
To stale't a little more.
  1 *Citizen.* Well, I'll hear it, sir: yet you must not
think to fob off our disgrace with a tale: but, an't please
you, deliver.
  Menenius. There was a time when all the
        body's members
Rebelled against the Belly; thus accused it:
That only like a gulf it did remain
I' th' midst o' th' body, idle and unactive,
Still cupboarding the viand, never bearing
100 Like labour with the rest; where th' other instruments
Did see and hear, devise, instruct, walk, feel,
And, mutually participate, did minister
Unto the appetite and affection common
Of the whole body. The Belly answered—
  1 *Citizen.* Well, sir, what answer made the Belly?
  Menenius. Sir, I shall tell you. With a kind of smile,
Which ne'er came from the lungs, but even thus—
For, look you, I may make the Belly smile
As well as speak—it tauntingly replied
110 To th' discontented members, the mutinous parts
That envied his receipt; even so most fitly
As you malign our senators for that
They are not such as you.
  1 *Citizen.*   Your Belly's answer—What?
The kingly crownéd head, the vigilant eye,
The counsellor heart, the arm our soldier,
Our steed the leg, the tongue our trumpeter,
With other muniments and petty helps
In this our fabric, if that they—
  Menenius.   What then?
'Fore me, this fellow speaks! what then? what then?

1 *Citizen.* Should by the cormorant Belly   120
     be restrained,
Who is the sink o' th' body,—
  Menenius.   Well, what then?
  1 *Citizen.* The former agents, if they did complain,
What could the Belly answer?
  Menenius.   I will tell you;
If you'll bestow a small (of what you have little)
Patience awhile, you'st hear the belly's answer.
  1 *Citizen.* You're long about it.
  Menenius.   Note me this, good friend;
Your most grave Belly was deliberate,
Not rash like his accusers, and thus answered:
'True is it, my incorporate friends,' quoth he,
'That I receive the general food at first,   130
Which you do live upon; and fit it is,
Because I am the storehouse and the shop
Of the whole body. But, if you do remember,
I send it through the rivers of your blood,
Even to the court, the heart, to th'seat o' th' brain;
And, through the cranks and offices of man,
The strongest nerves and small inferior veins
From me receive that natural competency
Whereby they live: and though that all at once,
You, my good friends'—this says the Belly, mark me— 140
  1 *Citizen.* Ay, sir; well, well.
  Menenius.   'Though all at once cannot
See what I do deliver out to each,
Yet I can make my audit up, that all
From me do back receive the flour of all,
And leave me but the bran.' What say you to't?
  1 *Citizen.* It was an answer. How apply you this?
  Menenius. The senators of Rome are this good Belly,
And you the mutinous members: for examine

Their counsels and their cares, digest things rightly
150 Touching the weal o'th' common, you shall find
No public benefit which you receive
But it proceeds or comes from them to you,
And no way from yourselves. What do you think,
You, the great toe of this assembly?

   1 *Citizen.* I the great toe! why the great toe?
   Menenius. For that, being one o'th' lowest,
      basest, poorest,
Of this most wise rebellion, thou goest foremost.
Thou rascal, that art worst in blood to run,
Lead'st first to win some vantage.
160 But make you ready your stiff bats and clubs:
Rome and her rats are at the point of battle;
The one side must have bale.

'*Enter Caius Marcius*'

                      Hail, noble Marcius!
  Marcius. Thanks. What's the matter, you
      dissentious rogues
That, rubbing the poor itch of your opinion,
Make yourselves scabs?

   1 *Citizen.*   We have ever your good word.
   Marcius. He that will give good words to thee
      will flatter
Beneath abhorring. What would you have, you curs,
That like nor peace nor war? the one affrights you,
The other makes you proud. He that trusts to you,
170 Where he should find you lions, finds you hares;
Where foxes, geese: you are no surer, no,
Than is the coal of fire upon the ice,
Or hailstone in the sun. Your virtue is
To make him worthy whose offence subdues him
And curse that justice did it. Who deserves greatness

Deserves your hate. And your affections are
A sick man's appetite, who desires most that
Which would increase his evil. He that depends
Upon your favours swims with fins of lead
And hews down oaks with rushes. Hang ye! Trust ye? 180
With every minute you do change a mind,
And call him noble that was now your hate,
Him vile that was your garland. What's the matter
That in these several places of the city
You cry against the noble Senate, who
(Under the gods) keep you in awe, which else
Would feed on one another? What's their seeking?
  Menenius. For corn at their own rates, whereof
      they say
The city is well stored.
  Marcius.   Hang 'em! They say!
They'll sit by th'fire, and presume to know   190
What's done i'th' Capitol: who's like to rise,
Who thrives and who declines; side factions and
     give out
Conjectural marriages, making parties strong,
And feebling such as stand not in their liking
Below their cobbled shoes. They say there's
     grain enough!
Would the nobility lay aside their ruth,
And let me use my sword, I'd make a quarry
With thousands of these quartered slaves, as high
As I could pick my lance.
  Menenius. Nay, these are all most
     thoroughly persuaded;   200
For though abundantly they lack discretion,
Yet are they passing cowardly. But, I beseech you,
What says the other troop?
  Marcius.   They are dissolved: hang 'em!

They said they were an-hungry; sighed forth proverbs—
That hunger broke stone walls, that dogs must eat,
That meat was made for mouths, that the gods sent not
Corn for the rich men only: with these shreds
They vented their complainings; which being answered,
And a petition granted them—a strange one,
210 To break the heart of generosity
And make bold power look pale—they threw their caps
As they would hang them on the horns o'th' moon,
Shouting their emulation.

 Menenius.   What is granted them?
 Marcius. Five tribunes to defend their vulgar wisdoms,
Of their own choice. One's Junius Brutus, one
Sicinius Velutus, and—I know not. 'Sdeath!
The rabble should have first unroofed the city,
Ere so prevailed with me: it will in time
Win upon power and throw forth greater themes
220 For insurrection's arguing.

 Menenius.   This is strange.
 Marcius. Go, get you home, you fragments!

    '*Enter a Messenger, hastily*'

Messenger. Where's Caius Marcius?
Marcius.   Here: what's the matter?
Messenger. The news is, sir, the Volsces are in arms.
Marcius. I am glad on 't: then we shall ha' means
  to vent
Our musty superfluity. See, our best elders.

Enter COMINIUS, TITUS LARTIUS, *and other Senators*;
 JUNIUS BRUTUS *and* SICINIUS VELUTUS

 I *Senator.* Marcius, 'tis true that you have lately
  told us;
The Volsces are in arms.

Marcius.   They have a leader,
Tullus Aufidius, that will put you to 't.
I sin in envying his nobility;
And were I anything but what I am,   230
I would wish me only he.
  Cominius.   You have fought together.
  Marcius. Were half to half the world by th' ears,
        and he
Upon my party, I'd revolt, to make
Only my wars with him. He is a lion
That I am proud to hunt.
  I *Senator.*   Then, worthy Marcius,
Attend upon Cominius to these wars.
  Cominius. It is your former promise.
  Marcius.   Sir, it is,
And I am constant. Titus Lartius, thou
Shalt see me once more strike at Tullus' face.
What, art thou stiff? stand'st out?
  Titus.   No, Caius Marcius; 240
I'll lean upon one crutch and fight with t'other
Ere stay behind this business.
  Menenius.   O, true-bred!
  I *Senator.* Your company to th' Capitol; where
        I know
Our greatest friends attend us.
  Titus.   [*to Cominius.*] Lead you on.
[*to Marcius.*] Follow Cominius; we must follow you;
Right worthy you priority.
  Cominius.   Noble Marcius!
  I *Senator.* [*to the citizens*] Hence to your homes;
        be gone!
  Marcius.   Nay, let them follow.
The Volsces have much corn; take these
        rats thither

To gnaw their garners. ['*citizens steal away*'];
    Worshipful mutineers,
250 Your valour puts well forth. Pray, follow.
                        All go but Sicinius and Brutus

  Sicinius. Was ever man so proud as is this Marcius?
  Brutus. He has no equal.
  Sicinius. When we were chosen tribunes for
    the people—
  Brutus. Marked you his lip and eyes?
  Sicinius.   Nay, but his taunts.
  Brutus. Being moved, he will not spare to gird
    the gods.
  Sicinius. Bemock the modest moon.
  Brutus. The present wars devour him! He is grown
Too proud to be so valiant.
  Sicinius.   Such a nature,
Tickled with good success, disdains the shadow
260 Which he treads on at noon. But I do wonder
His insolence can brook to be commanded
Under Cominius.
  Brutus.   Fame, at the which he aims,
In whom already he's well graced, can not
Better be held, nor more attained, than by
A place below the first: for what miscarries
Shall be the general's fault, though he perform
To th' utmost of a man; and giddy censure
Will then cry out of Marcius 'O, if he
Had borne the business!'
  Sicinius.   Besides, if things go well,
270 Opinion, that so sticks on Marcius, shall
Of his demerits rob Cominius.
  Brutus.   Come:
Half all Cominius' honours are to Marcius,
Though Marcius earned them not; and all his faults

To Marcius shall be honours, though indeed
In aught he merit not.
　Sicinius.　　　　　　Let's hence, and hear
How the dispatch is made; and in what fashion,
More than his singularity, he goes
Upon this present action.
　Brutus.　　　　　　Let's along.　　　　*[they go*

[1. 2.]　　　　*Corioli. The Senate-House*

'*Enter TULLUS AUFIDIUS, with Senators of Corioli*'

　1 *Senator.*　So, your opinion is, Aufidius,
That they of Rome are ent'red in our counsels,
And know how we proceed.
　Aufidius.　　　　　　Is it not yours?
What ever hath been thought on in this state
That could be brought to bodily act ere Rome
Had circumvention? 'Tis not four days gone
Since I heard thence: these are the words: I think
I have the letter here: yes, here it is:
[*reads*] 'They have pressed a power, but it is
　　　not known
Whether for east or west. The dearth is great;　　10
The people mutinous: and it is rumoured,
Cominius, Marcius your old enemy
(Who is of Rome worse hated than of you),
And Titus Lartius, a most valiant Roman,
These three lead on this preparation
Whither 'tis bent: most likely 'tis for you:
Consider of it.'
　1 *Senator.*　　Our army's in the field:
We never yet made doubt but Rome was ready
To answer us.

Aufidius.   Nor did you think it folly
20 To keep your great pretences veiled till when
They needs must show themselves; which in
          the hatching,
It seemed, appeared to Rome. By the discovery
We shall be short'ned in our aim, which was
To take in many towns ere almost Rome
Should know we were afoot.

    2 *Senator.*   Noble Aufidius,
Take your commission; hie you to your bands:
Let us alone to guard Corioli.
If they set down before 's, for the remove
Bring up your army; but I think you'll find
30 They've not prepared for us.

    Aufidius.   O, doubt not that;
I speak from certainties. Nay, more,
Some parcels of their power are forth already,
And only hitherward. I leave your honours.
If we and Caius Marcius chance to meet,
'Tis sworn between us we shall ever strike
Till one can do no more.

    All.   The gods assist you!
Aufidius. And keep your honours safe!
    1 *Senator.*   Farewell.
    2 *Senator.*   Farewell.
    All. Farewell.   [*they go*

[I. 3.]   *Rome. A room in Marcius' house*

'*Enter* VOLUMNIA *and* VIRGILIA, *mother and wife to
Marcius: they set them down on two low stools, and sew*'

Volumnia. I pray you, daughter, sing, or express
yourself in a more comfortable sort: if my son were my

husband, I should freelier rejoice in that absence wherein he won honour than in the embracements of his bed
where he would show most love. When yet he was but
tender-bodied, and the only son of my womb; when
youth with comeliness plucked all gaze his way; when,
for a day of kings' entreaties, a mother should not sell
him an hour from her beholding; I, considering how
honour would become such a person—that it was no 10
better than picture-like to hang by th'wall, if renown
made it not stir—was pleased to let him seek danger
where he was like to find fame. To a cruel war I sent
him, from whence he returned his brows bound with
oak. I tell thee, daughter, I sprang not more in joy at
first hearing he was a man-child than now in first seeing
he had proved himself a man.

Virgilia. But had he died in the business, madam,
how then?

Volumnia. Then his good report should have been my 20
son; I therein would have found issue. Hear me profess
sincerely: had I a dozen sons, each in my love alike,
and none less dear than thine and my good Marcius,
I had rather had eleven die nobly for their country than
one voluptuously surfeit out of action.

'*Enter a Gentlewoman*'

Gentlewoman. Madam, the Lady Valeria is come to
visit you.

Virgilia. Beseech you give me leave to retire myself.

Volumnia. Indeed, you shall not.
Methinks I hear hither your husband's drum; 30
See him pluck Aufidius down by th' hair;
As children from a bear, the Volsces shunning him.
Methinks I see him stamp thus, and call thus:
'Come on, you cowards! you were got in fear,

Though you were born in Rome.' His bloody brow
With his mailed hand then wiping, forth he goes,
Like to a harvest-man that's tasked to mow
Or all or lose his hire.

Virgilia. His bloody brow? O Jupiter, no blood!

40 *Volumnia.* Away, you fool! It more becomes a man
Than gilt his trophy. The breasts of Hecuba,
When she did suckle Hector, looked not lovelier
Than Hector's forehead when it spit forth blood
At Grecian sword, contemning. Tell Valeria
We are fit to bid her welcome.   [*Gentlewoman goes*

Virgilia. Heavens bless my lord from fell Aufidius!

Volumnia. He'll beat Aufidius' head below his knee,
And tread upon his neck.

Re-enter Gentlewoman with VALERIA and her Usher

Valeria. My ladies both, good day to you.

50 *Volumnia.* Sweet madam!

Virgilia. I am glad to see your ladyship.

Valeria. How do you both? you are manifest house-
keepers. What are you sewing here? A fine spot, in
good faith. How does your little son?

Virgilia. I thank your ladyship; well, good madam.

Volumnia. He had rather see the swords and hear a
drum than look upon his schoolmaster.

Valeria. O' my word, the father's son: I'll swear 'tis
a very pretty boy. O' my troth, I looked upon him
60 o' Wednesday half an hour together: has such a confirmed countenance! I saw him run after a gilded
butterfly; and when he caught it, he let it go again; and
after it again; and over and over he comes, and up
again; catched it again: or whether his fall enraged
him, or how 'twas, he did so set his teeth, and tear it;
O, I warrant, how he mammocked it!

Volumnia. One on's father's moods.

Valeria. Indeed, la, 'tis a noble child.

Virgilia. A crack, madam.

Valeria. Come, lay aside your stitchery; I must have 70
you play the idle huswife with me this afternoon.

Virgilia. No, good madam; I will not out of doors.

Valeria. Not out of doors!

Volumnia. She shall, she shall.

Virgilia. Indeed, no, by your patience; I'll not over
the threshold till my lord return from the wars.

Valeria. Fie, you confine yourself most unreasonably;
come, you must go visit the good lady that lies in.

Virgilia. I will wish her speedy strength, and visit her
with my prayers; but I cannot go thither.   80

Volumnia. Why I pray you?

Virgilia. 'Tis not to save labour, nor that I want love.

Valeria. You would be another Penelope; yet, they
say, all the yarn she spun in Ulysses' absence did but fill
Ithaca full of moths. Come; I would your cambric
were sensible as your finger, that you might leave
pricking it for pity. Come, you shall go with us.

Virgilia. No, good madam, pardon me; indeed, I will
not forth.

Valeria. In truth, la, go with me, and I'll tell you 90
excellent news of your husband.

Virgilia. O, good madam, there can be none yet.

Valeria. Verily, I do not jest with you; there came
news from him last night.

Virgilia. Indeed, madam?

Valeria. In earnest, it's true; I heard a senator speak
it. Thus it is: the Volsces have an army forth; against
whom Cominius the general is gone, with one part of
our Roman power: your lord and Titus Lartius are set
down before their city Corioli; they nothing doubt 100

prevailing, and to make it brief wars. This is true, on mine honour; and so, I pray, go with us.

Virgilia. Give me excuse, good madam; I will obey you in every thing hereafter.

Volumnia. Let her alone, lady; as she is now, she will but disease our better mirth.

Valeria. In troth, I think she would. Fare you well, then. Come, good sweet lady. Prithee, Virgilia, turn thy solemness out o' door, and go along with us.

110 *Virgilia.* No, at a word, madam; indeed, I must not. I wish you much mirth.

Valeria. Well then, farewell.   [*they go*

[1. 4.]   *Before the gates of Corioli*

Enter MARCIUS, TITUS LARTIUS, *Captains and Soldiers, with drum, trumpet, and colours. To them a Messenger*

Marcius. Yonder comes news: a wager they have met.

Lartius. My horse to yours, no.

Marcius.   'Tis done.

Lartius.   Agreed.

Marcius. Say, has our general met the enemy?

Messenger. They lie in view, but have not spoke
    as yet.

Lartius. So, the good horse is mine.

Marcius.   I'll buy him of you.

Lartius. No, I'll nor sell nor give him: lend you him
    I will

For half a hundred years. [*to the trumpeter*] Summon
    the town.

Marcius. How far off lie these armies?

Messenger.   Within this mile and half.

Marcius. Then shall we hear their 'larum, and
    they ours.
Now, Mars, I prithee, make us quick in work,   10
That we with smoking swords may march from hence
To help our fielded friends! Come, blow thy blast.

    '*They sound a parley. Enter two Senators
        with others, on the walls*'

Tullus Aufidius, is he within your walls?
  1 *Senator.* No, nor a man that fears you less than he;
That's lesser than a little. ['*drum afar off*'] Hark, our
    drums
Are bringing forth our youth. We'll break our walls
Rather than they shall pound us up: our gates,
Which yet seem shut, we have but pinned with rushes;
They'll open of themselves. ['*alarum far off*'] Hark
    you, far off!
There is Aufidius. List what work he makes   20
Amongst your cloven army.
  Marcius.   O, they are at it!
  Lartius. Their noise be our instruction. Ladders, ho!

    *The gates are flung open and the Volsces make a
        sally out upon them*

Marcius. They fear us not, but issue forth
    their city.
Now put your shields before your hearts, and fight
With hearts more proof than shields. Advance,
    brave Titus.
They do disdain us much beyond our thoughts,
Which makes me sweat with wrath. Come on,
    my fellows.
He that retires, I'll take him for a Volsce,
And he shall feel mine edge. [*he advances, fighting*

'*Alarum. The Romans are beat back to their trenches.*
Enter MARCIUS, cursing'

30   *Marcius.* All the contagion of the south light on you,
You shames of Rome! you herd of—Boils and plagues
Plaster you o'er, that you may be abhorred
Farther than seen, and one infect another
Against the wind a mile! You souls of geese
That bear the shapes of men, how have you run
From slaves that apes would beat! Pluto and hell!
All hurt behind! backs red, and faces pale
With flight and agued fear! Mend and charge home,
Or, by the fires of heaven, I'll leave the foe,
40 And make my wars on you. Look to't. Come on;
If you'll stand fast, we'll beat them to their wives,
As they us to our trenches.

'*Another alarum*'. *The Volsces fly*, '*and MARCIUS*
follows them to the gates'

So, now the gates are ope: now prove good seconds:
'Tis for the followers Fortune widens them,
Not for the fliers. Mark me, and do the like.

[enters the gates

  1 *Soldier.* Fool-hardiness; not I.
  2 *Soldier.* Nor I.   *[Marcius is shut in*
  1 *Soldier.* See, they have shut him in.
  All.   To th' pot, I warrant him.

['alarum continues'

'*Enter TITUS LARTIUS*'

  Lartius. What is become of Marcius?
  All.   Slain, sir, doubtless.
50 1 *Soldier.* Following the fliers a the very heels,
With them he enters; who, upon the sudden,

Clapped to their gates. He is himself alone,
To answer all the city.
  Lartius.   O noble fellow!
Who sensibly outdares his senseless sword,
And when it bows stand'st up! Thou art lost, Marcius!
A carbuncle entire, as big as thou art,
Were not so rich a jewel. Thou wast a soldier
Even to Cato's wish, not fierce and terrible
Only in strokes; but with thy grim looks and
The thunder-like percussion of thy sounds   60
Thou mad'st thine enemies shake, as if the world
Were feverous and did tremble.

The gates re-open, and 'MARCIUS, *bleeding, assaulted
by the enemy' is seen within*

  1 *Soldier.*   Look, sir.
  Lartius.   O, 'tis Marcius!
Let's fetch him off, or make remain alike.
           ['*they fight, and all enter the city*'

[1. 5.]   '*Certain Romans, with spoils' come
running from the city*

  1 *Roman.* This will I carry to Rome.
  2 *Roman.* And I this.
  3 *Roman.* A murrain on't! I took this for silver.
        [*sounds of the distant battle still heard*

    '*Enter* MARCIUS *and* TITUS' LARTIUS
with a trumpeter

  Marcius. See here these movers that do prize
    their honours
At a cracked drachma! Cushions, leaden spoons,
Irons of a doit, doublets that hangmen would
Bury with those that wore them, these base slaves,

Ere yet the fight be done, pack up. Down with them!
And hark, what noise the general makes! To him!
10 There is the man of my soul's hate, Aufidius,
Piercing our Romans: then, valiant Titus, take
Convenient numbers to make good the city;
Whilst I, with those that have the spirit, will haste
To help Cominius.

    Lartius.   Worthy sir, thou bleed'st;
Thy exercise hath been too violent
For a second course of fight.

    Marcius.   Sir, praise me not;
My work hath yet not warmed me. Fare you well:
The blood I drop is rather physical
Than dangerous to me. To Aufidius thus
20 I will appear, and fight.

    Lartius.   Now the fair goddess, Fortune,
Fall deep in love with thee; and her great charms
Misguide thy opposers' swords! Bold gentleman,
Prosperity be thy page!

    Marcius.   Thy friend no less
Than those she placeth highest! So farewell.

    Lartius. Thou worthiest Marcius!   [*Marcius goes*
Go, sound thy trumpet in the market-place;
Call thither all the officers o'th' town,
Where they shall know our mind. Away!

                               [*they hurry forth*

[1. 6.]   *Near the Roman camp*

'*Enter* COMINIUS, *as it were in retire, with soldiers*'

Cominius. Breathe you, my friends: well fought; we
    are come off
Like Romans, neither foolish in our stands

Nor cowardly in retire. Believe me, sirs,
We shall be charged again. Whiles we have struck,
By interims and conveying gusts we have heard
The charges of our friends. The Roman gods,
Lead their successes as we wish our own,
That both our powers, with smiling fronts encount'ring,
May give you thankful sacrifice!

'*Enter a Messenger*'

Thy news?

Messenger. The citizens of Corioli have issued,   10
And given to Lartius and to Marcius battle:
I saw our party to their trenches driven,
And then I came away.

Cominius.   Though thou speak'st truth,
Methinks thou speak'st not well. How long is't since?

Messenger. Above an hour, my lord.

Cominius. 'Tis not a mile; briefly we heard
   their drums.
How couldst thou in a mile confound an hour,
And bring thy news so late?

Messenger.   Spies of the Volsces
Held me in chase, that I was forced to wheel
Three or four miles about; else had I, sir,   20
Half an hour since brought my report.

MARCIUS is seen approaching

Cominius.   Who's yonder
That does appear as he were flayed? O gods!
He has the stamp of Marcius, and I have
Before-time seen him thus.

Marcius. [*shouts*]   Come I too late?

Cominius. The shepherd knows not thunder from
   a tabor

More than I know the sound of Marcius' tongue
From every meaner man.

  Marcius. [*at hand*]   Come I too late?

  Cominius. Ay, if you come not in the blood of others,
But mantled in your own.

  Marcius.   O, let me clip ye
30 In arms as sound as when I wooed; in heart
As merry as when our nuptial day was done,
And tapers burned to bedward!   [*they embrace*

  Cominius.   Flower of warriors!—
How is't with Titus Lartius?

  Marcius. As with a man busied about decrees:
Condemning some to death and some to exile;
Ransoming him or pitying, threat'ning th' other;
Holding Corioli in the name of Rome,
Even like a fawning greyhound in the leash,
To let him slip at will.

  Cominius.   Where is that slave
40 Which told me they had beat you to your trenches?
Where is he? call him hither.

  Marcius.   Let him alone;
He did inform the truth. But for our gentlemen,
The common file—a plague! tribunes for them!—
The mouse ne'er shunned the cat as they did budge
From rascals worse than they.

  Cominius.   But how prevailed you?

  Marcius. Will the time serve to tell? I do not think.
Where is the enemy? Are you lords o' th' field?
If not, why cease you till you are so?

  Cominius.   Marcius,
We have at disadvantage fought and did
50 Retire to win our purpose.

  Marcius. How lies their battle? know you on which side
They have placed their men of trust?

Cominius.   As I guess, Marcius,
Their bands i' th' vaward are the Antiates,
Of their best trust; o'er them Aufidius,
Their very heart of hope.

Marcius.   I do beseech you,
By all the battles wherein we have fought,
By th' blood we have shed together, by th' vows
We have made to endure friends, that you directly
Set me against Aufidius and his Antiates;
And that you not delay the present, but,   60
Filling the air with swords advanced and darts,
We prove this very hour.

Cominius.   Though I could wish
You were conducted to a gentle bath,
And balms applied to you, yet dare I never
Deny your asking: take your choice of those
That best can aid your action.

Marcius.   Those are they
That most are willing. If any such be here—
As it were sin to doubt—that love this painting
Wherein you see me smeared; if any fear
Lesser his person than an ill report;   70
If any think brave death outweighs bad life,
And that his country's dearer than himself;
Let him alone, or so many so minded,
Wave thus, to express his disposition,
And follow Marcius.

> [*'they all shout, and wave their swords; take
> him up in their arms, and cast up their caps'*

O me, alone! Make you a sword of me?
If these shows be not outward, which of you
But is four Volsces? none of you but is
Able to bear against the great Aufidius
A shield as hard as his. A certain number,   80

Though thanks to all, must I select from all: the rest
Shall bear the business in some other fight,
As cause will be obeyed. Please you to march;
And I shall quickly draw out my command,
Which men are best inclined.

  Cominius.   March on, my fellows:
Make good this ostentation, and you shall
Divide in all with us.   [*they march on*

[1. 7.]   *Before the gates of Corioli*

'*TITUS LARTIUS, having set a guard upon Corioli, going
with drum and trumpet toward COMINIUS and CAIUS
MARCIUS, enters with a Lieutenant, other Soldiers, and
a Scout*'

  Lartius. So, let the ports be guarded: keep your duties
As I have set them down. If I do send, dispatch
Those centuries to our aid; the rest will serve
For a short holding. If we lose the field,
We cannot keep the town.

  Lieutenant.   Fear not our care, sir.

  Lartius. Hence, and shut your gates upon 's.
Our guider, come; to th' Roman camp conduct us.
                          [*they march on*

[1. 8.]   *Near the Roman camp*

'*Alarum as in battle.*' '*Enter MARCIUS and AUFIDIUS*',
                from opposite sides

  Marcius. I'll fight with none but thee, for I do
     hate thee
Worse than a promise-breaker.

Aufidius.　　　　　　　　We hate alike:
Not Afric owns a serpent I abhor
More than thy fame and envy.　Fix thy foot.
　Marcius.　Let the first budger die the other's slave,
And the gods doom him after!
　Aufidius.　　　　　　　　If I fly, Marcius,
Holloa me like a hare.
　Marcius.　　　　Within these three hours, Tullus,
Alone I fought in your Corioli walls,
And made what work I pleased. 'Tis not my blood
Wherein thou seest me masked.　For thy revenge　　10
Wrench up thy power to th' highest.
　Aufidius.　　　　　　　Wert thou the Hector
That was the whip of your bragged progeny,
Thou shouldst not scape me here.

　　　'Here they fight, and certain Volsces come in
　　　　　　　the aid of Aufidius'

Officious, and not valiant, you have shamed me
In your condemnéd seconds.

　　'Marcius fights till they be driven' away 'breathless'

[1. 9.]　*'Flourish.　Alarum.　A retreat is sounded.'*
'Enter', from one side, 'COMINIUS with the Romans'; from
　the other side, 'MARCIUS, with his arm in a scarf'

　Cominius.　If I should tell thee o'er this thy day's work,
Thou't not believe thy deeds: but I'll report it
Where senators shall mingle tears with smiles;
Where great patricians shall attend, and shrug,
I' th' end admire; where ladies shall be frighted,
And, gladly quaked, hear more; where the dull tribunes,
That with the fusty plebeians hate thine honours,
Shall say against their hearts 'We thank the gods

Our Rome hath such a soldier.'
10 Yet cam'st thou to a morsel of this feast,
Having fully dined before.

'*Enter TITUS LARTIUS, with his power,*
from the pursuit'

Lartius. O general,
Here is the steed, we the caparison!
Hadst thou beheld—
Marcius. Pray now, no more: my mother,
Who has a charter to extol her blood,
When she does praise me grieves me. I have done
As you have done—that's what I can: induced
As you have been—that's for my country:
He that has but effected his good will
Hath overta'en mine act.
Cominius. You shall not be
20 The grave of your deserving; Rome must know
The value of her own: 'twere a concealment
Worse than a theft, no less than a traducement,
To hide your doings; and to silence that
Which, to the spire and top of praises vouched,
Would seem but modest: therefore, I beseech you,
In sign of what you are, not to reward
What you have done, before our army hear me.
Marcius. I have some wounds upon me, and
they smart
To hear themselves rememb'red.
Cominius. Should they not,
30 Well might they fester 'gainst ingratitude,
And tent themselves with death. Of all the horses—
Whereof we have ta'en good, and good store—of all
The treasure in this field achieved and city,
We render you the tenth; to be ta'en forth

Before the common distribution at
Your only choice.

Marcius.   I thank you, general;
But cannot make my heart consent to take
A bribe to pay my sword: I do refuse it,
And stand upon my common part with those
That have upheld the doing.   40

> ['*A long flourish. They all cry* Marcius!
>   Marcius! *cast up their caps and lances:*
>   *Cominius and Lartius stand bare*'

Marcius. May these same instruments which
        you profane
Never sound more! When drums and trumpets shall
I' th' field prove flatterers, let courts and cities be
Made all of false-faced soothing!
When steel grows soft as the parasite's silk,
Let him be made a coverture for th' wars!
No more, I say! For that I have not washed
My nose that bled, or foiled some debile wretch,
Which without note here's many else have done,
You shout me forth   50
In acclamations hyperbolical;
As if I loved my little should be dieted
In praises sauced with lies.

Cominius.   Too modest are you;
More cruel to your good report than grateful
To us that give you truly. By your patience,
If 'gainst yourself you be incensed, we'll put you
(Like one that means his proper harm) in manacles,
Then reason safely with you. Therefore, be it known,
As to us, to all the world, that Caius Marcius
Wears this war's garland: in token of the which,   60
My noble steed, known to the camp, I give him,
With all his trim belonging; and from this time,

For what he did before Corioli, call him,
With all th' applause and clamour of the host,
CAIUS MARCIUS CORIOLANUS.
 Bear th' addition nobly ever!

> ['*flourish; trumpets sound, and drums.*'

 All. Caius Marcius Coriolanus!

 Coriolanus. I will go wash;
And when my face is fair, you shall perceive
70 Whether I blush, or no. Howbeit, I thank you:
I mean to stride your steed, and at all times
To undercrest your good addition
To th' fairness of my power.

 Cominius.   So, to our tent;
Where, ere we do repose us, we will write
To Rome of our success. You, Titus Lartius,
Must to Corioli back: send us to Rome
The best, with whom we may articulate
For their own good and ours.

 Lartius.   I shall, my lord.

 Coriolanus. The gods begin to mock me. I, that now
80 Refused most princely gifts, am bound to beg
Of my lord general.

 Cominius.   Take't; 'tis yours. What is't?

 Coriolanus. I sometime lay here in Corioli
And at a poor man's house; he used me kindly.
He cried to me; I saw him prisoner;
But then Aufidius was within my view,
And wrath o'erwhelmed my pity. I request you
To give my poor host freedom.

 Cominius.   O, well begged!
Were he the butcher of my son, he should
Be free as is the wind. Deliver him, Titus.

90 *Lartius.* Marcius, his name?

 Coriolanus.   By Jupiter, forgot!

I am weary; yea, my memory is tired.
Have we no wine here?
  Cominius.   Go we to our tent:
The blood upon your visage dries; 'tis time
It should be looked to: come.   *[they go*

[1. 10.]   *The camp of the Volsces*

  '*A flourish. Cornets. Enter* TULLUS AUFIDIUS
     bloody, with two or three soldiers'

Aufidius. The town is ta'en!
  1 *Soldier.* 'Twill be delivered back on good condition.
  Aufidius. Condition!
I would I were a Roman; for I cannot,
Being a Volsce, be that I am. Condition!
What good condition can a treaty find
I' th' part that is at mercy? Five times, Marcius,
I have fought with thee; so often hast thou beat me;
And wouldst do so, I think, should we encounter
As often as we eat. By th' elements,   10
If e'er again I meet him beard to beard,
He's mine or I am his. Mine emulation
Hath not that honour in't it had; for where
I thought to crush him in an equal force,
True sword to sword, I'll potch at him some way,
Or wrath or craft may get him.
  1 *Soldier.*   He's the devil.
  Aufidius. Bolder, though not so subtle. My
    valour's poisoned
With only suff'ring stain by him; for him
Shall fly out of itself. Nor sleep nor sanctuary,
Being naked, sick, nor fane nor Capitol,   20

The prayers of priests nor times of sacrifice,
Embarquements all of fury, shall lift up
Their rotten privilege and custom 'gainst
My hate to Marcius. Where I find him, were it
At home, upon my brother's guard, even there,
Against the hospitable canon, would I
Wash my fierce hand in's heart. Go you to th' city;
Learn how 'tis held, and what they are that must
Be hostages for Rome.

  1 *Soldier*.   Will not you go?

30 *Aufidius*. I am attended at the cypress grove:
   I pray you—
'Tis south the city mills—bring me word thither
How the world goes, that to the pace of it
I may spur on my journey.

  1 *Soldier*.   I shall, sir.   [*they go*

 [2. 1.]   *Rome. A public place*

  '*Enter* MENENIUS, *with the two Tribunes of the
people,* SICINIUS, *and* BRUTUS'

 Menenius. The augurer tells me we shall have news
to-night.

 Brutus. Good or bad?

 Menenius. Not according to the prayer of the people,
for they love not Marcius.

 Sicinius. Nature teaches beasts to know their friends.

 Menenius. Pray you, who does the wolf love?

 Sicinius. The lamb.

 Menenius. Ay, to devour him, as the hungry plebeians
10 would the noble Marcius.

 Brutus. He's a lamb indeed, that baas like a bear.

Menenius. He's a bear indeed, that lives like a lamb. You two are old men: tell me one thing that I shall ask you.

Both. Well, sir.

Menenius. In what enormity is Marcius poor in, that you two have not in abundance?

Brutus. He's poor in no one fault, but stored with all.

Sicinius. Especially in pride.

Brutus. And topping all others in boasting. 　20

Menenius. This is strange now. Do you two know how you are censured here in the city—I mean of us o'th' right-hand file? do you?

Both. Why, how are we censured?

Menenius. Because you talk of pride now—will you not be angry?

Both. Well, well, sir, well.

Menenius. Why, 'tis no great matter; for a very little thief of occasion will rob you of a great deal of patience. Give your dispositions the reins, and be angry at your 30 pleasures; at the least, if you take it as a pleasure to you in being so. You blame Marcius for being proud?

Brutus. We do it not alone, sir.

Menenius. I know you can do very little alone; for your helps are many, or else your actions would grow wondrous single: your abilities are too infant-like for doing much alone. You talk of pride. O that you could turn your eyes toward the napes of your necks, and make but an interior survey of your good selves! O that you could! 　40

Both. What then, sir?

Menenius. Why, then you should discover a brace of unmeriting, proud, violent, testy magistrates (alias fools) as any in Rome.

Sicinius. Menenius, you are known well enough too.

Menenius. I am known to be a humorous patrician,
and one that loves a cup of hot wine with not a drop of
allaying Tiber in't; said to be something imperfect in
favouring the first complaint, hasty and tinder-like upon
50 too trivial motion; one that converses more with the
buttock of the night than with the forehead of the
morning. What I think I utter, and spend my malice
in my breath. Meeting two such wealsmen as you are—
I cannot call you Lycurguses—if the drink you give me
touch my palate adversely, I make a crooked face at it.
I cannot say your worships have delivered the matter
well, when I find the ass in compound with the major
part of your syllables; and though I must be content to
bear with those that say you are reverend grave men,
60 yet they lie deadly that tell you you have good faces.
If you see this in the map of my microcosm, follows it
that I am known well enough too? what harm can your
bisson conspectuities glean out of this character, if I be
known well enough too?

Brutus. Come, sir, come, we know you well enough.

Menenius. You know neither me, yourselves, nor any
thing. You are ambitious for poor knaves' caps and
legs: you wear out a good wholesome forenoon in
hearing a cause between an orange-wife and a faucet-
70 seller, and then rejourn the controversy of three-pence
to a second day of audience. When you are hearing a
matter between party and party, if you chance to be
pinched with the colic, you make faces like mummers,
set up the bloody flag against all patience, and, in roaring
for a chamber-pot, dismiss the controversy bleeding,
the more entangled by your hearing. All the peace you
make in their cause is calling both the parties knaves.
You are a pair of strange ones.

Brutus. Come, come, you are well understood to be

a perfecter giber for the table than a necessary bencher 80
in the Capitol.

Menenius. Our very priests must become mockers, if
they shall encounter such ridiculous subjects as you are.
When you speak best unto the purpose, it is not worth
the wagging of your beards; and your beards deserve
not so honourable a grave as to stuff a botcher's cushion
or to be entombed in an ass's pack-saddle. Yet you must
be saying Marcius is proud; who, in a cheap estimation,
is worth all your predecessors since Deucalion; though
peradventure some of the best of 'em were hereditary 90
hangmen. God-den to your worships: more of your
conversation would infect my brain, being the herdsmen
of the beastly plebeians. I will be bold to take my leave
of you.   [*Brutus and Sicinius stand 'aside'*

'*Enter VOLUMNIA, VIRGILIA, and VALERIA*'

How now, my as fair as noble ladies—and the moon,
were she earthly, no nobler—whither do you follow
your eyes so fast?

Volumnia. Honourable Menenius, my boy Marcius
approaches; for the love of Juno, let's go.

Menenius. Ha? Marcius coming home!   100

Volumnia. Ay, worthy Menenius; and with most
prosperous approbation.

Menenius. Take my cap, Jupiter, and I thank thee.
Hoo! Marcius coming home!

Virgilia. }
Valeria. } Nay, 'tis true.

Volumnia. Look, here's a letter from him: the state
hath another, his wife another; and, I think, there's one
at home for you.

Menenius. I will make my very house reel to-night.
A letter for me?   110

Virgilia. Yes, certain, there's a letter for you; I saw 't.

Menenius. A letter for me! it gives me an estate of seven years' health; in which time I will make a lip at the physician: the most sovereign prescription in Galen is but empiricutic, and, to this preservative, of no better report than a horse-drench. Is he not wounded? he was wont to come home wounded.

Virgilia. O, no, no, no.

Volumnia. O, he is wounded; I thank the gods for't.

120 *Menenius.* So do I too, if it be not too much. Brings a' victory in his pocket, the wounds become him.

Volumnia. On's brows, Menenius. He comes the third time home with the oaken garland.

Menenius. Has he disciplined Aufidius soundly?

Volumnia. Titus Lartius writes they fought together, but Aufidius got off.

Menenius. And 'twas time for him too, I'll warrant him that: an he had stayed by him, I would not have

been so fidiused for all the chests in Corioli, and the gold
130 that's in them. Is the Senate possessed of this?

Volumnia. Good ladies, let's go. Yes, yes, yes: the Senate has letters from the General, wherein he gives my son the whole name of the war: he hath in this action outdone his former deeds doubly.

Valeria. In troth, there's wondrous things spoke of him.

Menenius. Wondrous! ay, I warrant you, and not without his true purchasing.

Virgilia. The gods grant them true!

140 *Volumnia.* True! pooh-pooh!

Menenius. True! I'll be sworn they are true. Where is he wounded?—[*observing the tribunes*] God save your good worships! Marcius is coming home: he has more cause to be proud.—Where is he wounded?

Volumnia. I' th' shoulder and i' th' left arm: there will be large cicatrices to show the people, when he shall stand for his place. He received in the repulse of Tarquin seven hurts i' th' body.

Menenius. One i' th' neck, and two i' th' thigh— there's nine that I know.   150

Volumnia. He had before this last expedition twenty-five wounds upon him.

Menenius. Now it's twenty-seven: every gash was an enemy's grave. ['*A shout and flourish*'] Hark! the trumpets.

Volumnia. These are the ushers of Marcius. Before him he carries noise, and behind him he leaves tears: Death, that dark spirit, in's nervy arm doth lie, Which, being advanced, declines, and then men die.

'*A sennet. Trumpets sound. Enter* COMINIUS *the general and* TITUS LARTIUS; *between them,* CORIOLANUS, *crowned with an oaken garland; with Captains and Soldiers, and a Herald*'

Herald. Know, Rome, that all alone Marcius did fight 160
Within Corioli gates, where he hath won,
With fame, a name to Caius Marcius; these
In honour follows Coriolanus.
Welcome to Rome, renownéd Coriolanus! ['*flourish*'
All. Welcome to Rome, renownéd Coriolanus!
Coriolanus. No more of this, it does offend my heart;
Pray now, no more.
Cominius.   Look, sir, your mother!
Coriolanus.   O, ['*kneels*'
You have, I know, petitioned all the gods
For my prosperity!
Volumnia.   Nay, my good soldier, up;
My gentle Marcius, worthy Caius, and   170

By deed-achieving honour newly named—
What is it?—Coriolanus must I call thee?—
But, O, thy wife!

   Coriolanus.   My gracious silence, hail!
Wouldst thou have laughed had I come coffined home,
That weep'st to see me triumph? Ah, my dear,
Such eyes the widows in Corioli wear,
And mothers that lack sons.

   Menenius.   Now, the gods crown thee!

   Coriolanus. And live you yet? [*sees Valeria*] O my
      sweet lady, pardon.

   Volumnia. I know not where to turn: O, welcome
      home!

180 And welcome, General: and you're welcome all.

   Menenius. A hundred thousand welcomes.
          I could weep
And I could laugh, I am light and heavy. Welcome!
A curse begnaw the very root on's heart
That is not glad to see thee! You are three
That Rome should dote on: yet, by the faith of men,
We have some old crab-trees here at home that will not
Be grafted to your relish. Yet welcome, warriors:
We call a nettle but a nettle, and
The faults of fools but folly.

   Cominius.   Ever right.

190   *Coriolanus.* Menenius, ever, ever.

   Herald. Give way there, and go on.

   Coriolanus. [*to wife and mother*] Your hand,
      and yours!
Ere in our own house I do shade my head,
The good patricians must be visited;
From whom I have received not only greetings,
But with them change of honours.

   Volumnia.   I have lived

To see inherited my very wishes
And the buildings of my fancy: only
There's one thing wanting, which I doubt not but
Our Rome will cast upon thee.

  Coriolanus.   Know, good mother,
I had rather be their servant in my way   200
Than sway with them in theirs.

  Cominius.   On, to the Capitol!

    ['*Flourish; cornets. Exeunt in state, as before.*'
                  Brutus and Sicinius come forward

  Brutus. All tongues speak of him, and the
       bleared sights
Are spectacled to see him. Your prattling nurse
Into a rapture lets her baby cry
While she chats him: the kitchen malkin pins
Her richest lockram 'bout her reechy neck,
Clamb'ring the walls to eye him: stalls, bulks, windows,
Are smothered up, leads filled and ridges horsed
With variable complexions, all agreeing
In earnestness to see him: seld-shown flamens   210
Do press among the popular throngs, and puff
To win a vulgar station: our veiled dames
Commit the war of white and damask in
Their nicely-guarded cheeks to th' wanton spoil
Of Phœbus' burning kisses: such a pother,
As if that whatsoever god who leads him
Were slily crept into his human powers,
And gave him graceful posture.

  Sicinius.   On the sudden,
I warrant him consul.

  Brutus.   Then our office may
During his power go sleep.   220

  Sicinius. He cannot temp'rately transport his honours

From where he should begin and end, but will
Lose those he hath won.
    Brutus.   In that there's comfort.
    Sicinius.   Doubt not
The commoners, for whom we stand, but they
Upon their ancient malice will forget
With the least cause these his new honours; which
That he will give make I as little question
As he is proud to do't.
    Brutus.   I heard him swear,
Were he to stand for consul, never would he
230 Appear i' th' market-place, nor on him put
The napless vesture of humility;
Nor, showing, as the manner is, his wounds
To th' people, beg their stinking breaths.
    Sicinius.   'Tis right.
    Brutus. It was his word. O, he would miss it rather
Than carry it but by the suit of the gentry to him
And the desire of the nobles.
    Sicinius.   I wish no better
Than have him hold that purpose and to put it
In execution.
    Brutus.   'Tis most like he will.
    Sicinius. It shall be to him then as our good wills:
240 A sure destruction.
    Brutus.   So it must fall out
To him or our authorities. For an end,
We must suggest the people in what hatred
He still hath held them; that to's power he would
Have made them mules, silenced their pleaders and
Dispropertied their freedoms; holding them,
In human action and capacity,
Of no more soul nor fitness for the world
Than camels in the war, who have their provand

Only for bearing burthens, and sore blows
For sinking under them.

 Sicinius.   This, as you say, suggested 250
At some time when his soaring insolence
Shall touch the people—which time shall not want,
If he be put upon't, and that's as easy
As to set dogs on sheep—will be the fire
To kindle their dry stubble; and their blaze
Shall darken him for ever.

     '*Enter a Messenger*'

 Brutus.   What's the matter?
 Messenger. You are sent for to the Capitol.
   'Tis thought
That Marcius shall be consul.
I have seen the dumb men throng to see him and
The blind to hear him speak; matrons flung gloves, 260
Ladies and maids their scarfs and handkerchers,
Upon him as he passed; the nobles bended,
As to Jove's statue, and the commons made
A shower and thunder with their caps and shouts.
I never saw the like.

 Brutus.   Let's to the Capitol,
And carry with us ears and eyes for th' time,
But hearts for the event.

 Sicinius.   Have with you. [*they go*

[2. 2.] *Rome. The Senate House at the Capitol*

'*Enter two Officers, to lay cushions*'

1 *Officer*. Come, come, they are almost here. How many stand for consulships?

2 *Officer*. Three, they say: but 'tis thought of every one Coriolanus will carry it.

1 *Officer*. That's a brave fellow; but he's vengeance proud, and loves not the common people.

2 *Officer*. Faith, there hath been many great men that have flattered the people, who ne'er loved them; and there be many that they have loved, they know not 10 wherefore: so that, if they love they know not why, they hate upon no better a ground. Therefore, for Coriolanus neither to care whether they love or hate him manifests the true knowledge he has in their disposition; and out of his noble carelessness lets them plainly see't.

1 *Officer*. If he did not care whether he had their love or no, he waved indifferently 'twixt doing them neither good nor harm. But he seeks their hate with greater devotion than they can render it him, and leaves nothing undone that may fully discover him their opposite. 20 Now, to seem to affect the malice and displeasure of the people is as bad as that which he dislikes, to flatter them for their love.

2 *Officer*. He hath deserved worthily of his country; and his ascent is not by such easy degrees as those who, having been supple and courteous to the people, bonneted, without any further deed to have them at all, into their estimation and report. But he hath so planted his honours in their eyes and his actions in their hearts that for their tongues to be silent and not confess so 30 much were a kind of ingrateful injury; to report other-

wise were a malice that, giving itself the lie, would pluck
reproof and rebuke from every ear that heard it.

  1 *Officer.* No more of him; he's a worthy man. Make
way, they are coming.

'*A sennet. Enter the Patricians and the Tribunes of the
People, Lictors before them;* CORIOLANUS, MENENIUS,
COMINIUS *the Consul.* SICINIUS *and* BRUTUS *take their
places by themselves*'

  Menenius. Having determined of the Volsces, and
To send for Titus Lartius, it remains,
As the main point of this our after-meeting,
To gratify his noble service that
Hath thus stood for his country: therefore, please you
Most reverend and grave elders, to desire   40
The present consul, and last general
In our well-found successes, to report
A little of that worthy work performed
By Caius Marcius Coriolanus; whom
We met here both to thank and to remember
With honours like himself.

  1 *Senator.*   Speak, good Cominius:
Leave nothing out for length, and make us think
Rather our state's defective for requital
Than we to stretch it out. [*to the Tribunes*] Masters
    o' th' people,
We do request your kindest ears; and, after,   50
Your loving motion toward the common body,
To yield what passes here.

  Sicinius.   We are convented
Upon a pleasing treaty, and have hearts
Inclinable to honour and advance
The theme of our assembly.

  Brutus.   Which the rather

We shall be blessed to do, if he remember
A kinder value of the people than
He hath hereto prized them at.

Menenius.   That's off, that's off;
I would you rather had been silent. Please you
60 To hear Cominius speak?

Brutus.   Most willingly:
But yet my caution was more pertinent
Than the rebuke you give it.

Menenius.   He loves your people;
But tie him not to be their bedfellow.
Worthy Cominius, speak.

      ['*Coriolanus rises and offers to go away*'
        Nay, keep your place.

1 *Senator.* Sit, Coriolanus; never shame to hear
What you have nobly done.

Coriolanus.   Your Honours' pardon:
I had rather have my wounds to heal again
.Than hear say how I got them.

Brutus.   Sir, I hope
My words disbenched you not.

Coriolanus.   No, sir: yet oft,
70 When blows have made me stay, I fled from words.
You soothed not, therefore hurt not: but your people,
I love them as they weigh—

Menenius.   Pray now, sit down.

Coriolanus. I had rather have one scratch my head
 i' th' sun
When the alarum were struck than idly sit
To hear my nothings monstered.   [*he goes*

Menenius.   Masters of the people,
Your multiplying spawn how can he flatter—
That's thousand to one good one—when you
  now see

He had rather venture all his limbs for honour
Than one on's ears to hear it? Proceed, Cominius.
   Cominius.   I shall lack voice: the deeds of Coriolanus 80
Should not be uttered feebly.   It is held
That valour is the chiefest virtue and
Most dignifies the haver: if it be,
The man I speak of cannot in the world
Be singly counterpoised.   At sixteen years,
When Tarquin made a head for Rome, he fought
Beyond the mark of others: our then dictator,
Whom with all praise I point at, saw him fight,
When with his Amazonian chin he drove
The bristled lips before him: he bestrid   90
An o'erpressed Roman, and i' th' consul's view
Slew three opposers: Tarquin's self he met,
And struck him on his knee: in that day's feats,
When he might act the woman in the scene,
He proved best man i' th' field, and for his meed
Was brow-bound with the oak.   His pupil age
Man-ent'red thus, he waxéd like a sea;
And, in the brunt of seventeen battles since,
He lurched all swords of the garland.   For this last,
Before and in Corioli, let me say,   100
I cannot speak him home.   He stopped the fliers,
And by his rare example made the coward
Turn terror into sport: as weeds before
A vessel under sail, so men obeyed,
And fell below his stem.   His sword, death's stamp,
Where it did mark, it took; from face to foot
He was a thing of blood, whose every motion
Was timed with dying cries.   Alone he ent'red
The mortal gate of th' city, which he painted
With shunless destiny; aidless came off,   110
And with a sudden re-enforcement struck

Corioli like a planet. Now all's his,
When by and by the din of war 'gan pierce
His ready sense, then straight his doubled spirit
Re-quickened what in flesh was fatigate,
And to the battle came he; where he did
Run reeking o'er the lives of men, as if
'Twere a perpetual spoil: and till we called
Both field and city ours, he never stood
120 To ease his breast with panting.

    Menenius.   Worthy man!

   1 *Senator.* He cannot but with measure fit
      the honours
Which we devise him.

    Cominius.   Our spoils he kicked at,
And looked upon things precious as they were
The common muck of the world: he covets less
Than misery itself would give, rewards
His deeds with doing them, and is content
To spend the time to end it.

    Menenius.   He's right noble:
Let him be called for.

   1 *Senator.*   Call Coriolanus.

   Officer. He doth appear.

CORIOLANUS *returns*

130 *Menenius.* The Senate, Coriolanus, are well pleased
To make thee consul.

    Coriolanus.   I do owe them still
My life and services.

    Menenius.   It then remains
That you do speak to the people.

    Coriolanus.   I do beseech you
Let me o'erleap that custom, for I cannot
Put on the gown, stand naked, and entreat them,

For my wounds' sake, to give their suffrage: please you
That I may pass this doing.

  Sicinius.   Sir, the people
Must have their voices; neither will they bate
One jot of ceremony.

  Menenius.   Put them not to't.
Pray you, go fit you to the custom, and   140
Take to you, as your predecessors have,
Your honour with your form.

  Coriolanus.   It is a part
That I shall blush in acting, and might well
Be taken from the people.

  (*Brutus.*   Mark you that.

  Coriolanus. To brag unto them, 'Thus I did, and thus!'
Show them th' unaching scars which I should hide,
As if I had received them for the hire
Of their breath only!

  (*Menenius.*   Do not stand upon't.
[*aloud*] We recommend to you, tribunes of the people,
Our purpose to them: and to our noble consul   150
Wish we all joy and honour.

  Senators. To Coriolanus come all joy and honour!

              [*Flourish of cornets; all leave the Senate*
                    House but Sicinius and Brutus

Brutus. You see how he intends to use the people.

Sicinius. May they perceive's intent! He will
    require them,
As if he did contemn what he requested
Should be in them to give.

  Brutus.   Come, we'll inform them
Of our proceedings here. On th' market-place,
I know, they do attend us.   [*they follow*

'*Enter seven or eight Citizens*'

1 *Citizen*. Once, if he do require our voices, we ought
not to deny him.

2 *Citizen*. We may, sir, if we will.

3 *Citizen*. We have power in ourselves to do it, but it
is a power that we have no power to do: for if he show
us his wounds and tell us his deeds, we are to put our
tongues into those wounds and speak for them; so, if he
tell us his noble deeds, we must also tell him our noble
acceptance of them. <u>Ingratitude</u> is monstrous: and for
10 the multitude to be ingrateful, were to make a monster
of the multitude; of the which we being members,
should bring ourselves to be monstrous members.

1 *Citizen*. And to make us no better thought of, a
little help will serve; for once we stood up about the
corn, he himself stuck not to call us the many-headed
multitude.

3 *Citizen*. We have been called so of many; not that
our heads are some brown, some black, some abram,
some bald, but that our wits are so diversely coloured:
20 and truly I think, if all our wits were to issue out of one
skull, they would fly east, west, north, south, and their
consent of one direct way should be at once to all the
points o' th' compass.

2 *Citizen*. Think you so? Which way do you judge
my wit would fly?

3 *Citizen*. Nay, your wit will not so soon out as
another man's will; 'tis strongly wedged up in a blockhead; but if it were at liberty, 'twould, sure, southward.

2 *Citizen*. Why that way?

30 3 *Citizen*. To lose itself in a fog; where being three

parts melted away with rotten dews, the fourth would
return for conscience sake, to help to get thee a wife.

2 *Citizen*. You are never without your tricks: you
may, you may.

3 *Citizen*. Are you all resolved to give your voices?
But that's no matter, the greater part carries it. I say,
if he would incline to the people, there was never a
worthier man.

'*Enter* CORIOLANUS *in a gown of humility,*
with MENENIUS'

Here he comes, and in the gown of humility: mark his
behaviour. We are not to stay all together, but to come 40
by him where he stands, by ones, by twos, and by
threes. He's to make his requests by particulars; wherein
every one of us has a single honour, in giving him our
own voices with our own tongues: therefore follow me,
and I'll direct you how you shall go by him.

All. Content, content.   [*they go off*

Menenius. O sir, you are not right: have you
    not known
The worthiest men have done 't?

Coriolanus.   What must I say?—
'I pray, sir'—Plague upon't! I cannot bring
My tongue to such a pace. 'Look, sir, my wounds!   50
I got them in my country's service, when
Some certain of your brethren roared and ran
From th' noise of our own drums.'

Menenius.   O me, the gods!
You must not speak of that: you must desire them
To think upon you.

Coriolanus.   Think upon me! hang 'em!
I would they would forget me, like the virtues
Which our divines lose by 'em.

Menenius.   You'll mar all.
I'll leave you. Pray you, speak to 'em, I pray you,
In wholesome manner.   [*he goes*

Re-enter Second and Third Citizens

Coriolanus.   Bid them wash their faces,
60 And keep their teeth clean. So, here comes a brace.
You know the cause, sir, of my standing here.

3 Citizen. We do, sir; tell us what hath brought
you to't.

Coriolanus. Mine own desert.

2 Citizen. Your own desert?

Coriolanus. Ay, not mine own desire.

3 Citizen. How not your own desire?

Coriolanus. No, sir, 'twas never my desire yet to
trouble the poor with begging.

70 *3 Citizen.* You must think, if we give you any thing,
we hope to gain by you.

Coriolanus. Well then, I pray, your price o' th'
consulship?

3 Citizen. The price is, to ask it kindly.

Coriolanus. Kindly, sir, I pray let me ha't: I have
wounds to show you, which shall be yours in private.
[*to the Second Citizen*] Your good voice, sir; what say
you?

2 Citizen. You shall ha' it, worthy sir.

80 *Coriolanus.* A match, sir. There's in all two worthy
voices begged. I have your alms: adieu.

                    [*turns from them*

3 Citizen. But this is something odd.

2 Citizen. An 'twere to give again—but 'tis no matter.

                    [*they go*
'*Enter two other Citizens*'

Coriolanus. Pray you now, if it may stand with the

tune of your voices that I may be consul, I have here
the customary gown.

4 Citizen. You have deserved nobly of your country,
and you have not deserved nobly.

Coriolanus. Your enigma?

4 Citizen. You have been a scourge to her enemies, 90
you have been a rod to her friends. You have not indeed
loved the common people.

Coriolanus. You should account me the more virtuous,
that I have not been common in my love. I will, sir,
flatter my sworn brother, the people, to earn a dearer
estimation of them; 'tis a condition they account gentle:
and since the wisdom of their choice is rather to have
my hat than my heart, I will practise the insinuating
nod, and be off to them most counterfeitly; that is, sir,
I will counterfeit the bewitchment of some popular 100
man, and give it bountiful to the desirers. Therefore,
beseech you I may be consul.

5 Citizen. We hope to find you our friend; and therefore give you our voices heartily.

4 Citizen. You have received many wounds for your
country.

Coriolanus. I will not seal your knowledge with
showing them. I will make much of your voices and
so trouble you no farther.

Both Citizens. The gods give you joy, sir, heartily! 110
                                                 [they go

Coriolanus. Most sweet voices!
Better it is to die, better to starve,
Than crave the hire which first we do deserve.
Why in this woolvish toge should I stand here,
To beg of Hob and Dick that do appear
Their needless vouches? Custom calls me to't.
What custom wills, in all things should we do't,

The dust on antique time would lie unswept,
And mountainous error be too highly heaped
120 For truth to o'erpeer. Rather than fool it so,
Let the high office and the honour go
To one that would do thus. I am half through:
The one part suffered, the other will I do.

'*Enter three Citizens more*'

Here come moe voices.
Your voices! For your voices I have fought;
Watched for your voices; for your voices bear
Of wounds two dozen odd; battles thrice six
I have seen, and heard of; for your voices have
Done many things, some less, some more. Your voices!
130 Indeed, I would be consul.

    5 *Citizen*. He has done nobly, and cannot go without
any honest man's voice.

    6 *Citizen*. Therefore let him be consul: the gods give
him joy, and make him good friend to the people!

    All. Amen, amen. God save thee, noble consul!

                                 [*they go*

Coriolanus. Worthy voices!

    '*Enter* MENENIUS, *with* BRUTUS *and* SICINIUS'

Menenius. You have stood your limitation; and
      the tribunes
Endue you with the people's voice. Remains
That in th' official marks invested you
140 Anon do meet the Senate.

    Coriolanus.   Is this done?

    Sicinius. The custom of request you have discharged:
The people do admit you, and are summoned
To meet anon upon your approbation.

    Coriolanus. Where? at the Senate House?

Sicinius.   There, Coriolanus.

Coriolanus. May I change these garments?

Sicinius.   You may, sir.

Coriolanus. That I'll straight do, and, knowing
    myself again,

Repair to th' Senate House.

Menenius. I'll keep you company. Will you along?

Brutus. We stay here for the people.

Sicinius.   Fare you well.

                    [Coriolanus and Menenius depart

He has it now; and, by his looks, methinks   150
'Tis warm at's heart.

Brutus.   With a proud heart he wore

His humble weeds. Will you dismiss the people?

Citizens return

Sicinius. How now, my masters! have you chose
    this man?

1 *Citizen.* He has our voices, sir.

Brutus. We pray the gods he may deserve your loves.

2 *Citizen.* Amen, sir: to my poor unworthy notice,

He mocked us when he begged our voices.

3 *Citizen.*   Certainly;

He flouted us downright.

1 *Citizen.* No, 'tis his kind of speech—he did not
    mock us.

2 *Citizen.* Not one amongst us, save yourself, but says 160

He used us scornfully: he should have showed us

His marks of merit, wounds received for's country.

Sicinius. Why, so he did, I am sure.

All. No, no; no man saw 'em.

3 *Citizen.* He said he had wounds which he could
    show in private;

And with his hat, thus waving it in scorn,

'I would be consul,' says he: 'agéd custom,
But by your voices, will not so permit me;
Your voices therefore.' When we granted that,
170 Here was 'I thank you for your voices. Thank you,
Your most sweet voices. Now you have left your voices,
I have no further with you.' Was not this mockery?
    Sicinius. Why either were you ignorant to see't,
Or, seeing it, of such childish friendliness
To yield your voices?
    Brutus.   Could you not have told him—
As you were lessoned—when he had no power,
But was a petty servant to the state,
He was your enemy, ever spake against
Your liberties and the charters that you bear
180 I' th' body of the weal: and now, arriving
A place of potency and sway o' th' state,
If he should still malignantly remain
Fast foe to th' plebeii, your voices might
Be curses to yourselves? You should have said
That as his worthy deeds did claim no less
Than what he stood for, so his gracious nature
Would think upon you for your voices, and
Translate his malice towards you into love,
Standing your friendly lord.
    Sicinius.   Thus to have said,
190 As you were fore-advised, had touched his spirit
And tried his inclination; from him plucked
Either his gracious promise, which you might,
As cause had called you up, have held him to;
Or else it would have galled his surly nature,
Which easily endures not article
Tying him to aught: so, putting him to rage,
You should have ta'en th' advantage of his choler,
And passed him unelected.

Brutus.   Did you perceive
He did solicit you in free contempt
When he did need your loves; and do you think   200
That his contempt shall not be bruising to you
When he hath power to crush? Why, had your bodies
No heart among you? or had you tongues to cry
Against the rectorship of judgement?
     Sicinius.   Have you
Ere now denied the asker, and now again,
Of him that did not ask but mock, bestow
Your sued-for tongues?
     3 *Citizen.* He's not confirmed; we may deny him yet.
     2 *Citizen.* And will deny him:
I'll have five hundred voices of that sound.   210
     1 *Citizen.* I twice five hundred, and their friends to
         piece 'em.
     Brutus. Get you hence instantly, and tell
         those friends
They have chose a consul that will from them take
Their liberties, make them of no more voice
Than dogs that are as often beat for barking
As therefore kept to do so.
     Sicinius.   Let them assemble;
And, on a safer judgement, all revoke
Your ignorant election. Enforce his pride
And his old hate unto you: besides, forget not
With what contempt he wore the humble weed,   220
How in his suit he scorned you: but your loves,
Thinking upon his services, took from you
Th' apprehension of his present portance,
Which, gibingly, ungravely, he did fashion
After the inveterate hate he bears you.
     Brutus.   Lay
A fault on us, your tribunes, that we laboured,

No impediment between, but that you must
Cast your election on him.

  Sicinius.   Say you chose him
More after our commandment than as guided
230 By your own true affections; and that your minds,
Pre-occupied with what you rather must do
Than what you should, made you against the grain
To voice him consul. Lay the fault on us.

  Brutus. Ay, spare us not. Say we read lectures to you,
How youngly he began to serve his country,
How long continued; and what stock he springs of,
The noble house o' th' Marcians, from whence came
That Ancus Marcius, Numa's daughter's son,
Who after great Hostilius here was king;
240 Of the same house Publius and Quintus were,
That our best water brought by conduits hither;
[And Censorinus that was so surnamed]
And nobly naméd so, twice being censor,
Was his great ancestor.

  Sicinius.   One thus descended,
That hath beside well in his person wrought
To be set high in place, we did commend
. To your remembrances: but you have found,
Scaling his present bearing with his past,
That he's your fixéd enemy, and revoke
250 Your sudden approbation.

  Brutus.   Say you ne'er had done't—
Harp on that still—but by our putting on:
And presently, when you have drawn your number,
Repair to th' Capitol.

  Citizens.   We will so: almost all
Repent in their election.   [*they go*

  Brutus.   Let them go on;
This mutiny were better put in hazard

Than stay, past doubt, for greater:
If, as his nature is, he fall in rage
With their refusal, both observe and answer
The vantage of his anger.

  Sicinius.   To th' Capitol, come:
We will be there before the stream o' th' people; 260
And this shall seem, as partly 'tis, their own,
Which we have goaded onward.   [*they go*

[3. 1.]   *Rome. A street*

'*Cornets. Enter* CORIOLANUS, MENENIUS, *all the Gentry,*
COMINIUS, TITUS LARTIUS, *and other Senators*'

  Coriolanus. Tullus Aufidius then had made new head?
  Lartius. He had, my lord; and that it was
  which caused
Our swifter composition.
  Coriolanus. So then the Volsces stand but as at first;
Ready, when time shall prompt them, to make road
Upon's again.
  Cominius. They are worn, Lord Consul, so
That we shall hardly in our ages see
Their banners wave again.
  Coriolanus.   Saw you Aufidius?
  Lartius. On safeguard he came to me; and did curse
Against the Volsces, for they had so vilely   10
Yielded the town: he is retired to Antium.
  Coriolanus. Spoke he of me?
  Lartius.   He did, my lord.
  Coriolanus.   How? what?
  Lartius. How often he had met you, sword to sword;
That of all things upon the earth he hated

Your person most; that he would pawn his fortunes
To hopeless restitution, so he might
Be called your vanquisher.

   Coriolanus.   At Antium lives he?

   Lartius. At Antium.

   Coriolanus. I wish I had a cause to seek him there,
20 To oppose his hatred fully. Welcome home.

           '*Enter* SICINIUS *and* BRUTUS'

Behold, these are the tribunes of the people,
The tongues o' th' common mouth. I do despise them;
For they do prank them in authority,
Against all noble sufferance.

   Sicinius.   Pass no further.

   Coriolanus. Ha? what is that?

   Brutus. It will be dangerous to go on—no further.

   Coriolanus. What makes this change?

   Menenius. The matter?

   Cominius. Hath he not passed the noble and.
      the common?.

30 *Brutus.* Cominius, no.

   Coriolanus.   Have I had children's voices?

   1 *Senator.* Tribunes, give way; he shall to th'
      market-place.

   Brutus. The people are incensed against him.

   Sicinius.   Stop,
Or all will fall in broil.

   Coriolanus.   Are these your herd?
Must these have voices, that can yield them now,
And straight disclaim their tongues? What are
      your offices?
You being their mouths, why rule you not their teeth?
Have you not set them on?

   Menenius.   Be calm, be calm.

Coriolanus. It is a purposed thing, and grows by plot,
To curb the will of the nobility:
Suffer't, and live with such as cannot rule,   40
Nor ever will be ruled.

  Brutus.   Call't not a plot:
The people cry you mocked them; and of late,
When corn was given them gratis, you repined,
Scandaled the suppliants for the people, called them
Time-pleasers, flatterers, foes to nobleness.

  Coriolanus. Why, this was known before.

  Brutus.   Not to them all.

  Coriolanus. Have you informed them sithence?

  Brutus.   How! I inform them!

  Coriolanus. You are like to do such business.

  Brutus.   Not unlike
Each way to better yours.

  Coriolanus. Why then should I be consul? By   50
     yond clouds,
Let me deserve so ill as you, and make me
Your fellow tribune.

  Sicinius.   You show too much of that
For which the people stir: if you will pass
To where you are bound, you must inquire your way,
Which you are out of, with a gentler spirit,
Or never be so noble as a consul,
Nor yoke with him for tribune.

  Menenius.   Let's be calm.

  Cominius. The people are abused; set on.
     This palt'ring
Becomes not Rome; nor has Coriolanus·
Deserved this so dishonoured rub, laid falsely   60
I' th' plain way of his merit.

  Coriolanus.   Tell me of corn!
This was my speech, and I will speak't again—

Menenius. Not now, not now.

1 *Senator.*   Not in this heat, sir, now.

Coriolanus. Now, as I live, I will.
My nobler friends, I crave their pardons. For
The mutable, rank-scented meiny, let them
Regard me as I do not flatter, and
Therein behold themselves. I say again,
In soothing them, we nourish 'gainst our Senate

70 The cockle of rebellion, insolence, sedition,
Which we ourselves have ploughed for, sowed,
     and scattered,
By mingling them with us, the honoured number;
Who lack not virtue, no, nor power, but that
Which they have given to beggars.

Menenius.   Well, no more.

1 *Senator.* No more words, we beseech you.

Coriolanus.   How! no more!
As for my country I have shed my blood,
Not fearing outward force, so shall my lungs
Coin words till their decay against those measles,
Which we disdain should tetter us, yet sought

80 The very way to catch them.

Brutus.   You speak o' th' people,
As if you were a god, to punish; not
A man of their infirmity.

Sicinius.   'Twere well
We let the people know't.

Menenius.   What, what? his choler?

Coriolanus. Choler!
Were I as patient as the midnight sleep,
By Jove, 'twould be my mind!

Sicinius.   It is a mind
That shall remain a poison where it is,
Not poison any further.

Coriolanus.   Shall remain!
Hear you this Triton of the minnows? mark you
His absolute 'shall'?
 Cominius.   'Twas from the canon.
 Coriolanus.   'Shall'!   90
O good but most unwise patricians! Why,
You grave but reckless senators, have you thus
Given Hydra here to choose an officer,
That with his peremptory 'shall,' being but
The horn and noise o' th' monster's, wants not spirit
To say he'll turn your current in a ditch,
And make your channel his? If he have power,
Then vail your ignorance; if none, awake
Your dangerous lenity. If you are learned,
Be not as common fools; if you are not,   100
Let them have cushions by you. You are plebeians,
If they be senators; and they no less,
When, both your voices blended, the great'st taste
Most palates theirs. They choose their magistrate;
And such a one as he, who puts his 'shall,'
His popular 'shall', against a graver bench
Than ever frowned in Greece. By Jove himself,
It makes the consuls base! and my soul aches
To know, when two authorities are up,
Neither supreme, how soon confusion   110
May enter 'twixt the gap of both and take
The one by th' other.
 Cominius.   Well, on to th' market-place.
 Coriolanus. Whoever gave that counsel to give forth
The corn o' th' storehouse gratis, as 'twas used
Sometime in Greece—
 Menenius.   Well, well, no more of that.
 Coriolanus. Though there the people had more
  absolute power,

I say they nourished disobedience, fed
The ruin of the state.

   Brutus.   Why shall the people give
One that speaks thus their voice?

   Coriolanus.   I'll give my reasons,
120 More worthier than their voices. They know the corn
Was not our recompense, resting well assured
They ne'er did service for't. Being pressed to th' war,
Even when the navel of the state was touched,
They would not thread the gates; this kind of service
Did not deserve corn gratis. Being i' th' war,
Their mutinies and revolts, wherein they showed
Most valour, spoke not for them. Th' accusation
Which they have often made against the Senate,
All cause unborn, could never be the native
130 Of our so frank donation. Well, what then?
How shall this bosom multiplied digest
The Senate's courtesy? Let deeds express
What's like to be their words: 'We did request it;
We are the greater poll, and in true fear
They gave us our demands.' Thus we debase
The nature of our seats, and make the rabble
Call our cares fears; which will in time
Break ope the locks o' th' Senate and bring in
The crows to peck the eagles.

   Menenius.   Come, enough.
140 *Brutus.* Enough, with over measure.

   Coriolanus.   No, take more.
What may be sworn by, both divine and human,
Seal what I end withal! This double worship,
Where one part does disdain with cause, the other
Insult without all reason; where gentry, title, wisdom,
Cannot conclude but by the yea and no
Of general ignorance—it must omit

Real necessities, and give way the while
To unstable slightness. Purpose so barred, it follows
Nothing is done to purpose. Therefore, beseech you—
You that will be less fearful than discreet;   150
That love the fundamental part of state
More than you doubt the change on 't; that prefer
A noble life before a long, and wish
To jump a body with a dangerous physic
That's sure of death without it—at once pluck out
The multitudinous tongue; let them not lick
The sweet which is their poison. Your dishonour
Mangles true judgement, and bereaves the state
Of that integrity which should become't;
Not having the power to do the good it would,   160
For th' ill which doth control 't.

  Brutus.   Has said enough.
  Sicinius. Has spoken like a traitor and shall answer
As traitors do.
  Coriolanus.   Thou wretch, despite o'erwhelm thee!
What should the people do with these bald tribunes,
On whom depending, their obedience fails
To th' greater bench? In a rebellion,
When what's not meet, but what must be, was law,
Then were they chosen: in a better hour
Let what is meet be said it must be meet,
And throw their power i' th' dust.   170
  Brutus. Manifest treason!
  Sicinius.   This a consul? No.
  Brutus. The ædiles, ho!

            '*Enter an Ædile*'

                  Let him be apprehended.
  Sicinius. Go, call the people: [*Ædile goes*] in whose
    name myself

Attach thee as a traitorous innovator,
A foe to th' public weal. Obey, I charge thee,
And follow to thine answer.
   Coriolanus.   Hence, old goat!
   Senators, &c. We'll surety him.
   Cominius.   Agéd sir, hands off.
   Coriolanus. Hence, rotten thing! or I shall shake
      thy bones
Out of thy garments.
   Sicinius.   Help, ye citizens!

     'Enter a rabble of Plebeians with the Ædiles'

180 *Menenius.* On both sides more respect.
   Sicinius. Here's he that would take from you all
      your power.
   Brutus. Seize him, ædiles!
   Citizens. Down with him! down with him!
   2 Senator. Weapons, weapons, weapons!
                ['they all bustle about Coriolanus'
Cries. 'Tribunes!' 'Patricians!' 'Citizens!' 'What, ho!'
'Sicinius!' 'Brutus!' 'Coriolanus!' 'Citizens!'
'Peace, peace, peace!' 'Stay! hold! peace!'
   Menenius. What is about to be? I am out of breath.
Confusion's near. I cannot speak. You, tribunes
190 To th' people! Coriolanus, patience!
Speak, good Sicinius.
   Sicinius.   Hear me, people; peace!
   Citizens. Let's hear our tribune: peace!—Speak,
      speak, speak.
   Sicinius. You are at point to lose your liberties:
Marcius would have all from you; Marcius,
Whom late you have named for consul.
   Menenius.   Fie, fie, fie!
This is the way to kindle, not to quench.

1 *Senator.* To unbuild the city, and to lay all flat.

Sicinius. What is the city but the people?

Citizens.   True,
The people are the city.

Brutus. By the consent of all, we were established   200
The people's magistrates.

Citizens.   You so remain.

Menenius. And so are like to do.

Cominius. That is the way to lay the city flat,
To bring the roof to the foundation,
And bury all which yet distinctly ranges,
In heaps and piles of ruin.

Sicinius.   This deserves death.

Brutus. Or let us stand to our authority,
Or let us lose it. We do here pronounce,
Upon the part o' th' people, in whose power
We were elected theirs, Marcius is worthy   210
Of present death.

Sicinius.   Therefore lay hold of him;
Bear him to th' rock Tarpeian, and from thence
Into destruction cast him.

Brutus.   Ædiles, seize him!

Citizens. Yield, Marcius, yield!

Menenius.   Hear me one word;
Beseech you, tribunes, hear me but a word.

Ædiles. Peace, peace!

Menenius. [*to Brutus*] Be that you seem, truly your
          country's friend,
And temp'rately proceed to what you would
Thus violently redress.

Brutus.   Sir, those cold ways,
That seem like prudent helps, are very poisonous   220
Where the disease is violent. Lay hands upon him,
And bear him to the rock.

Coriolanus. [*'draws his sword'*]   No, I'll die here.
There's some among you have beheld me fighting:
Come, try upon yourselves what you have seen me.
    Menenius. Down with that sword! Tribunes,
        withdraw awhile.
    Brutus. Lay hands upon him.
    Menenius.   Help Marcius, help,
You that be noble; help·him, young and old!
    Citizens. Down with him, down with him!

    *'In this mutiny, the Tribunes, the Ædiles, and
            the people, are beat in'*

    Menenius. Go, get you to your house; be gone, away!
All will be naught else.
    2 *Senator.*   Get you gone.
230 *Coriolanus.*   Stand fast;
We have as many friends as enemies.
    Menenius. Shall it be put to that?
    1 *Senator.*   The gods forbid!
I prithee, noble friend, home to thy house;
Leave us to cure this cause.
    Menenius.   For 'tis a sore upon us
You cannot tent yourself: be gone, beseech you.
    Cominius. Come, sir, along with us.
    Coriolanus. I would they were barbarians, as
        they are,
Though in Rome littered; not Romans, as they
        are not,
Though calved i' th' porch o' th' Capitol.
    Menenius.   Be gone.
240 Put not your worthy rage into your tongue:
One time will owe another.
    Coriolanus.   On fair ground
I could beat forty of them.

Menenius.   I could myself
Take up a brace o' th' best of them; yea, the two tribunes.
Cominius. But now 'tis odds beyond arithmetic;
And manhood is called foolery when it stands
Against a falling fabric. Will you hence
Before the tag return? whose rage doth rend
Like interrupted waters, and o'erbear
What they are used to bear.
Menenius.   Pray you, be gone.
I'll try whether my old wit be in request   250
With those that have but little: this must be patched
With cloth of any colour.
Cominius. [*to Coriolanus*]   Nay, come away
                    [*Coriolanus and Cominius depart*
1 *Patrician.* This man has marred his fortune.
Menenius. His nature is too noble for the world: ✳
He would not flatter Neptune for his trident,
Or Jove for 's power to thunder. His heart's his mouth:
What his breast forges, that his tongue must vent;
And, being angry, does forget that ever
He heard the name of death.   [*noise of the people*
Here's goodly work!   *returning*
2 *Patrician.*   I would they were a-bed!   260
Menenius. I would they were in Tiber! What the
    vengeance,
Could he not speak 'em fair?

'*Enter* BRUTUS *and* SICINIUS, *with the rabble again*'

Sicinius.   Where is this viper
That would depopulate the city and
Be every man himself?
Menenius.   You worthy tribunes—
Sicinius. He shall be thrown down the Tarpeian-rock
With rigorous hands: he hath resisted law,

And therefore law shall scorn him further trial
Than the severity of the public power,
Which he so sets at nought.

 1 *Citizen.*   He shall well know
270 The noble tribunes are the people's mouths,
And we their hands.

 All the citizens. He shall, sure on't.

 Menenius.   Sir, sir—

 Sicinius. Peace!

 Menenius. Do not cry havoc, where you should
  but hunt
With modest warrant.

 Sicinius.   Sir, how comes't that you
Have holp to make this rescue?

 Menenius.   Hear me speak:
As I do know the consul's worthiness,
So can I name his faults.

 Sicinius.   Consul! what consul?

 Menenius. The consul Coriolanus.

 Brutus.   He consul!

 All the citizens. No, no, no, no, no.

 Menenius. If, by the tribunes' leave, and yours,
280 good people,
I may be heard, I would crave a word or two;
The which shall turn you to no further harm
Than so much loss of time.

 Sicinius.   Speak briefly then;
For we are peremptory to dispatch
This viperous traitor: to eject him hence
Were but our danger, and to keep him here
Our certain death: therefore it is decreed
He dies to-night.

 Menenius. Now the good gods forbid
That our renownéd Rome, whose gratitude

Towards her deservéd children is enrolled   290
In Jove's own book, like an unnatural dam
Should now eat up her own!

Sicinius. He's a disease that must be cut away.

Menenius. O, he's a limb that has but a disease;
Mortal, to cut it off; to cure it, easy.
What has he done to Rome that's worthy death?
Killing our enemies, the blood he hath lost—
Which I dare vouch is more than that he hath
By many an ounce—he dropped it for his country;
And what is left, to lose it by his country   300
Were to us all that do't and suffer it
A brand to th' end o' th' world.

Sicinius.   This is clean kam.

Brutus. Merely awry: when he did love his country,
It honoured him.

Sicinius.   The service of the foot.
Being once gangrened, is not then respected
For what before it was.

Brutus.   We'll hear no more.
Pursue him to his house and pluck him thence,
Lest his infection, being of catching nature,
Spread further.

Menenius.   One word more, one word!
This tiger-footed rage, when it shall find   310
The harm of unscanned swiftness, will, too late,
Tie leaden pounds to's heels. Proceed by process;
Lest parties—as he is beloved—break out,
And sack great Rome with Romans.

Brutus.   If it were so—

Sicinius. What do ye talk?
Have we not had a taste of his obedience?
Our ædiles smote? ourselves resisted? Come!

Menenius. Consider this: he has been bred i' th' wars

Since a' could draw a sword, and is ill schooled
320 In bolted language; meal and bran together
He throws without distinction. Give me leave,
I'll go to him, and undertake to bring him
Where he shall answer, by a lawful form,
In peace, to his utmost peril.
   1 *Senator.*   Noble tribunes,
It is the human way: the other course
Will prove too bloody; and the end of it
Unknown to the beginning.
   Sicinius.   Noble Menenius,
Be you then as the people's officer.
Masters, lay down your weapons.
   Brutus.   Go not home.
330 *Sicinius.* Meet on the market-place. We'll attend
     you there:
Where, if you bring not Marcius, we'll proceed
In our first way.
   Menenius.   I'll bring him to you.
   [*to the Senators*] Let me desire your company: he
     must come,
Or what is worst will follow.
   Senators.   Pray you, let's to him.
                                   [*they go*

[3. 2.]   *Rome. The house of Coriolanus*

      '*Enter* CORIOLANUS *with Nobles*'

  Coriolanus. Let them pull all about mine ears;
     present me
Death on the wheel or at wild horses' heels;
Or pile ten hills on the Tarpeian rock,
That the precipitation might down stretch
Below the beam of sight; yet will I still

Be thus to them.
  A Noble.   You do the nobler.
  Coriolanus. I muse my mother
Does not approve me further, who was wont
To call them woollen vassals, things created
To buy and sell with groats; to show bare heads   **10**
In congregations, to yawn, be still and wonder,
When one but of my ordinance stood up
To speak of peace or war.

'Enter VOLUMNIA'

               I talk of you:
Why did you wish me milder? would you have me
False to my nature? Rather say I play
The man I am.
  Volumnia.   O, sir, sir, sir,
I would have had you put your power well on,
Before you had worn it out.
  Coriolanus.   Let go.
  Volumnia. You might have been enough the man
     you are,
With striving less to be so: lesser had been   **20**
The thwartings of your dispositions, if
You had not showed them how ye were disposed
Ere they lacked power to cross you.
  Coriolanus.   Let them hang.
  Volumnia. Ay, and burn too.

'Enter MENENIUS with the Senators'

  Menenius. Come, come, you have been too rough,
     something too rough;
You must return and mend it.
  Senator.   There's no remedy,
Unless, by not so doing, our good city

Cleave in the midst and perish.

Volumnia.   Pray be counselled:
I have a heart as little apt as yours,
30 But yet a brain that leads my use of anger
To better vantage.

Menenius.   Well said, noble woman!
Before he should thus stoop to th' herd—but that
The violent fit o' th' time craves it as physic
For the whole state—I would put mine armour on,
Which I can scarcely bear.

Coriolanus.   What must I do?

Menenius. Return to th' tribunes.

Coriolanus.   Well, what then? what then?

Menenius. Repent what you have spoke.

Coriolanus. For them! I cannot do it to the gods;
Must I then do't to them?

Volumnia.   You are too absolute;
40 Though therein you can never be too noble
But when extremities speak. I have heard you say,
Honour and policy, like unsevered friends,
I' th' war do grow together: grant that, and tell me
In peace what each of them by th' other lose
That they combine not there.

Coriolanus.   Tush, tush!

Menenius.   A good demand.

Volumnia. If it be honour in your wars to seem
The same you are not, which for your best ends
You adopt your policy, how is it less or worse
That it shall hold companionship in peace
50 With honour as in war; since that to both
It stands in like request?

Coriolanus.   Why force you this?

Volumnia. Because that now it lies you on to speak
To th' people, not by your own instruction,

Nor by th' matter which your heart prompts you,
But with such words that are but roted in
Your tongue, though but bastards and syllables
Of no allowance to your bosom's truth.
Now, this no more dishonours you at all
Than to take in a town with gentle words,
Which else would put you to your fortune and   60
The hazard of much blood.
I would dissemble with my nature, where
My fortunes and my friends at stake required
I should do so in honour. I am in this,
Your wife, your son, these senators, the nobles;
And you will rather show our general louts
How you can frown than spend a fawn upon 'em
For the inheritance of their loves and safeguard
Of what that want might ruin.

Menenius.   Noble lady!
Come, go with us; speak fair: you may salve so,   70
Not what is dangerous present, but the loss
Of what is past.

Volumnia.   I prithee now, my son,
†Go to them with this bonnet in thy hand;
And thus far having stretched it, here be with them,
Thy knee bussing the stones—[*curtseys*] for in
     such business
Action is eloquence, and the eyes of th' ignorant
More learnéd than the ears. Waving thy head,
With often thus correcting thy stout heart
(Now humble as the ripest mulberry
That will not hold the handling), say to them,   80
Thou art their soldier, and being bred in broils
Hast not the soft way which, thou dost confess,
Were fit for thee to use, as they to claim,
In asking their good loves; but thou wilt frame

Thyself, forsooth, hereafter theirs, so far
As thou hast power and person.
   Menenius.   This but done,
Even as she speaks, why, their hearts were yours;
For they have pardons, being asked, as free
As words to little purpose.
   Volumnia.   Prithee now,
90 Go, and be ruled: although I know thou hadst rather
Follow thine enemy in a fiery gulf
Than flatter him in a bower.

'*Enter* COMINIUS'

                           Here is Cominius.
   Cominius. I have been i' th' market-place; and, sir,
      'tis fit
You make strong party, or defend yourself
By calmness or by absence: all's in anger.
   Menenius. Only fair speech.
   Cominius.   I think 'twill serve, if he
Can thereto frame his spirit.
   Volumnia.   He must, and will.
Prithee now, say you will, and go about it.
   Coriolanus. Must I go show them my un-
      barbéd sconce?
100 With my base tongue give to my noble heart
A lie that it must bear? Well, I will do't:
Yet, were there but this single plot to lose,
This mould of Marcius, they to dust should grind it,
And throw't against the wind. To th' market-place!
You have put me now to such a part which never
I shall discharge to th' life.
   Cominius.   Come, come, we'll prompt you.
   Volumnia. I prithee now, sweet son, as thou
      hast said

My praises made thee first a soldier, so,
To have my praise for this, perform a part
Thou hast not done before.

Coriolanus.   Well, I must do't.   110
Away, my disposition, and possess me
Some harlot's spirit! My throat of war be turned,
Which choiréd with my drum, into a pipe
Small as an eunuch or the virgin voice
That babies lulls asleep! The smiles of knaves
Tent in my cheeks, and schoolboys' tears take up
The glasses of my sight! A beggar's tongue
Make motion through my lips, and my armed knees,
Who bowed but in my stirrup, bend like his
That hath received an alms! I will not do't;   120
Lest I surcease to honour mine own truth,
And by my body's action teach my mind
A most inherent baseness.

Volumnia.   At thy choice then.
To beg of thee, it is my more dishonour
Than thou of them. Come all to ruin: let
Thy mother rather feel thy pride than fear
Thy dangerous stoutness, for I mock at death
With as big heart as thou. Do as thou list.
Thy valiantness was mine, thou suck'dst it from me,
But owe thy pride thyself.

Coriolanus.   Pray, be content: 130
Mother, I am going to the market-place;
Chide me no more. I'll mountebank their loves,
Cog their hearts from them, and come home beloved
Of all the trades in Rome. Look, I am going:
Commend me to my wife. I'll return consul;
Or never trust to what my tongue can do
I' th' way of flattery further.

Volumnia.   Do your will.   [*she goes*

Cominius. Away! the tribunes do attend you.
    Arm yourself
To answer mildly; for they are prepared
140 With accusations, as I hear, more strong
Than are upon you yet.
    Coriolanus. The word is 'mildly.' Pray you, let us go.
Let them accuse me by invention, I
Will answer in mine honour.
    Menenius.   Ay, but mildly.
    Coriolanus. Well, mildly be it then—mildly.
                              [*they go*

[3. 3.]   *Rome. The Forum*

'*Enter SICINIUS and BRUTUS*'

Brutus. In this point charge him home, that he affects
Tyrannical power. If he evade us there,
Enforce him with his envy to the people,
And that the spoil got on the Antiates
Was ne'er distributed.

'*Enter an Ædile*'

               What, will he come?
Ædile. He's coming.
Brutus.   How accompanied?
Ædile. With old Menenius and those senators
That always favoured him.
    Sicinius.   Have you a catalogue
Of all the voices that we have procured,
10 Set down by th' poll?
    Ædile.   I have; 'tis ready.
Sicinius. Have you collected them by tribes?
Ædile.   I have.

Sicinius. Assemble presently the people hither:
And when they hear me say 'It shall be so
I' th' right and strength o' th' commons,' be it either
For death, for fine, or banishment, then let them,
If I say 'Fine', cry 'Fine!' if 'Death', cry 'Death!'
Insisting on the old prerogative
And power i' th' truth o' th' cause.
    Ædile.   I shall inform them.
    Brutus. And when such time they have begun
       to cry,
Let them not cease, but with a din confused   20
Enforce the present execution
Of what we chance to sentence.
    Ædile.   Very well.
    Sicinius. Make them be strong, and ready for
       this hint,
When we shall hap to give't them.
    Brutus.   Go about it.   [*the Ædile goes*
Put him to choler straight. He hath been used
Ever to conquer and to have his worth
Of contradiction: being once chafed, he cannot
Be reined again to temperance; then he speaks
What's in his heart; and that is there which looks
With us to break his neck.
    Sicinius.   Well, here he comes.   30

'*Enter* CORIOLANUS, MENENIUS, *and* COMINIUS,'
         with Senators and Patricians

    Menenius. Calmly, I do beseech you.
    (*Coriolanus.* Ay, as an ostler, that for th' poorest piece
Will bear the knave by th' volume. [*aloud*] Th'
       honoured gods
Keep Rome in safety, and the chairs of justice
Supplied with worthy men! plant love among 's!

Throng our large temples with the shows of peace,
And not our streets with war!

1 *Senator.*   Amen, amen.

Menenius. A noble wish.

'*Enter the Ædile, with the Plebeians*'

Sicinius. Draw near, ye people.

40 *Ædile.* List to your tribunes. Audience! peace,
      I say!

Coriolanus. First, hear me speak.

Both Tribunes.   Well, say. Peace, ho!

Coriolanus. Shall I be charged no further than
      this present?
Must all determine here?

Sicinius.   I do demand,
If you submit you to the people's voices,
Allow their officers, and are content
To suffer lawful censure for such faults
As shall be proved upon you?

Coriolanus.   I am content.

Menenius. Lo, citizens, he says he is content.
The warlike service he has done, consider; think

50 Upon the the wounds his body bears, which show
Like graves i' th' holy churchyard.

Coriolanus.   Scratches with briers,
Scars to move laughter only.

Menenius.   Consider further,
That when he speaks not like a citizen,
You find him like a soldier: do not take
His rougher accents for malicious sounds,
But, as I say, such as become a soldier
Rather than envy you.

Cominius.   Well, well, no more.

Coriolanus. What is the matter

That, being passed for consul with full voice,
I am so dishonoured that the very hour   60
You take it off again?
   Sicinius.   Answer to us.
   Coriolanus. Say, then: 'tis true, I ought so.
   Sicinius. We charge you, that you have contrived
      to take
From Rome all seasoned office, and to wind
Yourself into a power tyrannical;
For which you are a traitor to the people.
   Coriolanus. How! traitor!
   Menenius.   Nay, temperately! your promise.
   Coriolanus. The fires i' th' lowest hell fold in
      the people!
Call me their traitor! Thou injurious tribune!
Within thine eyes sat twenty thousand deaths,   70
In thy hands clutched as many millions, in
Thy lying tongue both numbers, I would say
'Thou liest' unto thee with a voice as free
As I do pray the gods.
   Sicinius.   Mark you this, people?
   Citizens. To th' rock, to th' rock with him!
   Sicinius.   Peace!
We need not put new matter to his charge.
What you have seen him do and heard him speak,
Beating your officers, cursing yourselves,
Opposing laws with strokes, and here defying
Those whose great power must try him—even this,   80
So criminal and in such capital kind,
Deserves th' extremest death.
   Brutus.   But since he hath
Served well for Rome—
   Coriolanus.   What do you prate of service?
   Brutus. I talk of that that know it.

Coriolanus. You!

Menenius. Is this the promise that you made
    your mother?

Cominius. Know, I pray you—

Coriolanus.   I'll know no further.
Let them pronounce the steep Tarpeian death,
Vagabond exile, flaying, pent to linger
90 But with a grain a day, I would not buy
Their mercy at the price of one fair word,
Nor check my courage for what they can give,
To have't with saying 'Good morrow.'

Sicinius.   For that he has
(As much as in him lies) from time to time
Envied against the people, seeking means
To pluck away their power, as now at last
Given hostile strokes, and that not in the presence
Of dreaded justice, but on the ministers
That do distribute it—in the name o' th' people,
100 And in the power of us the tribunes, we,
Even from this instant, banish him our city,
In peril of precipitation
From off the rock Tarpeian, never more
To enter our Rome gates. I' th' people's name,
I say it shall be so.

Citizens. It shall be so, it shall be so! Let him away!
He's banished, and it shall be so.

Cominius. Hear me, my masters and my
    common friends—

Sicinius. He's sentenced; no more hearing.

Cominius.   Let me speak.
110 I have been consul, and can show for Rome
Her enemies' marks upon me. I do love
My country's good with a respect more tender,
More holy and profound, than mine own life,

My dear wife's estimate, her womb's increase
And treasure of my loins; then if I would
Speak that—
    Sicinius.   We know your drift. Speak what?
    Brutus. There's no more to be said, but he
      is banished
As enemy to the people and his country.
It shall be so.
    Citizens.   It shall be so, it shall be so.
    Coriolanus. You common cry of curs! whose
       breath I hate   120
As reek o' th' rotten fens, whose loves I prize
As the dead carcasses of unburied men
That do corrupt my air—I banish you.
And here remain with your uncertainty!
Let every feeble rumour shake your hearts!
Your enemies, with nodding of their plumes,
Fan you into despair! Have the power still
To banish your defenders, till at length
Your ignorance—which finds not till it feels,
Making but reservation of yourselves,   130
Still your own foes—deliver you as most
Abated captives to some nation
That won you without blows! Despising
For you the city, thus I turn my back:
There is a world elsewhere.
               [*he goes, followed by Cominius, Menenius,*
                       Senators and Patricians
    Ædile. The people's enemy is gone, is gone!
    Citizens. Our enemy is banished! he is gone!
      Hoo—oo! [*'they all shout, and throw up their*
                                     caps'
    Sicinius. Go see him out at gates, and follow him,
As he hath followed you, with all despite;

140 Give him deserved vexation. Let a guard
Attend us through the city.
    Citizens. Come, come, let's see him out at
      gates; come!
The gods preserve our noble tribunes! Come. [*they go*

    [4. 1.]   *Rome. Before a gate of the city*

'*Enter* CORIOLANUS, VOLUMNIA, VIRGILIA, MENENIUS,
    COMINIUS, *with the young Nobility of Rome*'

    Coriolanus. Come, leave your tears; a brief farewell!
      The beast
With many heads butts me away. Nay, mother,
Where is your ancient courage? you were used
To say extremity was the trier of spirits;
That common chances common men could bear;
That when the sea was calm all boats alike
Showed mastership in floating; fortune's blows,
When most struck home, being gentle wounded, craves
A noble cunning. You were used to load me
10 With precepts that would make invincible
The heart that conned them.
    Virgilia. O heavens! O heavens!
    Coriolanus.   Nay, I prithee, woman—
    Volumnia. Now the red pestilence strike all trades
      in Rome,
And occupations perish!
    Coriolanus.   What, what, what!
I shall be loved when I am lacked. Nay, mother,
Resume that spirit when you were wont to say,
If you had been the wife of Hercules,
Six of his labours you'ld have done, and saved

Your husband so much sweat. Cominius,
Droop not; adieu. Farewell, my wife, my mother: 20
I'll do well yet. Thou old and true Menenius,
Thy tears are salter than a younger man's,
And venomous to thine eyes. My sometime general,
I have seen thee stern, and thou hast oft beheld
Heart-hard'ning spectacles; tell these sad women
'Tis fond to wail inevitable strokes,
As 'tis to laugh at 'em. Mother, you wot well
My hazards still have been your solace: and
Believe't not lightly—though I go alone,
Like to a lonely dragon that his fen   30
Makes feared and talked of more than seen—your son
Will or exceed the common or be caught
With cautelous baits and practice.
   Volumnia.   My first son,
Whither wilt thou go? Take good Cominius
With thee awhile: determine on some course
More than a wild exposure to each chance
That starts i' th' way before thee.
   Virgilia.   O the gods!
   Cominius. I'll follow thee a month, devise with thee
Where thou shalt rest, that thou mayst hear of us
And we of thee: so, if the time thrust forth   40
A cause for thy repeal, we shall not send
O'er the vast world to seek a single man,
And lose advantage, which doth ever cool
I' th' absence of the needer.
   Coriolanus.   Fare ye well:
Thou hast years upon thee; and thou art too full
Of the wars' surfeits to go rove with one
That's yet unbruised: bring me but out at gate.
Come, my sweet wife, my dearest mother, and
My friends of noble touch; when I am forth,

50 Bid me farewell, and smile. I pray you, come.
While I remain above the ground you shall
Hear from me still, and never of me aught
But what is like me formerly.
  Menenius.   That's worthily
As any ear can hear. Come, let's not weep.
If I could shake off but one seven years
From these old arms and legs, by the good gods,
I'ld with thee every foot.
  Coriolanus.   Give me thy hand.
Come.   [*they go*

[4. 2.]   *Rome. A street near the gate*

  '*Enter the two Tribunes,* SICINIUS *and* BRUTUS,
                with the Ædile'

Sicinius. Bid them all home; he's gone, and we'll
    no further.
The nobility are vexed, whom we see have sided
In his behalf.
  Brutus.   Now we have shown our power,
Let us seem humbler after it is done
Than when it was a-doing.
  Sicinius.   Bid them home:
Say their great enemy is gone, and they
Stand in their ancient strength.
  Brutus.   Dismiss them home. [*the Ædile goes*
Here comes his mother.

  '*Enter* VOLUMNIA, VIRGILIA, *and* MENENIUS'

  Sicinius.   Let's not meet her.
  Brutus.   Why?

Sicinius. They say she's mad.

Brutus. They have ta'en note of us: keep on
    your way.   10

Volumnia. O, you're well met: th' hoarded plague
    o' th' gods

Requite your love!

Menenius.   Peace, peace, be not so loud.

Volumnia. If that I could for weeping, you
    should hear—

Nay, and you shall hear some. [*to Brutus*] Will you
    be gone?

Virgilia. [*to Sicinius*] You shall stay too. I would
    I had the power

To say so to my husband.

Sicinius.   Are you mankind?

Volumnia. Ay, fool; is that a shame? Note but
    this, fool.

Was not a man my father? Hadst thou foxship

To banish him that struck more blows for Rome

Than thou hast spoken words?

Sicinius.   O blessed heavens!   20

Volumnia. Moe noble blows than ever thou
    wise words;

And for Rome's good. I'll tell thee what—yet go!

Nay, but thou shalt stay too. I would my son

Were in Arabia, and thy tribe before him,

His good sword in his hand.

Sicinius.   What then?

Virgilia.   What then!

He'ld make an end of thy posterity.

Volumnia. Bastards and all.

Good man, the wounds that he does bear for Rome!

Menenius. Come, come, peace.

Sicinius. I would he had continued to his country   30

As he began, and not unknit himself
The noble knot he made.
   Brutus.   I would he had.
   Volumnia. 'I would he had!' 'Twas you incensed
      the rabble;
Cats, that can judge as fitly of his worth
As I can of those mysteries which heaven
Will not have earth to know.
   Brutus.   Pray, let's go.
   Volumnia. Now, pray, sir, get you gone;
You have done a brave deed. Ere you go, hear this:
As far as doth the Capitol exceed
40 The meanest house in Rome, so far my son—
This lady's husband here, this, do you see?
Whom you have banished—does exceed you all.
   Brutus. Well, well, we'll leave you.
   Sicinius.   Why stay we to be baited
With one that wants her wits?
   Volumnia.   Take my prayers with you.
                         [Tribunes go

I would the gods had nothing else to do
But to confirm my curses! Could I meet 'em
But once a day, it would unclog my heart
Of what lies heavy to't.
   Menenius.   You have told them home,
And by my troth you have cause. You'll sup with me?
50 *Volumnia.* Anger's my meat; I sup upon myself,
And so shall starve with feeding. Come, let's go:
Leave this faint puling, and lament as I do,
In anger, Juno-like. Come, come, come.
                      [Vol. and Vir. depart
   Menenius. Fie, fie, fie!   *[he follows*

[4. 3.] *A highway between Rome and Antium*

'*Enter a Roman and a Volsce*', *meeting*

Roman. I know you well, sir, and you know me: your name, I think, is Adrian.

Volsce. It is so, sir: truly, I have forgot you.

Roman. I am a Roman; and my services are, as you are, against 'em. Know you me yet?

Volsce. Nicanor? no.

Roman. The same, sir.

Volsce. You had more beard when I last saw you; but your favour is well approved by your tongue. What's the news in Rome? I have a note from the Volscian 10 state to find you out there: you have well saved me a day's journey.

Roman. There hath been in Rome strange insurrections; the people against the senators, patricians, and nobles.

Volsce. Hath been! is it ended then? Our state thinks not so: they are in a most warlike preparation, and hope to come upon them in the heat of their division.

Roman. The main blaze of it is past, but a small thing 20 would make it flame again; for the nobles receive so to heart the banishment of that worthy Coriolanus, that they are in a ripe aptness to take all power from the people and to pluck from them their tribunes for ever. This lies glowing, I can tell you, and is almost mature for the violent breaking out.

Volsce. Coriolanus banished!

Roman. Banished, sir.

Volsce. You will be welcome with this intelligence, Nicanor.   30

Roman. The day serves well for them now. I have heard it said the fittest time to corrupt a man's wife is when she's fall'n out with her husband. Your noble Tullus Aufidius will appear well in these wars, his great opposer, Coriolanus, being now in no request of his country.

Volsce. He cannot choose. I am most fortunate thus accidentally to encounter you: you have ended my business, and I will merrily accompany you home.

40 *Roman.* I shall, between this and supper, tell you most strange things from Rome; all tending to the good of their adversaries. Have you an army ready, say you?

Volsce. A most royal one; the centurions and their charges, distinctly billeted, already in th' entertainment, and to be on foot at an hour's warning.

Roman. I am joyful to hear of their readiness, and am the man, I think, that shall set them in present action. So, sir, heartily well met, and most glad of your 50 company.

Volsce. You take my part from me, sir; I have the most cause to be glad of yours.

Roman. Well, let us go together.   [*they go*

[4. 4.]   *Antium. Before Aufidius's house*

'*Enter* CORIOLANUS *in mean apparel, disguised and muffled*'

Coriolanus. A goodly city is this Antium. City,
'Tis I that made thy widows: many an heir
Of these fair edifices 'fore my wars
Have I heard groan and drop. Then know me not,

Lest that thy wives with spits and boys with stones
In puny battle slay me.

'*Enter a Citizen*'

Save you, sir.

Citizen. And you.

Coriolanus.　　　　Direct me, if it be your will,
Where great Aufidius lies. Is he in Antium?

Citizen. He is, and feasts the nobles of the state
At his house this night.

Coriolanus.　　　　Which is his house, beseech you? 10

Citizen. This here before you.

Coriolanus.　　　　　　Thank you, sir: farewell.

[*Citizen goes*

O world, thy slippery turns! Friends now fast sworn,
Whose double bosoms seem to wear one heart,
Whose hours, whose bed, whose meal and exercise
Are still together, who twin, as 'twere, in love
Unseparable, shall within this hour,
On a dissension of a doit, break out
To bitterest enmity: so fellest foes,
Whose passions and whose plots have broke their sleep
To take the one the other, by some chance,　　　　20
Some trick not worth an egg, shall grow dear friends
And interjoin their issues. So with me:
My birth-place hate I, and my love's upon
This enemy town. I'll enter: if he slay me,
He does fair justice; if he give me way,
I'll do his country service.　　　[*he enters the house*

[4. 5.] *Antium. A hall in Aufidius's house, with three doors, one right leading to the outer gate, one left leading to the buttery, etc; the third centre opening into the great chamber*

'*Music plays. Enter a Servingman*' *from the chamber*

1 *Servingman.* Wine, wine, wine! What service
    is there!
I think our fellows are asleep.   [*goes out left*

'*Enter another Servingman*' *from the chamber*

2 *Servingman.* Where's Cotus? my master calls for
him. Cotus!   [*returns*

'*Enter* CORIOLANUS' *from without*

Coriolanus. A goodly house. The feast smells well,
    but I
Appear not like a guest.

Re-enter 1 *Servingman with wine*

1 *Servingman.* What would you have, friend? whence
are you? Here's no place for you: pray go to the door!
          [*returns to the chamber*
Coriolanus. I have deserved no better entertainment,
10 In being Coriolanus.

Re-enter 2 *Servingman*

2 *Servingman.* Whence are you, sir? Has the porter
his eyes in his head that he gives entrance to such
companions? Pray get you out.
Coriolanus. Away!
2 *Servingman.* 'Away!' Get you away.
Coriolanus. Now thou'rt troublesome.
2 *Servingman.* Are you so brave? I'll have you talked
with anon.

Enter from the chamber 3 *Servingman with* 1 *Servingman*

3 *Servingman.* What fellow's this?

1 *Servingman.* A strange one as ever I looked on! 20
I cannot get him out o' th' house. Prithee call my
master to him.

3 *Servingman.* What have you to do here, fellow?
Pray you avoid the house.

Coriolanus. Let me but stand; I will not hurt your
hearth.

3 *Servingman.* What are you?

Coriolanus. A gentleman.

3 *Servingman.* A marv'llous poor one.

Coriolanus. True, so I am.   30

3 *Servingman.* Pray you, poor gentleman, take up
some other station; here's no place for you. Pray you
avoid. Come.

Coriolanus. Follow your function, go and batten on
cold bits.   ['*pushes him away from him*'

3 *Servingman.* What, you will not? Prithee, tell my
master what a strange guest he has here.

2 *Servingman.* And I shall. [*returns to the chamber*

3 *Servingman.* Where dwell'st thou?

Coriolanus. Under the canopy.   40

3 *Servingman.* Under the canopy!

Coriolanus. Ay.

3 *Servingman.* Where's that?

Coriolanus. I' th' city of kites and crows.

3 *Servingman.* I' th' city of kites and crows! What
an ass it is! then thou dwell'st with daws too?

Coriolanus. No, I serve not thy master.

3 *Servingman.* How, sir! do you meddle with my
master?

Coriolanus. Ay; 'tis an honester service than to meddle 50

C. – 10

with thy mistress. Thou prat'st, and prat'st; serve
with thy trencher. Hence! [*'beats him' from the room*

Enter AUFIDIUS *with* 2 *Servingman*

Aufidius. Where is this fellow?
2 *Servingman.* Here, sir. I'ld have beaten him like
a dog, but for disturbing the lords within.   [*returns*
Aufidius. Whence com'st thou? What wouldst thou?
    Thy name?
Why speak'st not? Speak, man. What's thy name?
  Coriolanus. [*unmuffling*]   If, Tullus,
Not yet thou know'st me, and, seeing me, dost not
Think me for the man I am, necessity
60 Commands me name myself.
    Aufidius.   What is thy name?
    Coriolanus. A name unmusical to the Volscians' ears,
And harsh in sound to thine.
    Aufidius.   Say, what's thy name?
Thou hast a grim appearance, and thy face
Bears a command in't; though thy tackle's torn,
Thou show'st a noble vessel. What's thy name?
    Coriolanus. Prepare thy brow to frown—know'st thou
    me yet?
    Aufidius. I know thee not. Thy name!
    Coriolanus. My name is Caius Marcius, who
    hath done
To thee particularly, and to all the Volsces,
70 Great hurt and mischief; thereto witness may
My surname, Coriolanus. The painful service,
The extreme dangers, and the drops of blood
Shed for my thankless country, are requited
But with that surname—a good memory
And witness of the malice and displeasure
Which thou shouldst bear me. Only that name remains:

The cruelty and envy of the people,
Permitted by our dastard nobles, who
Have all forsook me, hath devoured the rest;
And suffered me by th' voice of slaves to be   80
Whooped out of Rome. Now, this extremity
Hath brought me to thy hearth: not out of hope—
Mistake me not—to save my life; for if
I had feared death, of all the men i' th' world
I would have 'voided thee; but in mere spite,
To be full quit of those my banishers,
Stand I before thee here. Then if thou hast
A heart of wreak in thee, that wilt revenge
Thine own particular wrongs and stop those maims
Of shame seen through thy country, speed thee straight 90
And make my misery serve thy turn. So use it
That my revengeful services may prove
As benefits to thee; for I will fight
Against my cank'red country with the spleen
Of all the under fiends. But if so be
Thou dar'st not this and that to prove more fortunes
Thou'rt tired, then, in a word, I also am
Longer to live most weary, and present
My throat to thee and to thy ancient malice;
Which not to cut would show thee but a fool,   100
Since I have ever followed thee with hate,
Drawn tuns of blood out of thy country's breast,
And cannot live but to thy shame, unless
It be to do thee service.
  Aufidius.   O Marcius, Marcius!
Each word thou hast spoke hath weeded from my heart
A root of ancient envy. If Jupiter
Should from yond cloud speak divine things,
And say 'Tis true', I'ld not believe them more
Than thee, all noble Marcius. Let me twine

110 Mine arms about that body, where against
My grainéd ash an hundred times hath broke
And scarred the moon with splinters: here I clip
The anvil of my sword, and do contest
As hotly and as nobly with thy love
As ever in ambitious strength I did
Contend against thy valour. Know thou first,
I loved the maid I married; never man
Sighed truer breath; but that I see thee here,
Thou noble thing, more dances my rapt heart
120 Than when I first my wedded mistress saw
Bestride my threshold. Why, thou Mars, I tell thee,
We have a power on foot, and I had purpose
Once more to hew thy target from thy brawn,
Or lose mine arm for't. Thou hast beat me out
Twelve several times, and I have nightly since
Dreamt of encounters 'twixt thyself and me;
We have been down together in my sleep,
Unbuckling helms, fisting each other's throat;
And waked half dead with nothing. Worthy Marcius,
130 Had we no quarrel else to Rome but that
Thou art thence banished, we would muster all
From twelve to seventy, and pouring war
Into the bowels of ungrateful Rome,
Like a bold flood o'erbear't. O, come, go in,
And take our friendly senators by th' hands,
Who now are here, taking their leaves of me
Who am prepared against your territories,
Though not for Rome itself.
    Coriolanus.   You bless me, gods!
    Aufidius. Therefore, most absolute sir, if thou wilt have
140 The leading of thine own revenges, take
Th' one half of my commission, and set down—
As best thou art experienced, since thou know'st

Thy country's strength and weakness—thine own ways,
Whether to knock against the gates of Rome,
Or rudely visit them in parts remote
To fright them ere destroy. But come in:
Let me commend thee first to those that shall
Say yea to thy desires. A thousand welcomes!
And more a friend than e'er an enemy;
Yet, Marcius, that was much. Your hand:
　　　most welcome!　　　　　　　　　　　　150
　　　　　　[*leads him in.* '*Enter two of the Servingmen*'
1 *Servingman.* Here's a strange alteration!

2 *Servingman.* By my hand, I had thought to have
strucken him with a cudgel; and yet my mind gave me
his clothes made a false report of him.

1 *Servingman.* What an arm he has! he turned me
about with his finger and his thumb, as one would set
up a top.

2 *Servingman.* Nay, I knew by his face that there was
something in him; he had, sir, a kind of face, me-
thought—I cannot tell how to term it.　　　　160

1 *Servingman.* He had so, looking as it were—Would
I were hanged, but I thought there was more in him
than I could think.

2 *Servingman.* So did I, I'll be sworn: he is simply the
rarest man i' th' world.

1 *Servingman.* I think he is; but a greater soldier than
he, you wot one.

2 *Servingman.* Who, my master?

1 *Servingman.* Nay, it's no matter for that.

2 *Servingman.* Worth six on him.　　　　　　170

1 *Servingman.* Nay, not so neither: but I take him to
be the greater soldier.

2 *Servingman.* Faith, look you, one cannot tell how to
say that: for the defence of a town our general is excellent.

1 *Servingman*. Ay, and for an assault too.

'*Enter the third Servingman*'

3 *Servingman*. O slaves, I can tell you news—news, you rascals!

1, 2 *Servingmen*. What, what, what? Let's partake.

3 *Servingman*. I would not be a Roman, of all nations;
180 I had as lief be a condemned man.

1, 2 *Servingmen*. Wherefore? wherefore?

3 *Servingman*. Why, here's he that was wont to thwack our general—Caius Marcius.

1 *Servingman*. Why do you say 'thwack our general'?

3 *Servingman*. I do not say 'thwack our general', but he was always good enough for him.

2 *Servingman*. Come, we are fellows and friends. He was ever too hard for him; I have heard him say
190 so himself.

1 *Servingman*. He was too hard for him directly. To say the troth on't, before Corioli he scotched him and notched him like a carbonado.

2 *Servingman*. An he had been cannibally given, he might have broiled and eaten him too.

1 *Servingman*. But more of thy news?

3 *Servingman*. Why, he is so made on here within as if he were son and heir to Mars; set at upper end o' th' table; no question asked him by any of the senators but
200 they stand bald before him. Our general himself makes a mistress of him; sanctifies himself with's hand, and turns up the white o' th' eye to his discourse. But the bottom of the news is, our general is cut i' th' middle and but one half of what he was yesterday, for the other has half by the entreaty and grant of the whole table. He'll go, he says, and sowl the porter of Rome gates by

th' ears; he will mow all down before him, and leave
his passage polled.

2 *Servingman*. And he's as like to do't as any man I can
imagine.   210

3 *Servingman*. Do't! he will do't; for look you, sir, he
has as many friends as enemies; which friends, sir, as it
were, durst not—look you, sir—show themselves, as we
term it, his friends whilst he's in dejectitude.

1 *Servingman*. Dejectitude! what's that?

3 *Servingman*. But when they shall see, sir, his crest
up again and the man in blood, they will out of their
burrows, like conies after rain, and revel all with him.

1 *Servingman*. But when goes this forward?

3 *Servingman*. To-morrow, to-day, presently. You   220
shall have the drum struck up this afternoon; 'tis as it
were a parcel of their feast, and to be executed ere they
wipe their lips.

2 *Servingman*. Why, then we shall have a stirring
world again. This peace is nothing but to rust iron,
increase tailors, and breed ballad-makers.

1 *Servingman*. Let me have war, say I; it exceeds
peace as far as day does night; it's sprightly, waking,
audible, and full of vent. Peace is a very apoplexy,
lethargy; mulled, deaf, sleepy, insensible; a getter of   230
more bastard children than war's a destroyer of men.

2 *Servingman*. 'Tis so: and as war in some sort may be
said to be a ravisher, so it cannot be denied but peace is
a great maker of cuckolds.

1 *Servingman*. Ay, and it makes men hate one another.

3 *Servingman*. Reason: because they then less need
one another. The wars for my money. I hope to see
Romans as cheap as Volscians. They are rising, they are
rising.

1, 2 *Servingmen*. In, in, in, in!   [*they hasten in* 240

[4. 6.]   *Rome.   A public place*

'*Enter the two Tribunes,* SICINIUS *and* BRUTUS'

Sicinius. We hear not of him, neither need we
    fear him.
His remedies are tame. The present peace
And quietness of the people, which before
Were in wild hurry, here do make his friends
Blush that the world goes well; who rather had,
Though they themselves did suffer by't, behold
Dissentious numbers pest'ring streets than see
Our tradesmen singing in their shops, and going
About their functions friendly.
10 *Brutus.* We stood to't in good time.

'*Enter* MENENIUS'

                              Is this Menenius?
Sicinius. 'Tis he, 'tis he. O, he is grown most kind
Of late. Hail, sir!
Menenius.   Hail to you both!
Sicinius. Your Coriolanus is not much missed
But with his friends. The commonwealth doth stand,
And so would do, were he more angry at it.
Menenius. All's well; and might have been much
    better, if
He could have temporized.
Sicinius.   Where is he, hear you?
Menenius. Nay, I hear nothing: his mother and
    his wife
Hear nothing from him.

'*Enter three or four Citizens*'

Citizens. The gods preserve you both!

Sicinius.   God-den, our neighbours. 20

Brutus. God-den to you all, god-den to you all.

1 *Citizen*. Ourselves, our wives, and children, on
   our knees,

Are bound to pray for you both.

Sicinius.   Live, and thrive!

Brutus. Farewell, kind neighbours: we
     wished Coriolanus

Had loved you as we did.

Citizens.   Now the gods keep you!

Both Tribunes. Farewell, farewell. [*Citizens pass on*

Sicinius. This is a happier and more comely time

Than when these fellows ran about the streets

Crying confusion.

Brutus.   Càius Marcius was

A worthy officer i' th' war, but insolent,   30

O'ercome with pride, ambitious past all thinking,

Self-loving—

Sicinius.   And affecting one sole throne,

Without assistance.

Menenius.   I think not so.

Sicinius. We should by this, to all our lamentation,

If he had gone forth consul, found it so.

Brutus. The gods have well prevented it, and Rome

Sits safe and still without him.

'*Enter an Ædile*'

Ædile.   Worthy tribunes,

There is a slave, whom we have put in prison,

Reports the Volsces with two several powers

Are ent'red in the Roman territories,   40

And with the deepest malice of the war

Destroy what lies before 'em.

Menenius.   'Tis Aufidius,

Who, hearing of our Marcius' banishment,
Thrusts forth his horns again into the world,
Which were inshelled when Marcius stood for Rome,
And durst not once peep out.
   Sicinius.   Come, what talk you
Of Marcius?
   Brutus. Go see this rumourer whipped. It cannot be
The Volsces dare break with us.
   Menenius.   Cannot be!
50 We have record that very well it can;
And three examples of the like hath been
Within my age. But reason with the fellow,
Before you punish him, where he heard this,
Lest you shall chance to whip your information
And beat the messenger who bids beware
Of what is to be dreaded.
   Sicinius.   Tell not me:
I know this cannot be.
   Brutus.   Not possible.

       'Enter a Messenger'

   Messenger. The nobles in great earnestness
      are going
All to the Senate House: some news is come
60 That turns their countenances.
   Sicinius.   'Tis this slave—
Go whip him 'fore the people's eyes—his raising,
Nothing but his report.
   Messenger.   Yes, worthy sir,
The slave's report is seconded; and more,
More fearful, is delivered.
   Sicinius.   What more fearful?
   Messenger. It is spoke freely out of many mouths—
How probable I do not know—that Marcius,

Joined with Aufidius, leads a power 'gainst Rome,
And vows revenge as spacious as between
The young'st and oldest thing.
  Sicinius.   This is most likely!
  Brutus. Raised only that the weaker sort may wish   70
Good Marcius home again.
  Sicinius.   The very trick on't.
  Menenius. This is unlikely:
He and Aufidius can no more atone
Than violent'st contrarieties.

Enter a second Messenger

  2 *Messenger.* You are sent for to the Senate.
A fearful army, led by Caius Marcius
Associated with Aufidius, rages
Upon our territories, and have already
O'erborne their way, consumed with fire, and took
What lay before them.   80

'*Enter COMINIUS*'

  Cominius. O, you have made good work!
  Menenius.   What news? what news?
  Cominius. You have holp to ravish your own
      daughters and
To melt the city leads upon your pates,
To see your wives dishonoured to your noses—
  Menenius. What's the news? what's the news?
  Cominius. Your temples burnéd in their cement, and
Your franchises, whereon you stood, confined
Into an auger's bore.
  Menenius.   Pray now, your news?—
You have made fair work, I fear me.—Pray, your news?—
If Marcius should be joined wi' th' Volscians—
  Cominius.   If!   90

He is their god; he leads them like a thing
Made by some other deity than Nature,
That shapes man better; and they follow him
Against us brats with no less confidence
Than boys pursuing summer butterflies,
Or butchers killing flies.

  Menenius.   You have made good work,
You and your apron-men; you that stood so much
Upon the voice of occupation and
The breath of garlic-eaters!

  Cominius.   He will shake
100 Your Rome about your ears.

  Menenius.   As Hercules
Did shake down mellow fruit. You have made
   fair work!

  Brutus. But is this true, sir?

  Cominius.   Ay; and you'll look pale
Before you find it other. All the regions
Do smilingly revolt, and who resist
Are mocked for valiant ignorance,
And perish constant fools. Who is't can blame him?
Your enemies and his find something in him.

  Menenius. We are all undone, unless
The noble man have mercy.

  Cominius.   Who shall ask it?
110 The tribunes cannot do't for shame; the people
Deserve such pity of him as the wolf
Does of the shepherds; for his best friends, if they
Should say 'Be good to Rome,' they charged
   him even
As those should do that had deserved his hate,
And therein showed like enemies.

  Menenius.   'Tis true:
If he were putting to my house the brand

That should consume it, I have not the face
To say 'Beseech you, cease.' You have made
    fair hands,
You and your crafts! you have crafted fair!
  Cominius.   You have brought
A trembling upon Rome, such as was never   120
S' incapable of help.
  Both Tribunes.   Say not we brought it.
  Menenius. How! Was't we? We loved him, but,
    like beasts
And cowardly nobles, gave way unto your clusters,
Who did hoot him out o' th' city.
  Cominius.   But I fear
They'll roar him in again. Tullus Aufidius,
The second name of men, obeys his points
As if he were his officer. Desperation
Is all the policy, strength, and defence,
That Rome can make against them.

        'Enter a troop of Citizens'

  Menenius.   Here come the clusters.
And is Aufidius with him? You are they   130
That made the air unwholesome when you cast
Your stinking greasy caps in hooting at
Coriolanus' exile. Now he's coming,
And not a hair upon a soldier's head
Which will not prove a whip; as many coxcombs
As you threw caps up will he tumble down,
And pay you for your voices. 'Tis no matter;
If he could burn us all into one coal,
We have deserved it.
  Citizens. Faith, we hear fearful news.
  1 Citizen.   For mine own part, 140
When I said banish him, I said 'twas pity.

2 *Citizen.* And so did I.

3 *Citizen.* And so did I; and, to say the truth, so did
very many of us. That we did, we did for the best; and
though we willingly consented to his banishment, yet
it was against our will.

Cominius. You're goodly things, you voices!

Menenius.   You have made
Good work, you and your cry! Shall's to the Capitol?

Cominius. O, ay, what else?

                              [*Cominius and Menenius go*

150 *Sicinius.* Go masters, get you home; be not dismayed;
These are a side that would be glad to have
This true which they so seem to fear. Go home,
And show no sign of fear.

1 *Citizen.* The gods be good to us! Come, masters,
let's home. I ever said we were i'th' wrong when we
banished him.

2 *Citizen.* So did we all. But come, let's home.

                              [*Citizens disperse*

Brutus. I do not like this news.

Sicinius. Nor I.

160 *Brutus.* Let's to the Capitol. Would half my wealth
Would buy this for a lie!

Sicinius.   Pray, let us go.   [*they go*

[4. 7.] *A camp at a small distance from Rome*

'*Enter AUFIDIUS with his Lieutenant*'

Aufidius. Do they still fly to th' Roman?

Lieutenant. I do not know what witchcraft's in
        him, but
Your soldiers use him as the grace 'fore meat,
Their talk at table and their thanks at end;

And you are dark'ned in this action sir,
Even by your own.
  Aufidius.   I cannot help it now,
Unless by using means I lame the foot
Of our design. He bears himself more proudlier,
Even to my person, than I thought he would
When first I did embrace him; yet his nature   10
In that's no changeling, and I must excuse
What cannot be amended.
  Lieutenant.   Yet I wish, sir—
I mean for your particular—you had not
Joined in commission with him, but either
Had borne the action of yourself, or else
To him had left it solely.
  Aufidius. I understand thee well; and be thou sure,
When he shall come to his account, he knows not
What I can urge against him. Although it seems,
And so he thinks, and is no less apparent   20
To th' vulgar eye, that he bears all things fairly
And shows good husbandry for the Volscian state,
Fights dragon-like, and does achieve as soon
As draw his sword; yet he hath left undone
That which shall break his neck or hazard mine,
Whene'er we come to our account.
  Lieutenant. Sir, I beseech you, think you he'll
     carry Rome?
  Aufidius. All places yield to him ere he sits down,
And the nobility of Rome are his;
The senators and patricians love him too.   30
The tribunes are no soldiers, and their people
Will be as rash in the repeal, as hasty
To expel him thence. I think he'll be to Rome
As is the osprey to the fish, who takes it
By sovereignty of nature. First he was

A noble servant to them, but he could not
Carry his honours even. Whether 'twas pride,
Which out of daily fortune ever taints
The happy man; whether defect of judgement,
40 To fail in the disposing of those chances
Which he was lord of; or whether nature,
Not to be other than one thing, not moving
From th' casque to th' cushion, but commanding peace
Even with the same austerity and garb
As he controlled the war; but one of these—
As he hath spices of them all—not all,
For I dare so far free him—made him feared,
So hated, and so banished: but he has a merit
To choke it in the utt'rance. So our virtues
50 Lie in th' interpretation of the time;
And power, unto itself most commendable,
Hath not a tomb so evident as a chair
T' extol what it hath done.
One fire drives out one fire; one nail, one nail;
Rights by rights falter, strengths by strengths do fail.
Come, let's away. When, Caius, Rome is thine,
Thou art poor'st of all; then shortly art thou mine.

                          [they go

[5. 1.]   *Rome. A public place*

'*Enter* MENENIUS, COMINIUS, SICINIUS, BRUTUS,
the two Tribunes, with others'

Menenius. No, I'll not go: you hear what he
    hath said
Which was sometime his general, who loved him
In a most dear particular. He called me father;
But what o' that? Go you that banished him,

A mile before his tent fall down, and knee
The way into his mercy. Nay, if he coyed
To hear Cominius speak, I'll keep at home.

  Cominius. He would not seem to know me.

  Menenius.   Do you hear?

  Cominius. Yet one time he did call me by my name.
I urged our old acquaintance, and the drops   10
That we have bled together. 'Coriolanus'
He would not answer to; forbad all names;
He was a kind of nothing, titleless,
Till he had forged himself a name i' th' fire
Of burning Rome.

  Menenius.   Why, so! You have made good work!
A pair of tribunes that have wrecked fair Rome
To make coals cheap—a noble memory!

  Cominius. I minded him how royal 'twas to pardon
When it was less expected; he replied,
It was a bare petition of a state   20
To one whom they had punished.

  Menenius.   Very well.
Could he say less?

  Cominius. I offered to awaken his regard
For 's private friends: his answer to me was,
He could not stay to pick them in a pile
Of noisome musty chaff. He said 'twas folly,
For one poor grain or two, to leave unburnt
And still to nose th' offence.

  Menenius.   For one poor grain or two!
I am one of those; his mother, wife, his child,
And this brave fellow too, we are the grains: 30
You are the musty chaff, and you are smelt
Above the moon. We must be burnt for you.

  Sicinius. Nay, pray, be patient: if you refuse your aid
In this so never-needed help, yet do not

Upbraid's with our distress. But, sure, if you
Would be your country's pleader, your good tongue,
More than the instant army we can make,
Might stop our countryman.

    Menenius.   No, I'll not meddle.

    Sicinius. Pray you, go to him.

    Menenius.   What should I do?

40 *Brutus.* Only make trial what your love can do
For Rome, towards Marcius.

    Menenius.   Well, and say that Marcius
Return me, as Cominius is returned,
Unheard—what then?
But as a discontented friend, grief-shot
With his unkindness? Say 't be so?

    Sicinius.   Yet your good will
Must have that thanks from Rome after the measure
As you intended well.

    Menenius.   I'll undertake 't:
I think he'll hear me. Yet to bite his lip
And hum at good Cominius much unhearts me.

50 He was not taken well; he had not dined:
The veins unfilled, our blood is cold, and then
We pout upon the morning, are unapt
To give or to forgive; but when we have stuffed
These pipes and these conveyances of our blood
With wine and feeding, we have suppler souls
Than in our priest-like fasts: therefore I'll watch him
Till he be dieted to my request,
And then I'll set upon him.

    Brutus. You know the very road into his kindness,

60 And cannot lose your way.

    Menenius.   Good faith, I'll prove him,
Speed how it will. I shall ere long have knowledge
Of my success.   *[goes*

Cominius.   He'll never hear him.
Sicinius.   Not?
Cominius. I tell you he does sit in gold, his eye
Red as 'twould burn Rome, and his injury
The gaoler to his pity. I kneeled before him;
'Twas very faintly he said 'Rise;' dismissed me
Thus with his speechless hand. What he would do
†He sent in writing after me; what he would not,
†Bound with an oath to yield to his conditions:
So that all hope is vain,   70
Unless his noble mother, and his wife—
Who, as I hear, mean to solicit him
For mercy to his country. Therefore, let's hence,
And with our fair entreaties haste them on.

                                        [*they go*

[5. 2.]   *Entrance of the Volscian camp before Rome*

        '*Enter* MENENIUS *to the Watch on Guard*'

 1 *Watch.* Stay. Whence are you?
 2 *Watch.*   Stand, and go back.
Menenius. You guard like men, 'tis well; but, by
        your leave,
I am an officer of state, and come
To speak with Coriolanus.
 1 *Watch.*   From whence?
Menenius.   From Rome.
 1 *Watch.* You may not pass, you must return:
        our general
Will no more hear from thence.
 2 *Watch.* You'll see your Rome embraced with
        fire, before
You'll speak with Coriolanus.

Menenius.   Good my friends,
If you have heard your general talk of Rome
10 And of his friends there, it is lots to blanks
My name hath touched your ears: it is Menenius.

  1 *Watch.* Be it so; go back. The virtue of
    your name
Is not here passable.

  Menenius.   I tell thee, fellow,
Thy general is my lover. I have been
The book of his good acts whence men have read
His fame unparalleled—haply amplified;
†For I have ever varnishéd my friends
(Of whom he's chief) with all the size that verity
Would without lapsing suffer: nay, sometimes,
20 Like to a bowl upon a subtle ground,
I have tumbled past the throw, and in his praise
Have almost stamped the leasing: therefore, fellow,
I must have leave to pass.

  1 *Watch.* Faith, sir, if you had told as many lies in his
behalf as you have uttered words in your own, you
should not pass here; no, though it were as virtuous to
lie as to live chastely. Therefore go back.

  Menenius. Prithee, fellow, remember my name is
Menenius, always factionary on the party of your
30 general.

  2 *Watch.* Howsoever you have been his liar, as you
say you have, I am one that, telling true under him,
must say you cannot pass. Therefore go back.

  Menenius. Has he dined, canst thou tell? For I would
not speak with him till after dinner.

  1 *Watch.* You are a Roman, are you?

  Menenius. I am, as thy general is.

  1 *Watch.* Then you should hate Rome, as he does.
Can you, when you have pushed out your gates the very

defender of them, and in a violent popular ignorance 40
given your enemy your shield, think to front his
revenges with the easy groans of old women, the
virginal palms of your daughters, or with the palsied
intercession of such a decayed dotant as you seem to be?
Can you think to blow out the intended fire your city is
ready to flame in, with such weak breath as this? No,
you are deceived; therefore, back to Rome, and prepare
for your execution. You are condemned; our general
has sworn you out of reprieve and pardon.

Menenius. Sirrah, if thy captain knew I were here, he 50
would use me with estimation.

2 *Watch.* Come, my captain knows you not.

Menenius. I mean, thy general.

1 *Watch.* My general cares not for you. Back, I say;
go, lest I let forth your half-pint of blood. Back—that's
the utmost of your having. Back.

Menenius. Nay, but, fellow, fellow—

'*Enter* CORIOLANUS *with* AUFIDIUS'

Coriolanus. What's the matter?

Menenius. Now, you companion, I'll say an errand
for you; you shall know now that I am in estimation; 60
you shall perceive that a Jack guardant cannot office me
from my son Coriolanus. Guess but by my entertainment with him if thou stand'st not i' th' state of hanging,
or of some death more long in spectatorship and crueller
in suffering; behold now presently, and swoon for
what's to come upon thee. [*to Coriolanus*] The glorious
gods sit in hourly synod about thy particular prosperity,
and love thee no worse than thy old father Menenius
does! O my son, my son! thou art preparing fire for us;
look thee, here's water to quench it. I was hardly moved 70
to come to thee; but being assured none but myself

could move thee, I have been blown out of your gates
with sighs; and conjure thee to pardon Rome and thy
petitionary countrymen. The good gods assuage thy
wrath, and turn the dregs of it upon this varlet here;
this, who, like a block, hath denied my access to thee.

Coriolanus. Away!

Menenius. How! away!

Coriolanus. Wife, mother, child, I know not. My affairs

80 Are servanted to others. Though I owe
My revenge properly, my remission lies
In Volscian breasts. That we have been familiar,
Ingrate forgetfulness shall poison rather
Than pity note how much. Therefore be gone.
Mine ears against your suits are stronger than
Your gates against my force. Yet, for I loved thee,
Take this along; I writ it for thy sake,
And would have sent it. [*gives him a letter.*] Another
    word, Menenius,
I will not hear thee speak. [*turns away*] This
    man, Aufidius,

90 Was my beloved in Rome: yet thou behold'st.

Aufidius. You keep a constant temper.

                  [*Coriolanus and Aufidius go*

1 *Watch.* Now, sir, is your name Menenius?

2 *Watch.* 'Tis a spell, you see, of much power. You
know the way home again.

1 *Watch.* Do you hear how we are shent for keeping
your greatness back?

2 *Watch.* What cause, do you think, I have to swoon?

Menenius. I neither care for th' world nor your
general: for such things as you, I can scarce think there's
100 any, you're so slight. He that hath a will to die by himself
fears it not from another. Let your general do his worst.

For you, be that you are, long; and your misery increase
with your age! I say to you, as I was said to, Away!

[*goes*

1 *Watch.* A noble fellow, I warrant him.
2 *Watch.* The worthy fellow is our general: he's the
rock, the oak not to be wind-shaken.   [*they go*

[5. 3.]   *The tent of Coriolanus*

CORIOLANUS *seated before it, in a chair of state with*
AUFIDIUS *and others about him*

Coriolanus. We will before the walls of Rome
      to-morrow
Set down our host. My partner in this action,
You must report to th' Volscian lords how plainly
I have borne this business.
Aufidius.   Only their ends
You have respected; stopped your ears against
The general suit of Rome; never admitted
A private whisper—no, not with such friends
That thought them sure of you.
Coriolanus.   This last old man,
Whom with a cracked heart I have sent to Rome,
Loved me above the measure of a father,   10
Nay, godded me indeed. Their latest refuge
Was to send him; for whose old love I have—
Though I showed sourly to him—once more offered
The first conditions, which they did refuse
And cannot now accept; to grace him only
That thought he could do more, a very little
I have yielded to. Fresh embassies and suits,
Nor from the state nor private friends, hereafter

Will I lend ear to. [*shouting heard*] Ha! what shout
   is this?
20 Shall I be tempted to infringe my vow
In the same time 'tis made? I will not.

'*Enter*', *in mourning habits*, '*Virgilia, Volumnia,
Valeria, young Marcius, with Attendants*'

[*Aside*] My wife comes foremost; then the
   honoured mould
Wherein this trunk was framed, and in her hand
The grandchild to her blood. But out, affection!
All bond and privilege of nature, break!
Let it be virtuous to be obstinate.
What is that curtsy worth? or those doves' eyes,
Which can make gods forsworn? I melt, and am not
Of stronger earth than others. My mother bows;
30 As if Olympus to a molehill should
In supplication nod: and my young boy
Hath an aspect of intercession which
Great Nature cries 'Deny not.' Let the Volsces
Plough Rome, and harrow Italy: I'll never
Be such a gosling to obey instinct, but stand
As if a man were author of himself
And knew no other kin.
   Virgilia.   My lord and husband!
   Coriolanus. These eyes are not the same I wore
      in Rome.
   Virgilia. The sorrow that delivers us thus changed
40 Makes you think so.
   (*Coriolanus.* [*rising*] Like a dull actor now
I have forgot my part and I am out,
Even to a full disgrace. [*goes to her*] Best of my flesh,
Forgive my tyranny; but do not say,
For that, 'Forgive our Romans.' O, a kiss

Long as my exile, sweet as my revenge!
Now, by the jealous queen of heaven, that kiss
I carried from thee, dear, and my true lip
Hath virgined it e'er since. You gods! I prate,
And the most noble mother of the world
Leave unsaluted. Sink, my knee, i' th' earth; ['*kneels*' 50
Of thy deep duty more impression show
Than that of common sons.

    Volumnia.   O, stand up blest!
Whilst with no softer cushion than the flint
I kneel before thee, and unproperly
Show duty, as mistaken all this while
Between the child and parent.   [*kneels*

    Coriolanus.   What's this?
Your knees to me? to your corrected son?   [*raises her*
Then let the pebbles on the hungry beach
Fillip the stars; then let the mutinous winds
Strike the proud cedars 'gainst the fiery sun,   60
Murd'ring impossibility, to make
What cannot be, slight work.

    Volumnia.   Thou art my warrior;
I holp to frame thee. Do you know this lady?

    Coriolanus. The noble sister of Publicola,
The moon of Rome, chaste as the icicle
That's curdied by the frost from purest snow
And hangs on Dian's temple—dear Valeria!

    Volumnia. [*showing young Marcius*] This is a poor
      epitome of yours,
Which by th' interpretation of full time
May show like all yourself.

    Coriolanus.   The god of soldiers,   70
With the consent of supreme Jove, inform
Thy thoughts with nobleness, that thou mayst prove
To shame unvulnerable, and stick i' th' wars

Like a great sea-mark, standing every flaw,
And saving those that eye thee!
 Volumnia.   Your knee, sirrah.
 Coriolanus. That's my brave boy!
 Volumnia. Even he, your wife, this lady, and myself
Are suitors to you.
 Coriolanus.   I beseech you, peace!
Or, if you'ld ask, remember this before:
80 The thing I have forsworn to grant may never
Be held by you denials. Do not bid me
Dismiss my soldiers, or capitulate
Again with Rome's mechanics. Tell me not
Wherein I seem unnatural; desire not
T' allay my rages and revenges with
Your colder reasons.
 Volumnia.   O, no more, no more!
You have said you will not grant us any thing;
For we have nothing else to ask but that
Which you deny already. Yet we will ask,
90 That, if you fail in our request, the blame
May hang upon your hardness: therefore hear us.
 Coriolanus. Aufidius, and you Volsces, mark;
  for we'll
Hear nought from Rome in private. [*sits*]
  Your request?
 Volumnia. Should we be silent and not speak,
  our raiment
And state of bodies would bewray what life
We have led since thy exile. Think with thyself
How more unfortunate than all living women
Are we come hither; since that thy sight, which should
Make our eyes flow with joy, hearts dance
  with comforts,
100 Constrains them weep and shake with fear and sorrow,

Making the mother, wife, and child, to see
The son, the husband, and the father, tearing
His country's bowels out. And to poor we
Thine enmity's most capital: thou barr'st us
Our prayers to the gods, which is a comfort
That all but we enjoy. For how can we,
Alas, how can we for our country pray,
Whereto we are bound, together with thy victory,
Whereto we are bound? Alack, or we must lose
The country, our dear nurse, or else thy person,   110
Our comfort in the country. We must find
An evident calamity, though we had
Our wish, which side should win; for either thou
Must as a foreign recreant be led
With manacles thorough our streets, or else
Triumphantly tread on thy country's ruin,
And bear the palm for having bravely shed
Thy wife and children's blood. For myself, son,
I purpose not to wait on fortune till
These wars determine: if I can not persuade thee   120
Rather to show a noble grace to both parts
Than seek the end of one, thou shalt no sooner
March to assault thy country than to tread—
Trust to't, thou shalt not—on thy mother's womb,
That brought thee to this world.
   Virgilia.   Ay, and mine,
That brought you forth this boy, to keep your name
Living to time.
   Boy.   A' shall not tread on me;
I'll run away till I am bigger, but then I'll fight.
   Coriolanus. Not of a woman's tenderness to be,
Requires nor child nor woman's face to see.   130
I have sat too long.   [*rising*
   Volumnia.   Nay, go not from us thus.

If it were so that our request did tend
To save the Romans, thereby to destroy
The Volsces whom you serve, you might condemn us,
As poisonous of your honour: no; our suit
Is, that you reconcile them: while the Volsces
May say 'This mercy we have showed,' the Romans,
'This we received;' and each in either side
Give the all-hail to thee, and cry 'Be blest
140 For making up this peace!' Thou know'st, great son,
The end of war's uncertain; but this certain,
That, if thou conquer Rome, the benefit
Which thou shalt thereby reap is such a name
Whose repetition will be dogged with curses;
Whose chronicle thus writ: 'The man was noble,
But with his last attempt he wiped it out,
Destroyed his country, and his name remains
To th' ensuing age abhorred.' Speak to me, son:
Thou hast affected the fine strains of honour,
150 To imitate the graces of the gods;
To tear with thunder the wide cheeks o' th' air,
And yet to charge thy sulphur with a bolt
That should but rive an oak. Why dost not speak?
Think'st thou it honourable for a noble man
Still to remember wrongs? Daughter, speak you:
He cares not for your weeping. Speak thou, boy:
Perhaps thy childishness will move him more
Than can our reasons. There's no man in the world
More bound to 's mother, yet here he lets me prate
160 Like one i' th' stocks. Thou hast never in thy life
Showed thy dear mother any courtesy,
When she, poor hen, fond of no second brood,
Has clucked thee to the wars, and safely home
Loaden with honour. Say my request's unjust,
And spurn me back; but if it be not so,

Thou art not honest, and the gods will plague thee,
That thou restrain'st from me the duty which
To a mother's part belongs. He turns away:
Down, ladies; let us shame him with our knees.
To his surname Coriolanus 'longs more pride   170
Than pity to our prayers. Down: an end;

                            [*The four all kneel*

This is the last: so we will home to Rome,
And die among our neighbours. Nay, behold's!
This boy, that cannot tell what he would have,
But kneels and holds up hands for fellowship,
Does reason our petition with more strength
Than thou hast to deny 't. Come, let us go: [*They rise*
This fellow had a Volscian to his mother;
His wife is in Corioli, and his child
Like him by chance. Yet give us our dispatch.   180
I am hushed until our city be a-fire,   [*he turns*
And then I'll speak a little.

  Coriolanus. ['*Holds her by the hand, silent*']

                     O mother, mother!
What have you done? Behold, the heavens do ope,
The gods look down, and this unnatural scene
They laugh at. O my mother, mother! O!
You have won a happy victory to Rome;
But, for your son—believe it, O, believe it—
Most dangerously you have with him prevailed,
If not most mortal to him. But let it come.
Aufidius, though I cannot make true wars,   190
I'll frame convenient peace. Now, good Aufidius,
Were you in my stead, would you have heard
A mother less? or granted less, Aufidius?
  Aufidius. I was moved withal.
  Coriolanus.   I dare be sworn you were!

And, sir, it is no little thing to make
Mine eyes to sweat compassion. But, good sir,
What peace you'll make, advise me: for my part,
I'll not to Rome, I'll back with you; and pray you
Stand to me in this cause. O mother! wife!

[speaks with them apart

200 (*Aufidius.* I am glad thou hast set thy mercy and
thy honour
At difference in thee. Out of that I'll work
Myself a former fortune.
   Coriolanus. [*coming forward with Volumnia and*
      Virgilia]   Ay, by and by;
But we will drink together; and you shall bear
A better witness back than words, which we
On like conditions will have counter-sealed.
Come, enter with us. Ladies, you deserve
To have a temple built you. All the swords
In Italy, and her confederate arms,
Could not have made this peace.

[they enter the tent

[5.4.]   *Rome. A street not far from the gate*

'*Enter* MENENIUS *and* SICINIUS'

   Menenius. See you yond coign o' th' Capitol, yond
cornerstone?
   Sicinius. Why, what of that?
   Menenius. If it be possible for you to displace it with
your little finger, there is some hope the ladies of Rome,
especially his mother, may prevail with him. But I say
there is no hope in't: our throats are sentenced, and stay
upon execution.
   Sicinius. Is't possible that so short a time can alter the
10 condition of a man?

Menenius. There is difference between a grub and a butterfly; yet your butterfly was a grub. This Marcius is grown from man to dragon: he has wings; he's more than a creeping thing.

Sicinius. He loved his mother dearly.

Menenius. So did he me: and he no more remembers his mother now than an eight-year-old horse. The tartness of his face sours ripe grapes; when he walks, he moves like an engine and the ground shrinks before his treading. He is able to pierce a corslet with his eye, 20 talks like a knell, and his hum is a battery. He sits in his state as a thing made for Alexander. What he bids be done is finished with his bidding. He wants nothing of a god but eternity and a heaven to throne in.

Sicinius. Yes, mercy, if you report him truly.

Menenius. I paint him in the character. Mark what mercy his mother shall bring from him: there is no more mercy in him than there is milk in a male tiger; that shall our poor city find. And all this is 'long of you.

Sicinius. The gods be good unto us!   30

Menenius. No, in such a case the gods will not be good unto us. When we banished him, we respected not them; and, he returning to break our necks, they respect not us.

         '*Enter a Messenger*'

Messenger. Sir, if you'ld save your life, fly to
     your house:
The plebeians have got your fellow-tribune,
And hale him up and down; all swearing if
The Roman ladies bring not comfort home
They'll give him death by inches.

         '*Enter another Messenger*'

Sicinius.   What's the news?

40   2 *Messenger.* Good news, good news! The ladies
              have prevailed,
      The Volscians are dislodged, and Marcius gone.
      A merrier day did never yet greet Rome,
      No, not th' expulsion of the Tarquins.
         Sicinius.   Friend,
      Art thou certain this is true? Is't most certain?
         2 *Messenger.* As certain as I know the sun is fire.
      Where have you lurked, that you make doubt of it?
      Ne'er through an arch so hurried the blown tide,
      As the recomforted through the gates. Why, hark you!

         '*Trumpets, hautboys, drums, beat, all together*'

      The trumpets, sackbuts, psalteries, and fifes,
50   Tabors and cymbals, and the shouting Romans,
      Make the sun dance. ['*a shout*'] Hark you!
         Menenius.   This is good news.
      I will go meet the ladies. This Volumnia
      Is worth of consuls, senators, patricians,
      A city full; of tribunes such as you,
      A sea and land full. You have prayed well to-day:
      This morning for ten thousand of your throats
      I'ld not have given a doit. [*shouts, trumpets, etc. heard
              louder*] Hark, how they joy!
      Sicinius. First, the gods bless you for your tidings; next,
      Accept my thankfulness.
         2 *Messenger.*   Sir, we have all
60   Great cause to give great thanks.
         Sicinius.   They are near the city!
         2 *Messenger.* Almost at point to enter.
         Sicinius.   We will meet them,
      And help the joy.   [*they go towards the gate*

[5. 5.] *Enter in procession the Ladies with a great press
of Senators, Patricians and People*

1 *Senator.* Behold our patroness, the life of Rome!
Call all your tribes together, praise the gods,
And make triumphant fires; strew flowers before them.
Unshout the noise that banished Marcius,
Repeal him with the welcome of his mother;
Cry 'Welcome, ladies, welcome!'
  All.   Welcome, ladies,
Welcome!
      [*they pass on; 'a flourish with drums and trumpets'*

[5. 6.]   *Corioli. A public place*
   '*Enter TULLUS AUFIDIUS, with Attendants*'

Aufidius. Go tell the lords o' th' city I am here:
Deliver them this paper: having read it,
Bid them repair to th' market-place, where I,
Even in theirs and in the commons' ears,
Will vouch the truth of it. Him I accuse
The city ports by this hath entered, and
Intends t' appear before the people, hoping
To purge himself with words. Dispatch.
                    [*Attendants go*

'*Enter three or four Conspirators of AUFIDIUS' faction*'

Most welcome!
  1 *Conspirator.* How is it with our general?
  Aufidius.   Even so   10
As with a man by his own alms empoisoned,
And with his charity slain.
  2 *Conspirator.*   Most noble sir,

If you do hold the same intent wherein
You wished us parties, we'll deliver you
Of your great danger.

   Aufidius.   Sir, I cannot tell;
We must proceed as we do find the people.

   3 *Conspirator.* The people will remain uncertain whilst
'Twixt you there's difference; but the fall of either
Makes the survivor heir of all.

   Aufidius.   I know it,
20 And my pretext to strike at him admits
A good construction. I raised him, and I pawned
Mine honour for his truth; who being so heightened,
He watered his new plants with dews of flattery,
Seducing so my friends; and, to this end,
He bowed his nature, never known before
But to be rough, unswayable, and free.

   3 *Conspirator.* Sir, his stoutness
When he did stand for consul, which he lost
By lack of stooping—

   Aufidius.   That I would have spoke of.
30 Being banished for't, he came unto my hearth;
Presented to my knife his throat: I took him,
Made him joint-servant with me; gave him way
In all his own desires; nay, let him choose
Out of my files, his projects to accomplish,
My best and freshest men; served his designments
In mine own person; holp to reap the fame
Which he did end all his; and took some pride
To do myself this wrong: till at the last
I seemed his follower, not partner; and
40 He waged me with his countenance, as if
I had been mercenary.

   1 *Conspirator.*   So he did, my lord:
The army marvelled at it; and, in the last,

When he had carried Rome and that we looked
For no less spoil than glory—
  Aufidius.   There was it;
For which my sinews shall be stretched upon him.
At a few drops of women's rheum, which are
As cheap as lies, he sold the blood and labour
Of our great action: therefore shall he die,
And I'll renew me in his fall. But hark!

     '*Drums and trumpets sound, with great shouts
              of the people*'

  1 *Conspirator.* Your native town you entered like   50
      a post,
And had no welcomes home; but he returns,
Splitting the air with noise.
  1 *Conspirator.*   And patient fools,
Whose children he hath slain, their base throats tear
With giving him glory.
  3 *Conspirator.*   Therefore, at your vantage,
Ere he express himself or move the people
With what he would say, let him feel your sword,
Which we will second. When he lies along,
After your way his tale pronounced shall bury
His reasons with his body.
  Aufidius.   Say no more:
Here come the lords.   60

     '*Enter the Lords of the city*'

  Lords. You are most welcome home.
  Aufidius.   I have not deserved it.
But, worthy lords, have you with heed perused
What I have written to you?
  Lords.   We have.
  1 *Lord.*   And grieve to hear 't.

What faults he made before the last, I think
Might have found easy fines; but there to end
Where he was to begin, and give away
The benefit of our levies, answering us
With our own charge, making a treaty where
There was a yielding—this admits no excuse.

70 *Aufidius.* He approaches: you shall hear him.

'*Enter* CORIOLANUS, *marching with drum and colours;
the commoners being with him*'

Coriolanus. Hail, lords! I am returned your soldier;
No more infected with my country's love
Than when I parted hence, but still subsisting
Under your great command. You are to know
That prosperously I have attempted, and
With bloody passage led your wars even to
The gates of Rome. Our spoils we have brought home
Doth more than counterpoise a full third part
The charges of the action. We have made peace
80 With no less honour to the Antiates
Than shame to th' Romans; and we here deliver,
Subscribed by th' consuls and patricians,
Together with the seal o' th' senate, what
We have compounded on.

Aufidius.   Read it not, noble lords;
But tell the traitor in the highest degree
He hath abused your powers.

Coriolanus. Traitor! how now!

Aufidius.   Ay, traitor, Marcius!

Coriolanus.   Marcius!

Aufidius. Ay, Marcius, Caius Marcius! Dost
      thou think
I'll grace thee with that robbery, thy stol'n name
90 Coriolanus, in Corioli?

You lords and heads o' th' state, perfidiously
He has betrayed your business and given up,
For certain drops of salt, your city Rome,
I say 'your city', to his wife and mother;
Breaking his oath and resolution, like
A twist of rotten silk; never admitting
Counsel o' th' war; but at his nurse's tears
He whined and roared away your victory;
That pages blushed at him and men of heart
Looked wond'ring each at other.

  Coriolanus.   Hear'st thou, Mars? 100
  Aufidius. Name not the god, thou boy of tears!
  Coriolanus.   Ha!
  Aufidius. No more.
  Coriolanus. Measureless liar, thou hast made
      my heart
Too great for what contains it. 'Boy!' O slave!
Pardon me, lords, 'tis the first time that ever
I was forced to scold. Your judgements, my
      grave lords,
Must give this cur the lie: and his own notion—
Who wears my stripes impressed upon him; that
Must bear my beating to his grave—shall join
To thrust the lie unto him.   110

  1 Lord. Peace, both, and hear me speak.
  Coriolanus. Cut me to pieces, Volsces; men
      and lads,
Stain all your edges on me. 'Boy'! False hound!
If you have writ your annals true, 'tis there,
That, like an eagle in a dove-cote, I
Fluttered your Volscians in Corioli.
Alone I did it. 'Boy!'
  Aufidius.   Why, noble lords,
Will you be put in mind of his blind fortune,

Which was your shame, by this unholy braggart,
120 'Fore your own eyes and ears?

    The Conspirators.   Let him die for't.

    The People. 'Tear him to pieces.' 'Do it presently.'
'He killed my son.' 'My daughter.' 'He killed my
cousin Marcus.' 'He killed my father.'

    2 Lord. Peace, ho! no outrage: peace!
The man is noble, and his fame folds in
This orb o' th' earth. His last offences to us
Shall have judicious hearing. Stand, Aufidius,
And trouble not the peace.

    Coriolanus.   O that I had him,
With six Aufidiuses or more—his tribe,
130 To use my lawful sword!

    Aufidius.   Insolent villain!

    The conspirators. Kill, kill, kill, kill, kill him!

    The Conspirators draw, and kill Coriolanus:
        Aufidius stands on his body

    Lords.   Hold, hold, hold, hold!

    Aufidius. My noble masters, hear me speak.

    1 Lord.   O Tullus!

    2 Lord. Thou hast done a deed whereat valour
        will weep.

    3 Lord. Tread not upon him. Masters all, be quiet;
Put up your swords.

    Aufidius. My lords, when you shall know—as in
        this rage
Provoked by him, you cannot—the great danger
Which this man's life did owe you, you'll rejoice
That he is thus cut off. Please it your honours
140 To call me to your senate, I'll deliver
Myself your loyal servant, or endure
Your heaviest censure.

1 *Lord.*   Bear from hence his body,
And mourn you for him. Let him be regarded
As the most noble corse that ever herald
Did follow to his urn.
   2 *Lord.*   His own impatience
Takes from Aufidius a great part of blame.
Let's make the best of it.
   Aufidius.   My rage is gone,
And I am struck with sorrow. Take him up:
Help, three o' th' chiefest soldiers; I'll be one.
Beat thou the drum, that it speak mournfully: **150**
Trail your steel pikes. Though in this city he
Hath widowed and unchilded many a one,
Which to this hour bewail the injury,
Yet he shall have a noble memory.
Assist.

       ['*exeunt bearing away the body of Coriolanus;*
                     a dead march sounded']

THE COPY FOR
CORIOLANUS, 1623

The following is taken, with slight modifications and the addition of a few sentences at the end, from my introduction to a facsimile of the Folio text published in 1928 by Messrs Faber and Faber, and is here reprinted with the kind permission of Mr Richard de la Mare. Textual research since 1928 does not seem seriously to have called its conclusions in question, as may be seen by comparison with the section on *Coriolanus* in Sir Walter Greg's *The Shakespeare First Folio* (1955), which, however, readers will do well to consult and details from which will be found quoted in the Notes below.

* * *

Coriolanus has an indifferent reputation with most editors. 'The text', declared Clark and Wright, 'abounds with errors, due probably to the carelessness or the illegibility of the transcript from which it was printed.'[1] It certainly contains some fifty or sixty words which have been condemned as corrupt and corrected in most modern editions—at first sight a large number for one play. It also suffers, as we shall presently see, from a strange malady in the arrangement of the verse. Yet such things are as likely to occur in a play printed direct from the author's manuscript as in one printed from a transcript; and, in any case, if the compositors had a transcript before them for the printing of *Corio-*

---

[1] *The Cambridge Shakespeare* (2nd ed. 1892), vol. VI, p. x. It is interesting to note that in 1898 E. K. Chambers was inclined to agree with this verdict; see p. vii of his edition of *Coriolanus* in the Warwick Shakespeare.

lanus— as they may have done—it was probably a pretty faithful copy of the original, since both the virtues and the vices of the Folio text are more readily assignable to the hand of Shakespeare than to another's.

Among the virtues must be reckoned first of all the full and elaborate stage-directions, almost as full as those in *The Tempest*, and perhaps necessitated, as in 1921 I suggested the latter might have been,[1] by the author's absence in Stratford at the time the play was being rehearsed. It is interesting, too, to find that this elaborately prepared text heads the section of Folio tragedies (for *Troilus and Cressida* which now stands first was thrust in as an afterthought) just as *The Tempest* heads the section of Folio comedies. If the position of the latter was due to its excellence and beauty, is it not possible that the manuscript of *Coriolanus* seemed to possess similar qualities in the eyes of those responsible for the order of the plays in 1623? One thing may at least be said with some confidence. These stage-directions are not the additions of an editor. They are obviously directions actually written for performance. They may also have been in the same handwriting as the dialogue, since the misprints *Annius* for *Iunius* in the stage-direction at 1. 1. 225, and *Athica* for *Ithaca* in the dialogue at 1. 3. 85 raise suspicion that the same hand penned both words, a hand accustomed to form its capital *I* in a fashion that might lead an unwary compositor to read *A*.[2]

Another virtue of this text is the spelling. It is spelling which, as some of those familiar with Shakespearian primary texts will agree, is probably in part Shakespeare's own. All the more amusing, therefore, is

[1] See the 'Note on the Copy', p. 80, *The Tempest* (N.S.), 1921.

[2] See note 1. 6. 84. The alternative is to suppose that the compositor's italic upper case was 'foul'.

it to find that quite a fair proportion of the few dozen 'misprints' noted above as forming part of the charge against the Folio printers are nothing but Shakespearian spellings. Shakespeare for instance, like other scribes of his time, often preferred *-les* to *-lesse*, the alternative forms of the termination we now uniformly write *-less*. When therefore we read, at 2.1. 231,

> The Naples Vesture of Humilitie,

it is perhaps unfair to register the second word as a misprint because it suggests the name of an Italian town to some editors ignorant of Elizabethan orthography. But the spellings which will probably seem most strange to the modern reader's eye are the abbreviations, all thoroughly characteristic of a late Shakespearian play, and yet in large quantities carefully expanded by Shakespeare's editors. Expressions like *i'th*, *a'th*, *too'th*, *for'th*, *by'th*, *for't*, *th'accusation*, *too's* (=to his), *upon's* (=upon us), abound and should be retained,[1] especially in this breathless play where they contribute very materially to the total effect. As George Gordon, the first serious defender of the text among modern editors, has well written, 'It would be difficult to say how much of the original rapidity has been lost' by the expansion of these abbreviated forms in modern texts. The changes 'are slight in themselves, but spread them over two thousand lines of active speech, as the editors have done, and they tell. They are like grit on the wheel of the action. Everything moves a little slower on account of them.'[2]

In a word, the text is very far from being one of the worst in the Folio, as some would have us believe.

---

[1] In a more modern form, when necessary, to prevent misunderstanding.

[2] *Coriolanus*, ed. by G. S. Gordon (Oxford, 1911), p. xxii.

Compare it with *The Merry Wives* or *Measure for Measure* and it seems almost a paragon of perfection. On the other hand, its superficial defects make it a much more interesting study than some cleaner texts, the cleanliness of which we suspect to be that of a copyist who has in transcribing obliterated the traces of the original he worked from. Its punctuation—despite some serious lapses, most of them we presume due to lack of guidance in the copy—is on the whole quite respectable and in places brilliant. And even those misprints which are true errors are often illuminating for the glimpses they seem to give us of the original manuscript.

To take one or two instances. Four times the words 'one' and 'on' are confused (1. 1. 16; 1. 2. 4; 2. 2. 79; 3. 1. 143), and three times the word 'shout' appears in print as 'shoot' (1. 1. 213; 1. 9. 50; 5. 5. 4). Both errors are to be accounted for by peculiarities in Shakespeare's spelling, and parallels to them are to be found in the Quartos.[1] Again Shakespeare is known to have been careless in the formation of his letters like *m, n, u, i, a,* etc., involving minim-strokes, a carelessness which explains misprints such as 'taintingly' for 'tauntingly' (1. 1. 109) and 'Lucius' for 'Lartius' (1. 1. 238), while the misprint of 'change' for 'charge' (5. 3. 152) likewise springs from the similarity between Shakespeare's *r*'s and *n*'s. Another trick of Shakespearian penmanship was the practice of using a capital *C* initially, for no apparent reason save that it was an easy letter to form. No doubt the prompter at the Globe Theatre knew this and other idiosyncracies and was not put off by them. But a compositor might be led seriously astray by a capital of this kind, which he would be likely to

[1] E.g. *L.L.L.* (Q.) 4. 1. 147 S.D., 'shoot within'; 'on' for 'one' three times in *R.J.* (Q2); and 'one' for 'on' twice in *Ado* (Q.), twice in *R.J.* (Q2), etc.

take as marking the beginning of a new sentence. We have a clear case of this at 4. 1. 5, which should run:

That common chances common men could bear,

but which the Folio prints:

That common chances. Common men could beare,

Of the four words in this line beginning with *c* Shakespeare's pen (for Shakespeare's mind can scarcely be said to have been responsible) elected to spell one with a capital letter; small blame to the compositor for supposing a fresh sentence was intended and inserting a period. The foregoing illustration brings us to the most entertaining corruption in the whole text. Enter to Volumnia and Virgilia at 1. 3. 25 a waiting gentlewoman announcing the approach of Valeria. Whereupon follows Volumnia's discourse on the loveliness of bloody brows in men and warriors, a discourse which the Folio concludes thus:

> The brests of *Hecuba*
> When she did suckle *Hector*, look'd not louelier
> Then *Hectors* forhead, when it spit forth blood
> At Grecian sword. *Contenning*, tell *Valeria*
> We are fit to bid her welcome.

The last line but one, as Collier finally rectified it, should read:

At Grecian swords, contemning. Tell Valeria

But how came the Folio compositor to corrupt the text so absurdly? The answer, I think, is that Shakespeare led him astray first by beginning 'contemning' with his favourite capital *C*, and then by writing the *mn* with a minim short so that it became *nn*, the result being that the puzzled compositor took the word as the name of the gentlewoman, set it up in the appropriate italics, and inserted a period to make all well.

The most interesting irregularity in the F. text, however, is the apparently spasmodic misdivision of the verse lines. We get throughout a succession of patches in which the verse has been printed in lines that either exceed or fall short of the required length. Gordon, who makes a valiant attempt to justify the text here also, quotes these two passages from it:

I. 6. 55–9.

I do beseech you,
By all the Battailles wherein we haue fought,
By th' Blood we haue shed together,
By th' Vowes we haue made
To endure Friends, that you directly set me
Against *Affidious*, and his *Antiats*

I. 9. 13–17

Pray now, no more:
My Mother, who ha 's a Charter to extoll her Bloud,
When she do's prayse me, grieues me:
I haue done as you haue done, that's what I can,
Induc'd as you haue beene, that's for my Countrey:

and comments upon them and upon a similarly irregularly divided speech in *Macbeth*[1] as follows:

The abrupt irregular beat of their divisions is the beat which the voice follows and which the ear expects. This, we feel, is how a good actor would declaim them. Readers who read only with the eye, and who are better pleased by smoothness and regularity than by any irregularity however dramatic, should be reminded that, whatever audience Shakespeare wrote for, he did not write for them. He wrote for the stage, not for the study; for playgoers, not for poets; for the ear, not for the eye. He wrote to be heard.[2]

[1] 2. 2. 1–8.
[2] *Op. cit.* p. xx. Gordon wrote this in 1912, thirty-six years before Dr Flatter published *Shakespeare's Producing Hand.*

Yet he is obliged to admit that this only holds good for a small percentage of the irregular lines, while he seems to ignore the fact that the malady is generally confined to short speeches and is specially liable to occur at the beginning or end of speeches in rapid dialogue.

* * *

Indeed, I came to the conclusion, when I edited *Antony and Cleopatra* in 1950, a F. text similar in many respects to that of *Coriolanus*, that such misdivisions were almost, if not wholly, due to the printer. The first of Gordon's two illustrations, for example, contains the long verse line

> By th' Blood we haue shed together, by th' Vowes

which the compositor could not possibly squeeze into the F. column and had therefore to do as best he could with the lining for the rest of the speech.[1] Why he departed from normality in the second illustration it would be difficult to say but that he and not Shakespeare was responsible seems suggested by the fact that the irregularity is not confined to the speech quoted but embraces the first three and a half lines of the speech following. I think it very doubtful therefore whether we need look for the origin of this mislineation beyond Jaggard's printing-office and have found it safer in general to follow the traditional arrangement in the *Cambridge Shakespeare* (1892). I am not overlooking Professor G. B. Harrison's valiant attempt to justify the F. lineation of *Coriolanus*.[2] But at the risk of being set down with Aldis Wright as a slave of 'that inspiring

[1] This point was first made in an anonymous review of the 1928 facsimile of *Coriolanus* in the *Times Literary Supplement* of 8 March 1928, a review I discovered after his death to have been written by Alfred Pollard.

[2] 'A Note on *Coriolanus*', pp. 239–52, *Adams Memorial Studies* (1948).

instrument—the metronome' I find myself uncon-
vinced by the professor's elaborate exegesis of the opening fifty-three lines of 1. 9 in the F. text and observe
that he makes no reference to the problems of casting-
off, width of the double-column, etc., which faced
Jaggard's compositors when setting up Shakespeare's
verse in F. and undoubtedly account for a fair, if not
the major, proportion of the lineation in dispute.

Since I wrote in 1928 the possibility that the
prompter or bookholder might jot down supplementary
or alternative stage-directions in the margin of an author's
foul papers, as he read it through preparatory to the
construction of the prompt book, has become generally
recognised.[1] And Greg (*Sh.'s First Folio* pp. 405–6)
suggests that the 'Cornets' in F. at 1.10.1 and 2.1.201
may be such prompter's additions. To these I should
like to add 'Coriolanus stands' at 2.2.34 which is inconsistent with other S.D.s (presumably Sh.'s) in the
scene and looks like something tagged on to the general
entry at that point.

[1] The credit, such as it is, of first recognizing this
possibility can I believe be shared by Greg and myself.
See p. 111 of my *Richard II* (1932), p. 118 of my *Henry VI*
pt 3 (1952) and p. 30 of Greg's *Editorial Problem* (1942).

NOTES

All significant departures from F. are recorded; the name of the text or edition in which the accepted reading first appeared being placed in brackets. Such names followed by + (e.g. Mal.+ or Camb.+) mean that the reading has apparently been followed by all edd. since (e.g. Malone or Aldis Wright), while a formula like Al.<Theob. or Warb.+C. J. S. means that a modern ed. has revived an earlier reading. Line-numeration for references to plays not yet printed in this edition is that found in Bartlett's *Concordance* and the *Globe Shakespeare*.

F. stands for the First Folio (1623); G. for Glossary; O.E.D. for *The Oxford English Dictionary*; S.D. for stage-direction; S.H. for speech-heading; Sh. for Shakespeare and Shakesperian; Plut. or North for Plutarch's *Parallel Lives of Greeks and Romans* (*c.* A.D. 100), translated by Sir Thomas North, 1579 (vol. VIII of *North's Plutarch*, ed. George Wyndham 1895 in *The Tudor Translations*); sp.=spelling or spelt; common words (e.g. prob.=probably), names of characters, plays or poems by Sh. and titles of other well-known works are also abbreviated.

The following is a list of the books cited with abridged titles: Abbott=*A Sh. Grammar* by E. A. Abbott, 1869 (3rd ed., 1873); Al.=ed. of Sh. by Peter Alexander, 1951; Amyot=*Les vies des Hommes Illustres, Grecs et Romains* (transl. of Plut.) by Jacques Amyot, 1559; Anders=*Sh.'s Books*, by H. R. D. Anders, 1904; Arcadia=*The Countess of Pembroke's Arcadia*, by Sir Philip Sidney, 1590 (ed. Feuillerat, 1912); Bacon, *Adv. Learning*=*The Advancement of Learning*, by Francis Bacon, 1605; Baldwin=*Sh.'s Small Latine and Lesse Greeke*, by T. W. Baldwin, 2 vols., 1944; B.C.P.

=Book of Common Prayer; Beeching=ed. by H. C.
Beeching (*Henry Irving Sh.*), 1889 (and in *Falcon Sh.*),
1890; Ben Jonson=*Works of Ben Jonson*, ed. by C. H.
Herford and Percy Simpson, 11 vols., 1925–52 (*The
Silent Woman*, vol. v, 1938); Bond=*Works of John
Lyly*, ed. by R. W. Bond, 1902; Bradley=*Sh. Tragedy*,
by A. C. Bradley, 1904; Bradley, *Coriolanus* in Proc.
British Academy 1911–12, and in *A Miscellany*, 1929;
Brooke=ed. by C. Tucker Brooke (*Yale Sh.*, 1917 sqq.);
Browne, ed. Sayle=*Works of Sir Thomas Browne*, ed. by
Charles Sayle, 1912; Browne, *Vulgar Errors* = *Pseudo-
doxia Epidemica, or Enquiries into very many...commonly
presumed Truths*, by Sir Thomas Browne (*Works*, ed.
Geoffrey Keynes, vol. 2, 1928); Browne, *Rel. Med.*=
Religio Medici, by Sir Thomas Browne, 1642 (Golden
Treasury ed. 1901); Camb.=*The Cambridge Sh.* (2nd
ed. 1892) by W. Aldis Wright; Camden=*Remaines of
a Greater Worke, concerning Britaine, etc.*, by William
Camden, 1605; Cap.=ed. of Sh. by Edward Capell,
1768; Cap. *Notes*=*Notes on Sh.* by Edward Capell,
1794; Case=ed. by W. J. Craig and R. H. Case
(*Arden Sh.*), 1922; C.J.S.=ed. of Sh. by C. J. Sisson
[1954]; C.J.S., *N.R.*=*New Readings in Sh.*, by C. J.
Sisson (2 vols.), 1956; Clar.=ed. by W. Aldis Wright
(*Clarendon Sh.*), 1879; Coleridge=*Coleridge's Sh.
Criticism*, ed. by T. M. Raysor, 2 vols., 1930; Coll.=
ed. by J. P. Collier, 1844; Coll. ii=*Notes and Emenda-
tions to the Text of Sh.'s Plays*, 1853; Craig, see O.S.;
Deighton=ed. by K. Deighton, 1891; Delius=ed. of
Sh. by N. Delius (3rd ed.) 1872; Drayton, *Polyolbion*=
The Poly-Olbion, by Michael Drayton, ed. J. W.
Hebble (vol. 4 of Drayton's *Works*), 1933; Dyce=ed.
of Sh. by Alexander Dyce (5th ed.), 1886; E.D.D.=
The English Dialect Dictionary, by Joseph Wright,
1898–1905; Edwards=*Canons of Criticism*, by Thomas
Edwards (3rd ed.) 1750; E.K.C.=ed. by E. K.

Chambers (*Warwick Sh.*), 1898; Franz=*Die Sprache Shakespeares* (*Sh. Grammatik*, 4 Auflage), by Wilhelm Franz, 1939; Furn.=ed. in Variorum Sh., by H. H. Furness Jr.; 1913; G.-B.=*Prefaces to Sh.* (5th series), by H. Granville-Barker, 1947; G.G.=ed. by George S. Gordon, 1912; Greg, *Sh. F.F.*=*The Sh. First Folio*, by Sir W. W. Greg, 1955; Grosart=*The Works of Robert Greene*, ed. by A. B. Grosart (12 vols. *The Huth Library*) 1881–3; Han.=ed. of Sh. by Sir Thomas Hanmer, 1743–4; Herf.=ed. by C. H. Herford (*Eversley Sh.*), 1901; Hudson=ed. by H. N. Hudson (*Harvard Sh.*), 1879; J.=ed. of Sh. by Samuel Johnson, 1765; J.C.M.=J. C. Maxwell (privately); Kellett= *Suggestions: Literary Essays*, by E. E. Kellett, 1923; Knight=2nd ed. by C. Knight, 1865; Leo=*Sh. Notes* by F. N. Leo, 1885; Lettsom=*Critical Examination of the text of Sh.*, by W. N. Lettsom, 1860; Linthicum= *Costume in the Drama of Sh.*, by M. C. Linthicum, 1936; Madden=*The Diary of Master Silence*, by D. H. Madden, 1907; Mal.=James Boswell's Variorum ed. of *Malone's Sh.*, 1821; Mason=*Comments on the Several Editions of Sh.'s Plays*, by J. M. Mason, 1807; McK.=*The Works of Thomas Nashe*, ed. by R. B. McKerrow (5 vols.), 1904–10; *M.L.R.*= *Modern Language Review*; Moore Smith=private notes by G. C. Moore Smith; M.S.R.=Malone Society Reprint; Nashe, see McK.; Neils.=ed. by W. A. Neilson, 1906; Noble=*Sh.'s Biblical Knowledge*, by Richmond Noble, 1935; N.S.=*New Sh.* edition; O.D.E.P.=*Oxford Dictionary of English Proverbs*, 1948; On.=*A Sh. Glossary*, by C. T. Onions, 1911, 1919; O.S.=*The Oxford Sh.*, ed. by W. J. Craig, 1892; P. A. Daniel=*Notes and Conjectural Emendations...in Sh.'s Plays*, by P. A. Daniel, 1870; Palmer=*Political Characters in Sh.*, by John Palmer, 1945; Peele, *Alcazar*=*The Battle of Alcazar*, by

George Peele, 1594 (ed. W. W. Greg, M.S.R., 1907);
Pope = ed. of Sh. by Alexander Pope, 1723–5; *R.E.S.* =
Review of English Studies; R. G. W. = 2nd ed. of
Sh., by R. Grant White, 3 vols. 1883; Rowe = ed. of
Sh. by Nicholas Rowe, 1709, 1710, 1714; R.W.C. =
Man's Unconquerable Mind, by R. W. Chambers, 1939;
Schmidt = ed. by Alexander Schmidt, 1878; Schmidt,
Sh. Lex. = *Sh.-Lexicon*, by Alexander Schmidt, 3rd ed.,
1902; Sherman = ed. by S. P. Sherman (*Tudor Sh.*),
1912; *Sh. Eng.* = *Sh.'s England*, 1916; *Sh.'s Hand* =
Sh.'s Hand in the Play of Sir Thomas More, by A. W.
Pollard and others, 1923; Sherrington, *Jean Fernel* =
The Endeavour of Jean Fernel, by Sir Charles Sherrington, O.M., 1946; Staunton = ed. of Sh. by H. Staunton,
1882; Steev. = ed. of Johnson's Sh., by G. Steevens,
1773; *Tamb.* = *Tamburlaine the Great* (Parts 1 and 2),
by Christopher Marlowe, 1590 (ed. U. Ellis-Fermor,
1930); Theob. = ed. of Sh. by L. Theobald, 1733–40;
Tilley = *Dictionary of Proverbs in England in the Six-
teenth and Seventeenth Centuries*, by M. P. Tilley, 1950;
T.L.S. = *Times Literary Supplement*; Tyrwhitt = *Ob-
servations on Sh.*, by Thomas Tyrwhitt, 1766; Ver. =
ed. by A. W. Verity (*The Student's Sh.*), 1905; Walker
(A.) = *Textual Problems of the First Folio*, by Alice
Walker, 1953; Walker (W. S.) = *Critical Examination
of the Text of Sh.*, by Sidney Walker, 1860; Warb. =
ed. of Sh. by W. Warburton, 1747; Whitelaw = ed. by
R. Whitelaw (*Rugby* ed.), 1872; Wordsworth (Bp.) =
Sh.'s Knowledge and Use of the Bible, by Bishop
Charles Wordsworth, 1854; Wright, see Clar.

The names of some of those responsible for readings
or conjectures are taken from the Camb. Sh. *ad hoc.*

Names of the Characters. List first given imperfectly
by Rowe. Sh. took all the names from North's *Plutarch*
(Coriolanus) except Adrian and Nicanor in 4. 3 which

are hardly character names and occur in other of Plutarch's Lives. For spellings and misprints in F. see 'Note on Copy'. The mistake 'Velutus' for 'Bellutus' is North's. As the second name of Titus appears as Lartius, Latius, and Lucius in F., it is well to state that 'Lartius' is correct and appears so in North from Λαρτίος in Plutarch's Greek.

Punctuation. The punctuation of the present text is in general based upon the old *Cambridge Shakespeare,* revised, however, wherever necessary in the light of that of F. which is described on p. 133 above.

Stage-directions. See p. 131. A complete list of these will be found on pp. 404–6 of *The Shakespeare First Folio,* by Greg, who notes that some are 'obvious instructions for the producer', while some others 'look more like information supplied for the reader'. All F. S.Ds. are cited in the Notes and such, or such portions, as are used in the text are printed within inverted commas.

Acts and Scenes. The F. text is divided into five acts which have been generally followed by editor, but it contains no scene divisions, those found in this and most modern texts being derived from Pope or Capell.

I. I

S.D. *Loc.* (Camb.) *Entry* (F.).

16. *good* v. G. *on* (F 3) F. 'one' a common Sh. sp. Cf. 1. 2. 4, n. and above p. 133.

17–21. *If they...abundance* The general sense is: 'They will not give us, even of their superfluity, for we are too precious to them as we are; our poverty and the sight of our misery serve to emphasize by contrast their own plenty'. See G. 'guess', 'humanely', 'dear', 'object', 'particularize', 'inventory'.

18. *while...wholesome* before it goes bad.

23. *rakes* 'As lean as a rake' is still proverbial.

27. S.H. '*1 Citizen*' (Mal. conj.) F. '*All*'. E.K.C. notes that the speech, too long for a crowd, is part of a connected dialogue in which 1 Cit. attacks Cor. while 2 Cit. inclines to excuse him.

a very dog i.e. pitiless. Cf. *Gent.* 2. 3. 10, 'no more pity in him than a dog'.

32. *pays himself* sc. for his services to the country.

34. S.H. *2 Citizen* (Mal.) F. '*All*'. Cf. l. 27, n.

38. *partly to please...to be proud* (Cap.) F. 'to please...to be partly proud'. Most edd. follow F. explaining 'to be partly proud' as 'partly to be proud', invoking Abbott, §420 on adverbial transpositions and citing 1. 2. 24; 1. 3. 38; 5. 6. 78 below. But, as Cap. notes, this does not fit the context. 1 Cit. sets out by ascribing all Cor.'s actions to pride; and when 2 Cit. objects, he sticks to his point, 'with this slight difference —that, perhaps indeed the pleasing of his mother might be some motive...but pride was his chief'.

39. *to...virtue* i.e. his pride is as pre-eminent as his valour. Cf. North, p. 144, '*Virtus* in the Latin was as muche as valiantnes'.

41–2. *in...covetous* Cf. his attitude at 1. 5. 4–8; 1. 9. 37–40.

45. S.D. F. 'Showts within'. 49. S.D. (F.).

50–1. *one...people* Cf. North, p. 149, 'The Senate...dyd send unto them certaine of the pleasauntest olde men, and the most acceptable to the people among them. Of these Menenius Agrippa was...chief man'.

55. *bats and clubs* Weapons of London prentices.

59. *strong breaths* A frequent gibe in Sh. Cf. 3. 1. 66; 4. 6. 99, 131–2; *J. C.* 1. 2. 247, etc.

65. *For=As for* Cf. l. 71, 'For the dearth'.

71. *your impediment* any curb of yours. Cf. *Oth.*
5. 2. 266.

73. (*not arms*) The brackets are F.'s.

74. *transported* Used both in its fig. and its orig.
sense.

calamity sc. the famine (which has put them beside
themselves).

75. *Thither* To insurrection.

76. *helms* Cf. *2 H. VI.* 1. 3. 98, 'You... shall steer
the happy helm'. The figure suggests that Sh. images
'calamity' as a violent storm.

79–83. *Suffer us...the poor* Sh. here combines the
causes of two separate popular disturbances in Plutarch:
(i) (North, pp. 147–9) 'Now he [Cor.] being growen to
great credit and authoritie in Rome for his valliantnes,
it fortuned there grewe sedition in the cittie, bicause the
Senate dyd favour the riche against the people, who dyd
complaine of the sore oppression of usurers, of whom
they borrowed money.' And when the Senate, despite
the people's long and faithful service in the Sabine wars
failed to carry out their promises of redress they fell 'to
flat rebellion and mutine' and refused to muster when
the enemy next attacked the city, but withdrew there-
from to the Mons Sacer. All this caused disputes in the
Senate, Martius (Cor.) arguing that the 'lenitie that
was favored, was a beginning of disobedience, and that
the prowde attempt of the communaltie, was to
abolishe lawe, and to bring all to confusion'. Menenius
was sent to the people at Mons Sacer and they, 'pacified
by his tale of the belly', agreed to return to the city,
provided they should be allowed to choose 'yerely' five
'tribuni plebis' to defend the poor from violence and
oppression. Junius Brutus and Sicinius Vellutus, the first
tribunes chosen, had been 'the causers and procurers of
this sedition. Hereupon the cittie being growen againe
to good quiet and unitie, the people immediatly went to

the warres.' There follows the account of Cor. taking
Corioles and the defeat of the Volsces. (ii) (North
p. 156) Sedition at Rome by reason of famine.

91. *stale* (Theob.+edd. ex. Steev., O.S. and Case).
F. 'scale' wh. Steev. interprets 'disperse', 'give it a
wider meaning'. But this is beside the point of the
context. Note 'st' is easily misread 'sc' in secretary hand.

93. *disgrace* v. G.

93–4. *an't...deliver* go ahead if you want to.

95–145. See the three source versions cited in
Introd. §11.

100. *where* whereas.

102. *And, mutually participate*, (Mal.+most) F.
'And mutually participate', Knight 'And mutually
participate;'.

103. *affection* v. G.

105. *Well, sir,...belly?* 1 Cit. is impatient with
this tedious old gentleman.

106–7. *a kind of smile...lungs* North's 'the belly...
laughed at their folly' is too hearty for Sh.; his Belly
smiles, with lips curled, contemptuously. Cf. *A.Y.L.*
2. 7. 30, 'My lungs began to crow like chanticleer'.

109. *tauntingly* (F4+most) F. 'taintingly'—
a minim-error. Herf. defends F. and explains 'at-
taintingly', i.e. indicting them (in turn), wh. is both
far-fetched and unexampled, whereas 'tauntingly'
(v. G.) tells the actor how to speak the answer when it
comes (ll. 129 ff.).

111. *most fitly* Ironical.

113. *answer—What?* (Al.) F. 'answer: What'
Most edd. 'answer—what!' 1 Cit. is still more impatient; putting a stop to Men.'s innuendos (cf. l. 105,
n.), and then taking over the tale himself for a time.

114–18. *The kingly* etc. Kellett, p. 29, cites John
of Salisbury: 'The King indeed holds the place of head
in the state, subject to none but God' and so on.

115. *counsellor heart* Cf. Kellett, p. 29, 'in the med. writings on law or politics, it is almost always *cor* or *pectus* that is *Senatus*'; and Lewis and Short *Lat. Dict.* 'Cor' IIʙ. 'Acc. to the ancients (cf. Cic. Tusc. 1. 9. 18) as the seat of wisdom, understanding'. See l. 135, n., and 2. 3. 202–4 where 'heart' again = the seat of good counsel.

119. *'Fore me* etc. By my soul! this fellow can talk!

125. *you'st* (F.) Said to be a provincial contraction of 'you' (= thou) and 'shalt'. Cf. Marston, *Malcontent* 5. 4 (ed. H. H. Wood, 1, 211), 'Nay if youle dooes no good / Youst dooes no harme'.

126. *You're* (Cap.) F. 'Y'are' and so throughout.

127. *Your...belly* i.e. this belly we're talking about.

132. *the storehouse...shop* v. G. 'shop'. He thus 'politely rejects their description of him as "like a gulf"' (Ver.).

134. *I send...blood* Prob. suggested by Holland's trans. of Livy; cf. Introd. pp. xv–xvi. The process of nutrition as then understood is expounded at 5. 1. 51–4 and explained in Sherrington's *Jean Fernel* (1946), pp. 69–77.

135. *to th' seat o' th' brain* = to the throne i.e. the brain—'o' th' brain' being a genitive of definition (O.E.D. 'of' 23) like 'the city of London' as J.C.M. notes in *N. & Q.* Aug. 1953 (vol. 198, p. 329). Thus the Belly sends forward the nutrition it has received first to the court (i.e. the heart) then to the throne itself (i.e. the brain). Cf. 'the kingly crownéd head' (l. 114) and 'the counsellor heart' (l. 115). Both passages reflect the notions of class. and med. physio-psychology which regarded the heart as the court or council chamber of deliberation and the head the place where Reason had its throne, Reason the supreme authority in the 'little world of man'. Malone led opinion astray by taking 'court' and 'seat' in apposition, himself led

astray through misunderstanding Camden who read:
'Therefore they [the members] all with one accord
desired the advice of the Heart. There Reason layd
open before them', etc.—which, however, did not
imply that the heart had its seat in the brain.

137. *nerves* v. G.

139–40. *once, You, my good friends'—this...mark
me* Rowe (subst.); F. 'once / (You...belly) mark me';
Wright 'once', —You'...belly, mark me,—'.

144. *flour* (Knight) F. 'flowre'. The two senses
were still both spelt 'flower' in J.'s *Dict.* Here fig. =
the finest extract.

149. *digest* (F 3) F. 'disgest'—a freq. 16 and 17 c.
form.

158. *rascal* v. G. *in blood* v. G. 'blood'. A sporting
metaphor, usually explained as an allusion to deer (see
Madden, pp. 228–9). But a 'rascal' might also be a
hound. O.E.D. (4 c) cites fr. a trans. of Caius' *Dogs*
(1576) 'Some be called fine dogs...some mongrels or
rascals'. This makes sense of ll. 156 ff., as J. saw. He
paraphrased the passage: 'Thou that art a hound, or
running dog of the lowest breed, lead'st the pack, when
anything is to be gotten.' If 1 Cit. was played by the
very lean Sincklo the term 'rascal' would be esp. apt.
Cf. *2 H. IV* (N.S.), 5. 4. S.D. n. The part would 'double'
easily with that of Sic. (see 2. 1. 13, n; 3. 1. 176, n).

162. S.D. (F.).

163. *Thanks.* Cap., G.-B. (p. 53), and Palmer
(p. 255) all note the curtness of this reply, his first
utterance—and a pregnant entry.

164–5. *That...scabs* 'In two lines he declares that
their grievances are only skin-deep, that they are self-
caused, and that they themselves are filthy fellows,
"scabs".' (G.G.).

164. *the poor...opinion* Cf. R. W. C. p. 235 ff. and G.
'opinion'.

165. *Make...scabs* Might='make scabs for yourselves' but 'make yourselves into scabs' is more pointed.
Cf. *Ado* 3. 3. 98, *Tw. N.* 2. 5. 75 for 'scab' as a term
of abuse.

166. *thee* (F.) Dyce conj. 'ye'—poss. misread as
'thee'. But it may be theatrically more effective if Cor.
rounds upon the aggressive 1 Cit. and silences him—
for ever!

168. *affrights you* Plut., on the contrary, describes
the people as serving 'faithfully' in the wars against the
Sabines and shewing 'the woundes and cuttes...they
had receyved in many battells, fighting for defence of
their countrie and common wealth'; and only provoked
to rebellion by the ingratitude of the Senate who allowed
usurers to sell them as slaves (North, pp. 147–8). Only
once (p. 150) does he speak of part of the Roman army
turning their backs. Cf. 1. 4. 30, n.

169. *proud* i.e. high-spirited curs (v. G.) and so 'ungovernable and prone to sedition; mark enough of their
not liking peace when they were so ready to break it'
(Cap.). It is what *they* call Cor. (v. ll. 33, 38).

171. *geese: you are no* (Theob.+) F. 'Geese you are:
No' *no surer*=disappearing as rapidly (Clar.).

172. *the coal...ice* For a prob. allusion to the
Great Frost of 1607–8 first pointed out in 1878 by
J. W. Hales, v. his *Notes and Essays on Sh.* p. 292,
see Introd. p. x.

173. *hailstone* Cf. *Wiv.* 1. 3. 80 'Rogues, hence,
avaunt; vanish like hailstones, go' [Clar.].

173–6. *Your virtue...hate. And* (punct. J.D.W.)
i.e. Your special quality is on the one hand to do honour
to the criminal, cursing the justice that punishes him,
and on the other to give hatred to the man who deserves
honour. F. punct. 'Your vertue...did it. Who...hate:
and'—which breaks the thread of Cor.'s tumultuous
speech. Their virtue is to love the good and hate the

bad, like a sick man who refuses wholesome food and craves for what is unwholesome or 'Like rats that ravin down their proper bane' (*Meas.* 1. 2. 125). *Ant.* 1. 2. 193–5; 1. 4. 42, cited by Case, express an opposite not a parallel.

176. *affections* v. G.

180. *Hang ye! Trust ye?* Coleridge plausibly conj. transposition.

183. *was* Anon. conj. 'wore' in Cap.'s copy of F3. [Camb.]. But 'your garland' describes Cor. himself.

184. *in these several places* Cf. ll. 46–7. Plut. says nothing about riots at different parts of the city.

187. *Would feed on one another* The same line in a similar context occurs in the Shn. 'Three Pages of Sir Thomas More', as was pointed out by R. W. C. p. 228; cf. *Sh.'s Hand*, p. 158.

188–9. *For corn...stored* Cf. North, p. 156, 'Sedition at Rome by reason of famine' and p. 160, 'Great store of corne brought to Rome'. For *at their own rates* v. pp. 160–1.

190. *They'll...fire* Cf. North, p. 158 'the home-tarriers and housedoves that kept Rome still' (i.e. that remained in Rome).

192. *side factions* v. G. 'side'.

194–5. *feebling...shoes* sc. speaking of those they don't like as if they were dirt beneath their ill-made shoes. Cf. G. 'feeble', 'cobbled'.

197. *quarry* v. G.

198. *quartered* sc. by his sword.

200. *all most* (Coll.) F. (+most edd.) 'almost'; Furn. accepts Coll.

201–2. *discretion...cowardly* Glancing at the prov. 'Discretion is the better part of valour'. Cf. *1 H. IV*, 5. 4. 119–20.

203. *the other troop* Cf. 1. 1. 46.

204. *an-hungry* Prob. a provincialism. He 'mocks

their homely speech as he mocks their homely proverbs.'
(G.G.).

205. *hunger...walls* a hungry man sticks at nothing;
cf. Tilley, H 811 *dogs...eat* cf. Tilley, D 533 (cites
no parallel) *meat...mouths* cf. Tilley, M 828 (cites no
parallel); *the gods...only* not in Tilley.

210. *To break...generosity* 'Enough to break the
hearts of all true-born gentlemen' (G.G.), v. G.
'generosity'. J.'s 'To give the final blow to the nobles'
is more likely.

211. *threw their caps* Action referred to also at
2. 1. 103, 264; 4. 6. 131–2, 136; *2 H. VI*, 4. 8. 15;
3 H. VI, 2. 1. 196; *R. III*. 3. 7. 35; *Ham.* 4. 5. 107;
Ant. 4. 12. 12.

213. *Shouting* (Pope+) F. 'Shooting'; Cf. 1. 9.
50, n., and p. 133.

emulation The simplest and obvious meaning is
rivalry [i.e. 'each of them striving to shout harder than
the rest' Mal.], O.E.D. 3 glosses it 'grudge against the
superiority of others' which is what Cor. accused them
of in ll. 190–95 and Ver. explains 'malicious triumph'.
But as Case notes the feeling now uppermost is exulta-
tion at their success.

214. *Five tribunes* etc. Here Sh. follows Plut. closely.

215–16. *Junius Brutus, one... and—I* (S. Walker
conj.) F. 'Iunius Brutus,...and I'. The 'one' fills out
the line and is needed for the sense, while the break
after 'and' brings out a point, noticed, I think, only by
Ver., viz.: 'Plut. does not mention more than two
names, and Sh. cleverly turns the omission into an
illustration of Cor.'s contempt for the people and all
that concerns them. Similarly in 1. 9. 90 he cannot call
to mind the name of his humble benefactor.' But this
last merits a different explanation, for which see note
ad loc. Rowe (+most edd.) prints a dash after 'not',
which now becomes otiose and misleading.

216. *Sicinius Velutus* 'Should properly be Sicinus Bellutus' (Greg, *Sh. F.F.* p. 406). But it is 'Sicinius Vellutus' in North (p. 149).

217. *unroofed* (Theob. +edd. 'unroof'd') F. 'vnroo'st'.

218-20. *it will...arguing* In North, p. 148, Cor. maintains that 'the lenitie that was favored' by some senators in respect of the oppression of the people by usurers (cf. l. 80), would be 'a beginning of disobedience, and that the prowde attempt of the communaltie was to abolish lawe, and to bring all to confusion'.

win upon power i.e. 'take advantage of the power already won to win more' E.K.C.

220. *For...arguing* 'For insurgents to debate upon' (Mal.).

221. S.D. (F.).

223. *Volsces* (edd.) F. 'Volcies'.

224-5. *means...superfluity* A common sentiment at this period. Cf. Nashe, *Pierce Penilesse* (McK. i. 211) 'There is a certaine waste of the people for whome there is no vse but warre: and these men must haue some employment still to cut them off', etc. See also North, p. 156 (near foot) where the 'mutinous and seditious persones' are called the city's 'superfluous ill humours'— wh. prob. suggested this to Sh.

225. S.D. (Camb.<Mal.+Cap.) F. 'Enter Sicinius Velutus, Annius Brutus Cominisn, Titus Lartius, with other Senatours'. N.B. 'Annius'=a misreading of Junius. Cf. Greg *Sh. F.F.* p. 406, and above p. 131.

227. *They have a leader* Plut. does not mention Auf. until Cor. deserts to Corioli.

229. *I sin in envying* Cf. *1 H. IV*, 1. 1. 78-9. Envy is one of the Seven Deadly Sins in the Catholic Church.

231. *together* (Cap +many) F. 'together?'. Com. could not have been ignorant of the fact (see 1. 10. 7-8)

and it is better to take it as 'a soldier's explanation of
Cor.'s praise' (Beeching). See also ll. 238–9 below,
which surely make Com.'s ignorance impossible.

238. *Lartius* (Rowe) F. 'Lucius'—carelessness
typical of Comp. B.

240. *stiff* sc. with age (cf. ll. 241–2). Clar. explains
'obstinate' and for 'stand'st out' compares *Tw. N.*
3. 3. 35 'only myself stood out'. But this is Cor.'s
banter with his old comrade and Clar.'s *cannot* be the
primary meaning. Note Tit.'s deference to the younger
soldier in ll. 245–6; he is beginning to feel a little past
it and salutes with delight the rising star.

244–5. S.D.s (Camb.<Mal.'s conj.) F. omits.
Theob.+18th c. edd. also omit, but insert a comma
after 'Follow', which makes Tit. address 'Lead you
on' to 1 Sen. and 'Follow...priority' to Com. But this
renders Com.'s reply 'Noble Martius' (F.) absurd, so
that they were obliged to read 'Noble Lartius'. The
Camb. S.D.s avoid textual change and give manifestly
better drama.

246. *Right...priority* Well do you deserve pride of
place!

Marcius (F. 'Martius') Theob.'s 'Lartius' would
make the line a tribute to Tit.'s generosity. But F.
implies that Com. takes Cor. by the hand to walk with
him, instead of after him as Tit. bids. The mutual
courtesies of these soldier-men are very attractive.

247. S.D. (Rowe) F. omits.

248. *The Volsces...corn* Cf. North, pp. 157–8,
'Martius...dyd ronne certen forreyes into the dominion
of the Antiates, where he met with great plenty of corne,
and had a marvelous great spoyle'. The Antiates were
the men of Antium, the Volscian capital.

249. S.D. (F.) F. prints this after the 'exeunt' for
Martius, etc. But clearly his taunt: 'Worshipful mutineers', etc. (v. G. 'worshipful') should relate to 'steal

away'. *mutineers* (Rowe) F. 'mutiners'. Cf. 'mutineere' at *Tp.* 3. 2. 36 (F.) v. G.

250. *puts well forth* makes a fine show. v. G. 'put'. *Pray follow* Is this still addressed (ironically) to the citizens; or does Cor. turn to Tit. and other senators? The capital is F.'s but preceded by a colon.

S.D. (J.D.W.) F. 'Citizens ſteele away. Manet Sicin. & Brutus'. v. l. 249, S.D., n.

254. *his lip* Case cites *Tw. N.* 3. 1. 147–8; *Wint.* 1. 2. 373.

256. *the modest moon* bashful and reserved Diana.

257. *him! He* (Han.+many) F. 'him, he'. Much debated ($3\frac{1}{2}$ pp. in Furn.). Mal. defends F. and takes 'The present wars' as referring to Cor.'s military reputation, because of which he is eaten up with pride. But as Clar. points out, 'it is difficult to see how "the present wars" (cf. l. 278 "this present action") in which Cor. had not yet been engaged can denote military reputation derived from past achievement'. And E.K.C. interprets 'He is...valiant' as 'Such valour coupled with such pride, is dangerous'—clearly right. Thus ll. 257–8 = May he perish in the coming war! It is dangerous when a man of so much arrogance is such a good soldier (after Warb.). But perh. 'to be so valiant' means 'of being so valiant' (Cap.).

259. *success* v. G. *disdains...noon* = disdains the very ground he walks on, because one has no shadow at noon.

260–75. *But I do wonder...merit not* They attribute their own meanness to Cor. and the absurdity of their charges underlines for the audience his freedom from envy and personal ambition. The like charges are brought against Antony (*Ant.* 3. 1. 11–27) but with truth.

261. *commanded* v. G.

263. *whom* 'In l. 262 he thinks of Fame as an

object aimed at: "which" therefore. In l. 263 he thinks of Fame as a person, whose good graces Cor. has won: "whom" therefore' (G.G.).

267. *giddy censure* i.e. people who jump to conclusions.

270. *Opinion* Here used in the double sense of (*a*) reputation, honour, and·(*b*) the public opinion that confers, or 'sticks', it on him.

271. *demerits* v. G. *Come* = I'd go further.

277. *his singularity* Two poss. interpretations: (i) his personal valour (E.K.C.), which gives us 'with what force—over and above his own great self—he takes the field' (Whitelaw), and (ii) 'his own singularity of disposition' (Steev.) which gives us 'in what manner, beyond his usual peculiarity of character, he enters upon the war i.e. whether with an exceptional manifestation of pride' (Ver.). I prefer the second.

I. 2

S.D. *Loc.* (<Pope 'Corioli'; Cap. 'The Senate-House'). *Entry* (<F. reading 'Coriolus'; v.l. 27, n.).

4. *hath* (F2) F. 'haue' Edd. conj. that 'what' = 'what things', but more likely 'haue' is a comp.'s slip. *on* (F3) F. 'one' cf. I. I. 16, n.

13. F. brackets.

24. *ere almost Rome* v. G. 'almost'.

27. *Let us alone to* = Trust us to. Cf. *Tw. N.* 3. 4. 187. *Corioli* To be pron. Coríoli (not Corióli). 'F. Corioles' (<North) and so throughout, exc. when misprinted.

28. *set down before* = besiege *for the remove* = to raise the siege (cf. *Ven.* 423 and *Rom.* 5. 3. 237). Both technical terms.

30. *They've* (Rowe) F. 'Th'haue'—and so throughout. *prepared* cf. 'preparation' (l. 15). 'Prepare' often = 'prepare for war' in Sh. (e.g. below 4. 5. 137).

1. 3

S.D. *Loc.* (<Rowe 'Rome'; Cap. 'A room', etc.)
Entry (F.).

2. *comfortable* v. G.

8. *should*=would.

10. *such a person* 'one of such a goodly exterior'
(Clar.) *it*=person.

11. *hang by the wall* become merely ornamental.
Clar. glosses 'to be useless or neglected' and cites
Cym. 3. 4. 52, *Meas.* 1. 2. 163: but this does not suit
'picture-like' or 'person'.

12. *made...stir* did not give it life and motion.

13. *a cruel war* i.e. the battle of Lake Regillus,
against the Tarquins, where Cor. 'being but a stripling',
was 'crowned with a garland of oken boughes' for
saving the life of a fellow-soldier. See North, p. 145.
But Sh. takes the oaken garland as crowning the bravest
soldier in the field. Cf. 2. 1. 122; 2. 2. 96.

25. S.D. (F.) i.e. a waiting-gentlewoman. Cf.
l. 48 S.D. 'her Usher'. Their dress would denote their
rank and lead an audience to infer that Volumnia was
a great lady.

32. *from* Sh. starts the line with the gen. idea of
children flying from a bear and completes it with
'shunning him'.

37–8. *Like...hire* A glimpse of piece-work in the
fields round Stratford. Cf. *Troil.* 5. 5. 24–5.

41. *trophy* v. G.

41–2. *The breasts,* etc. This fine stroke in Sh.'s
portrait of a Roman matron was omitted by Bp. Wordsworth (1854) 'on the score of delicacy', though not by
Dr Bowdler in his *Family Shakespeare* (1807)—a little
chapter in the history of British prudery [Furn.].

42. *Hector* The name recalls Homer and leads on to
the Corioli sc.s wh. recall the *Iliad.*

44. *At Grecian sword, contemning. Tell Valeria* (Camb., after Leo. who omits the comma.) F. 'At Grecian sword. *Contenning*, tell *Valeria*'—where 'Contenning' seems to be the name of the gentle-woman. F2 reads 'swords contending', Cap. 'swords contending', Coll. ii (1856) 'swords contemning' (anticipated in 1805 by Seymour's conj.). Thus gradually is Sh.'s text cleansed.

45. S.D. (<F. 'Exit Gent.'.)

48. S.D. (Mal.) F. 'Enter Valeria with an Vsher, and a Gentlewoman'. v. G. 'usher'.

52. *you are manifest house-keepers* 'you have clearly settled down for a morning indoors'; cf. *Cym.* 3. 3. 1 'a goodly day not to keep house' (E.K.C.). *manifest* Because they sit sewing. Cf. l. 53.

53. *spot* pattern, v. G. and *Oth.* 3. 3. 436–7, n.

58. *the father's son* etc. Vol.'s 'One on's father's moods' (l. 67) assures us that the picture of the son tearing a butterfly to pieces with his teeth is intended to underline the brutality of the father. E.K.C. sees symbolism in it also: 'as the child pursues the gilded butterfly, so the father pursues his ideal of honour, and, in the end, after a check, himself "mammocks" it'; while *gilded* 'hints at the superficial glamour of Cor.'s ideal'. I find all this far-fetched.

84. *yarn* F. 'yearne'.

85. *Ithaca* (F 3) F. 'Athica'; see p. 131 *moths* v. G. and *Oth.* 1. 3. 256. The quibble refers to the suitors who consumed Ulysses's goods at Ithaca.

101. *make...wars* make a short engagement of it. 'War' often 'means fighting generally. Cf. 5. 3. 190' (G.G.), and is often pl. where we should use the sing.

106. *disease our better mirth* spoil our enjoyment which will be better without her. Characteristic Sh. construction, in which a proleptic usage facilitates compression. Clar. cites *Mac.* 1. 6. 3; 3. 4. 76, and G.G.

R II, 5. 2. 38, 'To whose high will we bound our calm contents'.

110. *at a word* in short, once for all.

1. 4–1. 5

These scenes, dealing with the capture of Corioli, follow Plut. closely (North, pp. 150–54) exc. for a slight change in the episode of the Volscian prisoner, the introduction of a duel with Auf., and some compression of time. 'Cor. stands forth as the champion of Rome. His intrepid personal valour twice turns the fortunes of the day. Like an Homeric chieftain he meets the leader of the enemy in single combat. His single-eyed pursuit of honour bespeaks our enthusiasm. This day's deeds make him a hero, putting him on such a level that his ultimate failure shall appear as a real tragedy' (E.K.C.).

1. 4

S.D. *Loc.* (J.D.W. after Cap. 'Trenches before Corioli'). *Entry* (J. D.W.) F. 'Enter Martius, Titus Lartius, with Drumme and Colours, with Captaines and Souldiers, as before the City Corialus: to them a Messenger'.

2–7. *My horse...years* This wager seems suggested by the gift of the horse (North, p. 153). Cf. 1. 9. 61–2, n.

7. *Summon* to a parley. S.D. (J. D.W.).

9. *hear their 'larum* A hint to the audience, i.e. to explain alarums (v. G.) 'afar off' (l. 19; 1. 5. 3 S.D.).

12. *fielded*=at the main battle-field. S.D. (F.).

14. *that fears you less* (F.) J. conj. 'that fears you more' or 'but fears you less'—which is what Sh. meant. Mal. notes 'The text, I am confident, is right,

our author almost always entangling himself when he uses *less* and *more*'.

15. S.D. (F.).

17. *pound up* shut us up like cattle; v. G.

19. S.D. (F.).

21. *cloven* Proleptic = which is being hacked to pieces.

22. S.D. (J. D.W.) F. 'Enter the Army of the Volsces'—a *stage*-direction, suggesting a sudden entry of the 'fielded' Volscian army, and confusing to a reader.

29. S.D. i (J.D.W.) ii (F.) F. having given Marc. no 'exit', it is not clear what happens to him during the 'alarum' (which here = a stage-battle of some duration). Poss. he chases a party of Volsces through one of the stage-doors (the gates of Corioli being the entrance to the inner stage) and returns to find the Romans on the main stage at bay. F. also leaves the movements of Tit. obscure.

30. *All the contagion* etc. 'Marcius' language reminds one of a boating coach in a temper and rather out of breath' (E.K.C.), or of a choleric N.C.O. The sole justification for this in North is that when 'the Coriolans had the better and drave the Romaines backe againe into the trenches' Marcius stopped the rot 'crying out to the Romaines that had turned their backes and calling them againe to fight with a lowde voyce' (p. 150).

the contagion...light on you Cf. Caliban's curse (*Tp.* 1. 2. 324 'A south-west blow on ye / And blister you all o'er!' and *Cym.* 2. 3. 131, 'The south fog rot him!'. The warm S.-W. wind brought fogs laden, it was supposed, with pestilence.

31. *you herd of—Boils* (J.) F. 'you Heard of Byles'. 'Byles' or 'biles' was the old form. For 'herd' cf. 3. 1. 33; 3. 2. 32.

32–4. *abhorred...wind* i.e. that your stink may proclaim your loathsome presence before you come in sight and be so powerful as to infect others when the wind blows the other way.

37. *All hurt behind!* Case cites *Mac.* 5. 8. 46.

38. *agued fear* Cf. *R. II*, 3. 2. 190 'This ague-fit of fear'. *home* v. G.

39. *the fires of heaven* sun, moon and stars.

39–40. *I'll leave...you* Poss. touch of tragic irony.

42. *trenches* (Clar.) F. 'trenches followes' F2 (+Camb.+most) 'trenches followed'. Lettsom conj. (+some) 'trenches: follow me'. Coll. ii 'trenches. Follow'. F. gives the context thus:

> Come on,
> If you'l stand fast, wee'l beate them to their Wiues,
> As they vs to our Trenches followes.
> *Another Alarum, and Marcius followes them to*
> *gates, and is shut in.*
> So, now the gates are ope: now proue good Seconds,
> 'Tis for the followers Fortune, widens them,
> Not for the flyers: Marke me, and do the like.
> *Enter the Gati.*
> *1 Sol.* Foole-hardinesse, not I.
> *2 Sol.* Nor I.
> *1 Sol.* See they haue shut him in. *Alarum continues*
> *All.* To th'pot I warrant him. *Enter Titus Lartius*

Clearly the long misplaced S.D. is Sh.'s general account of what happens, and left for the prompter to sort out. This, I suggest, he proceeds to do with 'Enter the Gates' (misprinted 'Gati.') at l. 45. But something happens between ll. 45–6, viz. 'another alarum' (another pitched battle) at the end of which the Volsces fly and the town gates open to receive them, while Marcius pursues at their heels. Clar. suggests that the 'followes' (in l. 42) has prob. crept into the text from the neighbouring S.D. And G.-B. (p. 61)

observes: 'Neither sense nor verse accommodates it.'
I suppose rather that like 'Enter the Gates' (l. 45) it is
a prompter's S.D. to the actor playing Marcius.

S.D. (Camb.) For F. see above.

44–5. *'Tis for...fliers* His words in Plut. are 'that
fortune had opened the gates of the cittie, more for the
followers, then the flyers' (North, p. 151).

S.D. (Camb.) <F. 'Enter the Gati'.

47. S.D. (Dyce<F. see above).

48. *To th' pot* v. G. 'pot'. S.D.s (F.) The 'alarum'
is now heard from within the gates.

54. *Who...sword*='Who though himself sensitive
to pain seems stouter than his senseless sword; for it may
bend, he will not'. Steev. cites from *Arcadia*: 'Their
very armour by piece-meale fell away from them; and
yet their flesh abode the wounds constantly as though
it were lesse sensible of smart than the senseless armour'
(ed. 1593, p. 317).

stand'st (F.+Case; Al.; C.J.S.) Rowe (+most)
'stands'. 'Thou' is the subj. implied.

55. *lost* (Singer; Coll.) F. (+most) 'left'. 'Thou
wast a soldier', etc. (ll. 57–62) is Tit.'s epitaph, while
the 'carbuncle' (l. 56) has obviously been 'lost' not 'left'
by Rome. Cf. 'one entire...chrysolite' and 'a pearl richer
than all his tribe' (*Oth*. 5. 2. 148, 349–50)—both lost.

57. *Were* (F3) F. 'Weare'.

58. *Cato's* (Theob.<North) F. '*Calues*' Cf. North,
p. 150: 'For he was even such another, as Cato would
have a souldier and a captaine to be: not only terrible,
and fierce to laye about him, but to make the enemie
afeard with the sound of his voyce, and grimnes of his
countenaunce.' But the comparison, apt as an aside by
an historian writing c. A.D. 120 becomes absurd when
placed in the mouth of a contemp. of Cor. who lived
250 years before Cato; and Sh. may well have been
laughed at by Ben Jonson about it.

62. **S.D.** (J. D.W.) F. 'Enter Martius bleeding, assaulted by the Enemy'—i.e. fighting a rearguard action.

63. *make remain alike* 'stay with him, share his fate' (E.K.C.). S.D. (F.). This prob. denotes another stage-battle until the Volsces are driven back again into Corioli.

1. 5

S.D. *Loc.* No change needed; most edd. (<Cap.) read 'Within Corioli. A street.' *Entry* (J.D.W.) F. 'Enter certaine Romanes with spoiles'.

3. S.D.i (J.D.W.) F. 'Alarum continues still a-farre off.' The noises off keep the audience conscious of the main battle in progress. S.D. ii <F. 'Enter Martius, and Titus with a Trumpet'.

4. *movers* Ironical—'idle fellows who are loitering when they should be moving' (E.K.C.) v. G. No ref. to moving plunder. Cf. North, p. 151: 'The cittie being taken in this sorte, the most parte of the souldiers beganne incontinently to spoyle, to carie awaye, and to looke up the bootie they had wonne. But Martius was marvelous angry with them, and cried out on them, that it was no time now to looke after spoyle...whilest the other Consul and their fellowe cittizens peradventure were fighting with their enemies.'

honours (J.D.W.<Rowe ii, Pope, J.) F. (+Mal.; Camb., etc.) 'hours'. J. praised this 'improvement', remarking that had 'a modern editor' made it he 'would have spent half a page in ostentation of his sagacity'. Mal. restored F., adding 'Dr. J., too hastily I think, approves the alteration', while Steev. saw 'hours' as a reflexion of North's 'it was no time now', etc. [v. last n.]. Yet it is not their waste of time but their baseness that infuriates him, the fact that they value this cheap booty above the glory of battle: it is only at l. 9 that the sound

of distant battle reminds him of Com. and Auf. The words 'honour' and 'hour' are confused again at *Rom*. 1. 3. 67, 68 and at *Tim*. 3. 1. 54.

5. *drachma* (Badham, Singer ii) F. 'Drachme'. A Gk. coin which Sh. took to be a Roman one, prob. because he found it in Plut. s account of Caesar's will (v. *J. C*. 3. 2. 244, n.).

6. *Irons of a doit*=Swords and daggers at a farthing a-piece. *doublets* A 16th c. garment in which both North and Sh. clothe Caesar (*J. C*. 1. 2. 266, n.) and Sylvester clothes Adam! *hangmen* Whose perquisites were the clothes of their victims.

11. *Piercing* He recalls a Volscian's boast at 1. 4. 20–1.

12. *make good* v. G.

18. *physical* v. G. Cf. *J. C*. 2. 1. 261. Blood-letting was the sovereign remedy with doctors of that age.

21. *charms* v. G.

23–4. *Thy friend...highest* 'May she be no less a friend to thee than to those whom', etc. (Clar.).

25. S.D. (after Cap.).

28. S.D. (J.D.W.) F. 'Exeunt'.

1. 6

S.D. *Loc*. (after Pope 'The Roman Camp'). *Entry* (F.) 'in retire'=fighting a rear-guard action. Com.'s encouragement to his retreating troops is in contrast with Cor.'s in the like case at 1. 4. 30 ff. He is a good general; Cor. is not.

1. *Breathe* v. G. *come off* v. G.

4. *struck* v. G.

5. *By*— (i) at, (ii) by means of. *gusts* sc. of wind.

6. *The Roman gods* (F.) Han. (+many) 'ye Roman

Gods'. For 'The' with the vocative see Franz, § 261 and J.C.M.'s note on *Per*. 3. 1. 1. in this ed.

7. *successes* v. G.

8. *powers* v. G.

9. S.D. (F.).

16. *briefly* not long since, v. G.

21. S.D. (J.D.W.) F. 'Enter Martius'.

22. *flayed* sc. as bloody as a newly skinned carcass in a butcher's shop.

24. S.D. (J.D.W.) Dyce '[within]'—but Marc. is seen in l. 21.

27. *man* Han. regularised to 'man's' unnecessarily. S.D. (J.D.W.).

30–1. *woo'ed; in heart As* (Theob.+) F. 'woo'd in heart; As'.

32. S.D.   (J.D.W.)   *warriors!*—(J.D.W.)   F. 'warriors'.

36. *Ransoming...pitying* i.e. releasing one for ransom or remitting it for pity.

38–9. *Even...will* Cf. Sh.'s Addition to *Sir Thomas More* ll. 121–2 (in mod. sp.):

> And lead the majesty of law in liom
> To slip him like a hound;

Shr. 5. 2. 52; *1 H.IV*, 1. 3. 275; *H.V, Prol*. 1, 6–7; 3. 1. 31–2; *J. C*. 3. 1. 274. Clar. cites *The Gentleman's Recreation* (1721), p. 11: 'We let slip a Grey-Hound, and cast of (=off) a Hound. The string wherewith we lead a Grey-Hound is called a Lease; and for a Hound, a Lyome.'

38. *fawning* Cf. Spurgeon, *Sh.'s Imagery*, pp. 195–9.

42–3. *But for...file* = 'Had it not been for our fine rank and file, we should not have been beaten.' He becomes speechless for a moment, as usual, when thinking of the plebs. 'Gentlemen' is surely a scornful attribute of 'the common file'—'the would-be gentle-

men', Miss Porter well interprets it. [Furn.] There is
no distinction, as some edd. (e.g. Clar.) think, between
the gentry and the rest.

44. *budge* v. G. Does not actually=flee. But Sh.
nearly always uses it of cowardly yielding or giving
back in fight.

45. *rascals* Cf. 1. 1. 158, n.

51–5. *How lies...of hope* Cf. North (p. 152):
'Martius asked him howe the order of their enemies
battell was, and on which side they had placed their
best fighting men. The Consul made him aunswer, that
he thought the bandes which were in the voward of
their battell, were those of the Antiates, whom they
esteemed to be the warlikest men, and which for valiant
corage would geve no place, to any of the hoste of their
enemies. Then prayed Martius to be set directly against
them.'

51. *which* (Mal.) F. 'w^c' F 2 'what'.

53. *Antiates* (Pope) F. 'Antients' (in rom.)—but
the comp. gets it right ('*Antiats*') in l. 59.

54. *Aufidius* F. '*Auffidious*'—spelt '*Affidious*' in l. 59.
N.B. Plut. introduces him first on p. 168 as the chief
man in Antium.

60. *delay the present* 'make any delay now' (Case);
v. G. 'present'.

61. *advanced* v. G.

62. *prove* v. G.

70. *Lesser* (F 3) F. 'Lessen'.

75. S.D. (F.).

76. *O me, alone*!...*me?* (punct. Cap.+most) F. 'Oh
me alone, make you a sword of me:' The chief crux of
the text, many emendations proposed. Tucker Brooke
(<conj. by Style, *ap.* Camb.) assigns to *soldiers*. Yet
Cap.'s punct. seems to make all well. But he notes: 'The
first part of this line should be uttered in a tone of
surprize, expressive of the speaker's taking shame upon

himself for having thought that but one man might offer, v. l. 73; the latter part of it changes to another of pleasantry, and is address'd to the soldiers who have got him up in their arms' (*Notes on Sh*. 1774, p. 83). Rather, I think, the first half is a protest against the notion that he alone deserves 'chairing'. Cf. ll. 67–8, and 1. 9. 13–9. Deighton's conj. 'Of me alone make you a sword? of me?' is attractive.

77. *outward* = insincere (Case).

83. *As...obeyed* As occasion shall prescribe.

84. *I shall* (Hudson < Cap. conj.) F. (+ most edd.) 'foure shall'. Poss. capital 'I' in Sh.'s hand mistaken for the numeral '4'. See the first 'I' in l. 58 of Sh.'s 'Three Pages' (reproduced by Maunde Thompson as the last 'I' on Plate VII in *Sh.'s Hand*.) which resembles a roman 'A' and might explain the misprints 'Annius' for 'Iunius' (1. 1. 225, S.D.) and 'Athica' for 'Ithica' (1. 3. 85); cf. 'Note on Copy', p. 131. It is 'I select' in l. 81 and must surely be 'I draw out my command' (= I select my commando) here. Cor. is not the man to depute so vital a choice to 'four' unnamed officers.

85. *Which...inclined* In apposition to 'command'.

86. *this ostentation* this parade before Cor.

87. *Divide in all* Share the booty. S.D. (J.D.W.) F. 'Exeunt'.

1.7

S.D. *Loc.* (< Cap. 'the gates of Corioli') *Entry* (< F.). Greg (*Sh. F.F.* p. 406) notes that this S.D. 'is really a summary of what he [Tit.] says in this short scene. It might well have been copied in from the author's plot or scenario'.

7. S.D. (J.D.W.) F. 'Exit. Alarum, as in Battaile' (v. next sc.).

1. 8

Loc. (J.D.W.<Pope 'The Roman Camp'). Clearly we are supposed to return to approx. the same loc. as in 1. 6.; and F. 'Alarum, as in Battaile' (1. 7. 4. S.D.), warns the audience that Cor. and the Antiates are hard at it. *Entry* (Cap.) F. 'Enter Martius and Auffidius at seueral doores'.

1–2. *I do hate thee...We hate alike* Cf. Plut.'s account of Cor.'s desertion to the Volsces (North, pp. 168–9): 'Martius knewe very well, that Tullus [Aufidius] dyd more malice and envie him, then he dyd all the Romaines besides: bicause that many times in battells where they met, they were ever at the encounter one against another, like lustie coragious youthes, striving in all emulation of honour, and had encountered many times together. In so muche, as besides the common quarrell betweene them, there was bred a marvelous private hate one against another'.

4. *fame and envy* = detested reputation. Hendiadys. Cf. G. 'envy'. *Fix thy foot* Cf. *Ant.* 3. 7. 66 'fighting foot to foot'.

7. *Holloa me like a hare* i.e. pursue me with holloaing as huntsmen do, 'Having the fearful flying hare in sight' (*3 H. VI*, 2. 5. 130). For the hare as the extreme type of cowardice, cf. 1. 1. 170, above, *Tw. N.* 3. 4. 385, 'more a coward than a hare', and *Cym.* 4. 4. 37.

11. *Wrench...highest* Cf. *Mac.* 1. 7. 60 'screw your courage to the sticking point'; and my note there. *Hector* Cf. 1. 3. 42, n.

12. *the whip...progeny* the scourge with which your boasted ancestry the Trojans chastised the Greeks. Aeneas the reputed founder of Rome was Priam's son.

13 and 15. S.D.s (<F.) More descriptive S.D.s implying stage fights of some minutes. F. prints them

as one S.D. at l. 13 and edd. follow. But it is obvious
that Auf.'s address to the Volscians precedes their being
'driven in breathless', where I read 'away' for F. 'in',
which means 'into the tiring-house'.

14. *Officious* v. G.

15. *In your...seconds* 'By seconding me in such a
damned cowardly fashion' (E.K.C.).

I. 9

S.D. *Loc.* Pope rightly continues the scene, since
Cor. clearly is meant to return from chasing Auf. and the
Volscians. Cap.+subs. edd. read 'The Roman Camp'.
Entry (<F. wh. reads 'at one Doore' for 'from one
side' and 'At another Doore' for 'from the other side'.
For 'retreat' cf. *2 H. IV*, 4. 3. 69–70, '*John*. Now,
have you left pursuit? *West*.. Retreat is made and
execution stayed'. It is sounded by Tit. (cf. l. 11, S.D.).

2. *Thou't* (F.) Abbrev. of coll. 'thou woot'. Cf.
Ham. 5. 1. 269, n.

4. *shrug* sc. with incredulity.

6. *gladly quaked* delightfully agitated. Ver. compares
Desdemona listening to Oth.'s 'travel's history'. *dull*
v. G.

7. *fusty* smelly; v. G. *plebeians* Accented 'plébeians'
(Abbott § 492); cf. 3. 1. 101; 5. 4. 36.

10. *Yet cam'st...feast*=Yet this feast was but a
morsel compared with the large dinner you had eaten
before (in Corioli). *of*=in. Cf. *All's*, 1. 1. 7; 5. 3. 1.
Tit. emphasises the point in ll. 11–12.

11. S.D. (<F., but adding 'Lartius').

12. *Here...caparison* i.e. 'This man performed the
action, and we only filled up the show' (J.). This '*odd
encomium*' (J.)—surely apt enough in a soldier's mouth
—seems like the wager at 1. 4. 1–6 to have been
suggested by North as cited in ll. 61–2 b below.

14. *has a charter* is privileged.

19. *Hath...act* 'Has done more than I have, for I have not done all I would' (E.K.C.).

20. *the grave* etc. Cf. *Son.* 17. 3.

21. *her own* i.e. her own sons.

24. *the spire and top of praises vouched*='if proclaimed in the very highest terms of praise'. Cf. North, p. 153, 'whose valliantnes he commended beyond the moone'.

25. *but modest* only moderate praise.

26–7. *In sign...hear me* i.e. 'Listen! What I am going to say [in ll. 32–6] is no adequate reward, but the least acknowledgment possible' (C. B. Young).

29. *Should they not* i.e. be remembered.

30. *'gainst* v. G. 'against'.

31. *tent...death* cure themselves by killing you. Cf. 3. 1. 234–5.

31–6. *Of all the horses...choice* Versified North. Cf. p. 153: 'So in the ende he willed Martius, he should choose out of all the horses they had taken of their enemies, and of all the goodes they had wonne (whereof there was great store) tenne of every sorte which he liked best, before any distribution should be made to other'.

31–2. *horses—Whereof...store—of all* (Al.) Rowe 'horses, Whereof...store, of all'. F. 'Horses, Whereof... good, and good store of all'.

40. *upheld* (J.D.W.<Cap.) F. (+all edd.) 'beheld' —suggests that they stood by and looked on, which is imposs., since Cor. cannot be sarcastic at this point. *upheld*=supported, sustained. Cf. *3 H. VI*, 3. 3. 106–7; *M. V.* 5. 1. 215, etc. S.D. (F.).

46. *a coverture* (Tyrwhitt+most) F. 'an Ouerture' =a misprint influenced maybe by (1) the musical context, and (2) an initial 'C', often written as a rounded capital, not unlike an 'O', in Sh.'s hand (v. *Sh.'s Hand.*,

pp. 115–16, and Plate VII). Cf. 'couercame' for 'ouercame' in *L.L.L.* (Q) 4. 1. 69. Tyrwhitt also conj. 'it' for 'him' (=silk) in the same line, and this may be right too ('him' being then explained as a press-reader's miscorrection to agree with 'parasite'), for though 'him' might refer to an inanimate obj. in 16th-17th c. English, I know of no other ex. in Sh. By 'steel' I take it Cor. refers to the 'caps and lances'. To paraphrase Cor's. outburst—'If you are going to degrade war's instruments in this way never let me hear them again! When drums and trumpets come to be used for flattery, let nothing but hypocrisy and sycophancy be heard in courts and cities, and when steel grows soft as the parasite's silk doublet, let silk be used as armour.' Moore Smith (priv.) conj. 'an officer', wh. makes 'him' refer to 'parasite' and wd be attractive if it had more graphical support.

50. *shout* (F4) F. 'shoot'. Cf. 1. 1. 213, n. and p. 133. *shout. . .forth*=acclaim me.

52. *dieted*=lit. fed, hence (here) fattened, v. G. For 'dieted in' (=dieted with or by) cf. *Comp.* 261 'dieted in grace'; *sauced* (v. G.) carries on the metaphor. Cf. *Cym.* 4. 2. 50–1 (of cooking) 'He...sauced our broths as Juno had been sick And he her dieter'.

53–8. *Too modest...with you* Com. half playfully, but firmly, reminds the young hero that he is speaking to his general.

55. *give* v. G. *patience* He emphasises the word.

57. *means his proper harm* has suicidal intentions.

61–2. *My noble steed...belonging* Cf. North, p. 153, 'he gave him...a goodly horse with a capparison, and all furniture to him'—for wh. v. also 1. 4. 2–7, n. *trim belonging*=either 'fine trappings' or 'the accoutrement pertaining to it'—both words being either adj. or sb.

65 and 67. *Caius Marcius* (after Rowe). F. 'Marcus Caius'. Cf. 2. 1. 162–3 and 2. 2. 44. Plut. digresses for a whole page (pp. 154–5) to explain the Roman

fashion in names, so that Sh. had no excuse for going wrong. Is the aberration due to some editorial interference in the F. text? The queer case of 2. 1. 162–3 suggests it.

66. *addition* v. G. S.D. (F.).

72. *undercrest* Prob. an invented word; not found elsewhere (v. O.E.D.) 'support as if it were my crest, i.e. to act up to it and so justify its bestowal on me' (Ver.).

73. *To...power* 'as well as I fairly can' (Clar.). I prefer 'as spotlessly as I can', after Schmidt, who thinks Cor. still has 'fair' (l. 69) in mind.

77. *the best* sc. the leading men of Corioli.

articulate v. G.

83. *And at* (Han.) F. (+most) 'At' *poor man's* North (p. 154) tells us he was 'an honest wealthie man'. By making him 'poor' Sh. shows us that the hero is not contemptuous of poverty as such. The forgetfulness of the name is one of Sh.'s natural touches, 'the amnesia of an exhausted man' (Case). Cf. 1. 1. 215–16, n.

89. *free as the wind* Cf. *A.Y.L.* 2. 7. 47–9; *Tp.* 1. 2. 497–8.

I. 10

S.D. *Loc.* (Camb. after Pope). *Entry* (F.) The 'flourish' no doubt heralds the entry of Aufidius. 'Cornets'. Acc. to W. J. Lawrence the use of cornets points to performance at the Blackfriars Theatre (*Sh.'s Workshop*, 1928, pp. 48–64, esp. 60–64.)

2. *on good condition* on favourable terms. Cf. 1. 9. 77–8.

4–5. *I would...I am* 'As a Volsce, I can only be a defeated man, and that Aufidius can never be.' An ironical clue by Sh. to Cor. becoming a Volsce later; and almost an echo of 1. 1. 230–1.

5. *Condition!* F. 'Condition?'

5–6. *Condition!...condition* For the word-play v. G.

7. *the part that is at mercy* the conquered side. For 'at mercy' or 'in mercy' (*Lr.* 1. 4. 328) v. G. 'mercy'.

12. *Mine emulation* etc. Cf. 1. 8. 14–15. The debasement in character of the frustrated Auf. is a foretaste of similar development in the frustrated Cor.

13. *where*=whereas.

15. *potch* v. G. 'A purposely mean word as the context requires' (Ver.)—bitterly spoken in self-contempt.

17–19. *My valour's...itself* (<F. subs.) Pope (+some 19th c. edd.) 'My valour (poisoned...by him) for him...itself'—wh. is attractive. *fly...itself* 'discard its natural character' (Ver.). After 'stain' (v. G.) the astrol. notion of 'start from its sphere' is prob. in Sh.'s mind. Cf. *Son.* 35. 3. 'Clouds and eclipses stain both sun and moon'.

19–27. *Nor sleep...in's heart* Cf. Laertes' vow of revenge at *Ham.* 4. 7. 125–6.

20. *naked* defenceless.

23. *rotten* corrupt with age.

25. *upon...guard* 'with my brother posted to protect him' (J.).

26. *the hospitable canon* Cf. *Mac.* 1. 6. 12–16.

30. *attended* v. G. *cypress* (Rowe) F. 'Cyprus'.

31. *'Tis south...mills* Clar. notes that in these touches of local colour Sh. often has London in mind and that there were certainly four flour mills on the South Bank close to the Globe Theatre.

32–3. *that...journey* that I may not be left behind by the speed of events.

S.D. none in F.

2. I

S.D. *Loc.* (Cap.) *Entry* (F.).

1 ff. Men. 'finds it...amusing to "toast" the tribunes....Just so might a genial Pall Mall club man and a couple of London county-councillors satirize each other to-day' (E.K.C. 1898).

11. *baas* F. 'baes'.

13. *old men* If Sic. was played by Sinklo ('doubling' in 1. 1. as 1 Cit.; v. 1. 1. 158, n; 3. 1. 176, n.) who was an adult player in 1590, he must have been an old man in 1608–9.

16. *In...in* Characteristic Sh. repetition, natural also in mod. speech. Cf. Abbott, §407.

19–20. *in pride...in boasting* Cf. the exhibition of his great modesty in sc. 1. 9.

23. *o' th' right hand file*=belonging to the place of honour in the ranks of the army. Cf. G. 'file'.

28. *'tis...matter* if you *do* get angry; for a very little trifle will put you out.

29. *thief of occasion* Cf. the use of 'of' in 'city of London'; Cf. 1. 1. 135, n.

30. *dispositions...pleasures* Plur. because Men. is addressing two persons. Cf. 2. 3. 200, 221 ('loves') [G.G.] and 3. 1. 7 'our ages'.

36. *single* v. G.

38–9. *turn your eyes...interior survey* Alluding to the fable 'that every man has a bag hanging before him, in which he puts his neighbour's faults, and another behind him, in which he stows his own' (J.). See Aesop, *Phoedrus IV*. ix and Horace, *Satires*, II, iii, 299. Furn. objects that an 'interior survey' cannot refer to an *exterior* bag. But Sh. does not mention any bag, though he may well have the fable in mind, and psychologises it by adapting it to self-examination. Baldwin, *Sh.'s Small Latin*, II, 544–5, suggests that he may have come across in Erasmus, *Adagia* (1574, p. 177) the following couplet by Persius:

> Ut nemo in sese temptat descendere, nemo,
> Sed praecedenti spectatur mantua tergo.

43. *magistrates* (*alias fools*) Sh.'s audience prob. took the tribunes to=London J.P.s, and Men.'s comments to reflect the gen. attitude of gentry (esp. Inns of Court students) to such officials. Cf. Sh.'s treatment of Justice Shallow in *2 H. IV*.

45. *known well enough*=pretty notorious.

46. *patrician* F. 'Patritian' (ital.)—elsewhere always 'Patrician' (rom.).

47–8. *hot wine...allaying Tiber in't* Alluding 'to the popular mulled wine of Sh.'s day' (Furn.). Cf. Falstaff 'Go, brew me a pottle of sack, finely' (*Wiv.* 3. 5. 28) and *M. V.* 2. 2. 183–4; 'allay with some cold drops of modesty Thy skipping spirit'.

48–9. *something...complaint* i.e. rather inclined, when on the bench, to dispatch cases too rapidly. Cf. the tedious long-windedness of the tribunes over cases before them (ll. 68–71).

50. *too trivial motion* 'too trifling provocation' (Case). He was apt to be quarrelsome in his cups; 'hasty and tinder-like' implies outbursts of anger. Cf. G. 'motion', 'hasty', 'tinder-like'.

50–1. *converses* v. G. *the buttock...night* Cf. Armado: 'in the posteriors of this day' *L.L.L.* 5. 1. 85–6 [Mal.].

53. *wealsmen* i.e. 'devoted to the public good' (O.E.D.).

54. *Lycurguses* i.e. wise legislators: v. G. Sh. could learn of his 'great wisdom' from Plutarch, e.g. North i. 162. And ll. 53–4 sound like an echo of North, 1. 23: 'Lycurgus...beganne to devise howe to alter the whole government of the common weale', i.e. he was an innovating wealsman like the tribunes.

54–5. *if the drink...at it* i.e. 'if I don't like what you say, my looks mark my displeasure' (Case).

56. *cannot say* (Cap.) F. 'I can say'; Theob.'s 'can't' is accepted by most edd.; but doubtful if this contraction was in use before the 18th c.

57–8. *the ass...syllables* 'an element of the fool in all you say' (Herf.) is the gen. sense, but there is prob. some quibble on *as* and *ass*, so far undiscovered; perhaps grammatical, perhaps 'a pun on the last syllables (-us) of their names' (Sherman *ap*. Furn.).

60. *tell you you have* (Pope+) F. 'tell you have'.

61. *in the map...microcosm* sc. in my face, 'which is to the "microcosm" man what a map is to the "macrocosm" the world' (E.K.C.). Cf. G. 'map'.

62. *known...too* Cf. Sic. at l. 45. The phrase rankles.

63. *bisson* (Theob.) F. 'beesome' *bisson conspectuities* blear-eyed clearsightedness (Theob.) v. G. Cf. *Ham*. (Q2) 2. 2. 510 'Bison rehume'. He bamboozles them.

65. *we know* 'we' is emphatic.

67–8. *for...caps and legs* 'to be bowed and scraped to' (E.K.C.). (Cf. *Tim*. 3. 6. 96 'cap-and-knee slaves'.)

68. *wholesome* 'which might be spent more profitably' (Schmidt). One knows what Men. would consider a profitable forenoon. *hearing a cause* North (p. 149) calls the 'tribuni plebis' 'magistrates' (v. G.), but this did not mean justices, though Sh. prob. took it as such; cf. l. 43, n.

69. *faucet* (Neilson)—the mod. sp. F. 'fosset'— wh. most edd. follow. v. G.

70. *rejourn...threepence* adjourn the hearing of a three-penny-ha'penny dispute.

72. *party*=litigant v. G.

73. *make faces like mummers* The point is that mummers or performers in a dumb-show did not speak but conveyed their meaning by facial expression.

74. *set...flag*=declare war; cf. *H. V*, 1.2. 101, 'unwind your bloody flag'. Prob. alluding also to getting red in the face with the 'pinch'.

75. *bleeding* 'i.e. without having, as it were, dressed or cured it' (Schmidt).

80. *a perfecter...bencher* more successful as a witty diner-out than valuable as a senator.

82. *become mockers* i.e. cease being serious and take to scoffing.

83. *subjects* v. G.

86. *stuff...cushion* Cf. *Ado*, 3. 2. 42–3, 'the old ornament of his cheek hath already stuffed tennis-balls' and Lyly's *Midas*, v. ii (Bond's *Lyly*, iii. 157) 'a dozen of beards to stuffe two dozen of cushions'. [Clar.]. *a botcher's cushion* The cushion, I suppose, upon which a mender of old clothes or cobbler sat at work.

88. *in a cheap estimation* at the lowest computation. *since Deucalion* since the Flood.

92. *conversation* society; v. G.

94. S.D. (i) (Theob.) F. 'Bru. and Scic. Aside'; (ii) (F.).

95–7. *How now* etc. Men. is clearly a ladies' man: *the moon* etc. i.e. Diana. A delicate tribute to their chastity. *follow...fast* Case cites *Oth.* 2. 1. 36–8, 'Let's to the seaside', etc.

101–2. *with...approbation* with confirmation of the tidings of greatest success.

103. *take my cap* Like a schoolboy. Cf. 1. 1. 211, n. *Jupiter* the king of heaven—a reply to her 'Juno'.

112. *gives...estate of* endows me with. On. glosses 'estate' here 'state, condition'; the mod. meaning is more pregnant.

113. *make a lip at* cock a snook at. v. G. 'lip'.

115. *empiricutic* F. 'Emperickqutique' v. G. The usual form was 'empiric' or 'empirical', a term of contempt for doctors who based their methods on the results of observation and experiment, and not on Galenic 'philosophical' principles. Cf. G. 'Galen'. O.E.D. cites Bacon *Adv. Learn*. 1, 8, 'It is accounted an errour to commit a naturall bodie to Emperique Phisitians', etc.

121. *pocket, the* (Han.) F. (+most) 'Pocket? the'— Unlike Vol., the old soldier Men., does not believe in the absolute virtue of wounds; but wounds, if got in victorious fight, are good trophies. Han.'s comma also renders Vol.'s reply easier.

122. *brows, Menenius* (J. <Theob.). F. (+most) 'Browes: Menenius'. The victory is on his brows not in his pocket, she retorts, though exultantly. The F. punct. of ll. 121–2 might suggest that the wounds were on his forehead! And Men. does not need to be told that it's the *third* time; the words are merely expository of 'On's brows'.

124. *disciplined...soundly* = given...a sound thrashing.

129. *fidiused* i.e. aufidius-ed. Edd. cite 'I'll prat her' (*Wiv*, 4. 2. 178) and 'I'll fer him' (*H. V*, 4. 4. 29).

140. *pooh-pooh* (Cap.) F. (+most) 'pow waw'.

142. S.D. (J.D.W.) Theob. (+most) 'To the tribunes'.

143–4. *more...proud* Cf. above ll. 19 ff.

149–50. *One...nine* He begins checking her figures by counting up those he knows of; first aloud, then to himself, and concludes 'there's *nine* (not seven) that *I* know'. But there were other campaigns besides that against the Tarquins; so she goes on 'He had', etc.

153. *twenty-seven* He accepts her figure and adds the two new ones (l. 149).

154. S.D. (F.).

159. *advanced* uplifted. *declines* falls; cf. *Ham*. 2:

2. 492. 'Her son to kill his enemy has nothing to do but lift his hand and let it fall' (J.).

S.D. (<F.)—printing 'Latius' for 'Lartius'.

162–3. *Caius Marcius; these* | *In...Coriolanus* (Steev.+most) F. '*Martius Caius*: | *These in... Martius Caius Coriolanus*'. The accepted reading is clearly correct. Mal. conj. that the original names, accidentally transposed in l. 162, were then caught by the comp.'s eye and repeated in l. 163. But this does not explain the like transposition at 1. 9. 65, 67; 2. 2. 44 (all in conjunction with 'Coriolanus'). The error is the stranger that elsewhere 'Caius Martius' always appears in the correct order.

163. *In honour* etc. 'The third foot is completed by a pause, to give due emphasis to the resounding name wh. follows' (E.K.C.).

164. S.D. < (F. 'Sound. Flourish.')

166. *it does offend my heart* Surely meant to be genuine. Cf. Introd. pp. xxviii, ff.

167. S.D. (F.)—at l. 169. It was customary in Sh.'s age for sons to kneel and ask their mother's blessing when greeting them. Cf. *R. III*, 2. 2. 105.

171. *deed-achieving honour* Not 'honour that achieves deeds' but 'honour achieved by deeds'. Schmidt cites *Lucr.* 993 'an unrecalling crime'='a crime that cannot be recalled'. *achieving* is gerundive.

173. *My gracious silence*=my lovely silence. Cf. G. 'gracious'.

178. *Cor.* (Theob.+) F. '*Com.*' *And live you yet?* A jocular question. Cf. *Ado*, 1. 1. 114. S.D.(J.D.W. after Theob.) G.G. suggests that he may be addressing his wife, asking her to forgive him jesting at her tears. But could he call her 'my sweet *lady*'?

179. *I know...turn* T. Brooke (1924) suggests assigning this to *Cor.*, thus adding a dramatic turn to the reunion of family and friends.

180. *you're* F. 'y'are'. Most mod. edd. 'ye're'.

183. *begnaw the* (J.D.W.<Craig 'begnaw at') F. 'begin at'. 'Begnaw' being a trans. vb. cannot be followed by 'at', but otherwise Craig's emendation seems palmary. Cf. *R. III*, 1. 3. 222, 'the worm of conscience still begnaw thy soul!' *Tim.* 4. 3. 49, 'The canker gnaw thy heart!' and *Oth.* 2. 1. 291; 4. 2. 137; *Tit.* 3. 1. 262.

184. *You* (F2) F. 'Yon'.

187. *to your relish* i.e. so as to bear fruit 'of your flavour'—not 'to your taste' (E.K.C.). 'They will have more of your sweet in their bitter' (G.G.). *Yet* Pope om. perhaps rightly.

188–9. *We call...folly* i.e. 'poor things, they are what they are, and cannot help it' (Ver.).

189–90. *Ever right...ever* 'Right as usual', says Com.; and Cor. 'Menenius, as ever'.

195. *change of honours* i.e. a new set of honours. Cf. 'changes of raiment' at Judges xiv. 12; Zech. iii. 4; and 'double change of brav'ry', i.e. two splendid new dresses (*Shr.* 4. 3. 57).

197. *buildings* The fig. inheritance of landed property (l. 196) is thus extended. She is like an exultant heir newly come into a long dreamed of inheritance.

200–1. *I had...theirs* 'A significant foreshadowing' (Ver.). But also an important clue to character; note the distinction between servant and *sway* (v. G.). He does not *want* to be a consul (magistrate): he is quite content to go on serving Cominius as a soldier man. And as the words are not public but privately spoken to his mother they must be genuine. Cf. Introd. p. xxv.

201. S.D. (i) (F.) (ii) (Theob.) F. 'Enter Brutus and Scicinius'.

202 ff. With this description of a (London) crowd in (London) streets cf. *J. C.* 1. 1. 41–51; *R. II*, 5. 2. 1–21.

204. *rapture* (F.)—'a state of passionate excitement: a paroxysm, fit' (O.E.D. 5 c, citing this and, from 1634, 'in rage and sudden rapture').

205. *chats him* gossips about him.

205–6. *pins...neck* to protect it from the cold wind.

208. *ridges horsed* Spectators sat astride the ridges of the roofs.

209. *with variable complexions* by people of the most varied kind. See G. 'complexion'.

210. *flamens* F. 'Flamins' Sh. prob. has in mind religious recluses, though the epithet *seld-shown* was also apt to the Roman 'flamens'. Edd. suggest he may have learnt about them from Plut.'s *Life of Numa* [North, 1, 175], but the name must have been familiar to all educated persons in his day (cf. *Tim.* 4. 3. 156; Drayton's *Polyolbion*, VIII, 48, 322) and was often applied to the pre-Christian priesthood in ancient Britain.

211–12. *puff...station* App.=get out of breath trying to secure a good place in the crowd. But 'puff' is odd and not again in Sh. in this sense.

213. *the war of white and damask* A commonplace. Cf. *Ven.* 346, *Lucr.* 71, and *Shr.* 4. 5. 30 'such war of white and red within her cheeks'.

214. *guarded* (J.D.W.<conj. Lettsom) F. (+most) 'gawded'—an easy misreading of 'garded'. 'Nicely-guarded' = carefully protected by 'sun-expelling masks'. Cf. *Gent.* 4. 4. 151. E.K.C. glosses 'nicely gawded' as 'carefully adorned' and G.G. as 'daintily done up'. But 'commit...to th' wanton spoil of Phoebus' burning kisses'—Cf. *Ant.* 1. 5. 28 'with Phoebus' amorous pinches black'—lends strong support to 'guarded'.

216–17. *As if...powers* Mal. cites *Ant.* 4. 8. 24. 'he hath fought today As if a god in hate of mankind had Destroyed in such a shape'.

218. *posture* v. G.

221. *transport his honours* etc. Cf. G. 'transport' and 4. 7. 36–7 'he could not | Carry his honours even'.

222. *From…end* i.e. 'from where he should begin to where he should end. The word "transport" includes the ending as well as the beginning' (Mal.)— citing *Cym.* 3. 2. 62–4 'the gap | That we shall make in time from our hence-going | And our return'.

223–4. *Doubt…but they* i.e. 'Doubt not but that the commoners' (G.G.).

226. *which* sc. 'cause'.

227. *give make* (J.D.W.<Pope). F. 'giue them, make'. The 'them' is superfluous in sense and metre.

228. *As*=As that.

231. *The napless…humility* Sh.'s gloss on a misunderstanding by North of a passage in Amyot. Plutarch says: 'It was the custom with those who stood for the office [of consul] to greet their fellow-citizens and solicit their votes, descending into the forum in their toga, without a tunic under it. This was either because they wished the greater humility of their garb to favour their solicitations, or because they wished to display the tokens of their bravery, in case they bore wounds' [Loeb: *Plut. Lives*, IV, 149]. Translating this, Amyot writes of 'une robe simple…sans saye dessous' and refers to it later as 'si humble habit'; phrases which North renders 'a poore gowne…without any coate underneath', and 'in suche meane apparell' (p. 158).

napless (Rowe) F. 'Naples'—a common sp. Cf. 'Note on Copy', p. 132. 'Napless' implies a threadbare woollen garment and Sh. seems to have supposed that Cor. assumed a garb like that worn by the plebeians (and Eliz. poorer classes). Cf. 2. 2. 135, n.; 2. 3. 114, n.; 3. 2. 9.

234–5. *he would* etc. he would rather go without it than win it except by the request of the patricians. v. G. 'carry'.

239. *wills:* (Al.<F. 'wills;') Most edd. 'wills,'—
J. 'will's,' and though Mal. reads 'wills:' he takes
'good wills' as the plur. of 'good-will'. As Mason
however rightly saw, 'good' is the subj., 'wills' its
pred. and 'A sure destruction' what their 'good' wills
or requires.

241. *For an end* i.e. to this end. Schmidt+Case
explain 'In short', a possible but less attractive sense.

242. *suggest* v. G.

243. *still* always.

248. *the war* (Han.+most) F. 'their Warre' E.K.C.
and Al. accept, but it is awkward with 'their provand'
in the same line.

252. *touch* (Han.+most) F. 'teach'. Mal. interprets F. 'instruct the people in their duty to their
rulers', G.G. similarly as 'lecture them, as he does in
1.1.166, ff.'; and C.J.S. as 'teach the people their time
for revolt'. But these, the last esp., are surely too far-
fetched for spectators to follow, whereas 'touch' =
touch to the quick, wound their feelings (cf. O.E.D.
25) exactly fits the context, and is freq. with Sh.

254. *the fire* (J.D.W.<Pope) F. (+most) 'his fire'.
The 'fire' is not Cor.'s 'insolence' but the suggestions
of the tribunes, which once ablaze *darkens* him; 'his' is
therefore doubly ruled out. Cap. conj. 'as fire', but
that would make 'the ass' too much 'in compound'
with Sic.'s 'syllables' (v. 2. 1. 57). Comp. *B* is esp.
careless with these little words; cf. nn. at 1. 9. 83; 2.
1. 56, 60, 183, 227, 248, etc.

256. S.D. (F.).

260–2. *matrons...passed* Sh. attributes the customs
of his age to ancient Rome [Mal.] *flung* F. 'flong'.

266. *th' time* the present.

267. *the event* its consequences. S.D. (<F.
'Exeunt'.)

2. 2

S.D. *Loc.* (<Cap.) See G. 'Capitol' *Entry*<F., 'Enter two Officers, to lay Cushions, as it were, in (=as if in) the Capitoll.' It was customary in Sh.'s day to 'lay cushions' for dignitaries on solemn occasions. Cf. 3. 1. 101, n., 4. 7. 43, *Ham.* 5. 2. 222 S.D. and the comic touch in *Ado* 4. 2. 2. (a police court case).

7. *hath* (F.+Al.; C.J.S.) F4 (+most) 'have'.

16. *waved* v. G. Indic. for subjunc.; cf. Abbott, §361 (who prints 'waived'). The form 'wave' for 'waver' is well attested, but not found in Sh. elsewh. Perh. he wrote 'waverd' and the comp. omitted 'r'.

24. *ascent* (F2) F. 'assent'. *degrees* v. G.

25–7. *bonneted, without...at all, into* (Al.<Delius) F. 'Bonnetted, without...deed, to haue...at all into'— which most edd. follow (omitting the comma after 'deed') and Mal. paraphrases: 'They humbly took off their bonnets without any further deed whatsoever done in order to *have* them, that is, to insinuate themselves into the good opinion of the people.' Al.'s punct. gives us 'They did nothing but go bonnet in hand to win popular support'. Cf. 3. 2. 72, 'go to them with this bonnet in thy hand', and *R. II*, 1. 4. 31, 'Off goes his bonnet to an oyster-wench'.

27. *estimation* v. G. *report* v. G.

33. *of him* (F.) Is not 'of them' more apt?—dismissing his detractors.

34. S.D. (<F.)—but F. continues 'Coriolanus stands' which (perh., meant to imply he was not a senator as yet) is inconsistent with its S.D. at l. 64 'Coriolanus rises' etc., and so Rowe omitted it. Al. (<Neilson) retains both S.D.s and resolves the inconsistency by adding an inconsequent S.D. 'Coriolanus sits' at l. 46. Ll. 68–9 prove the S.D. at l. 64. The words are prob. a prompter's jotting; see p. 137 above.

38. *gratify* v. G. *that*=who.

39. *stood for* v. G. 'stand' (iv).

42. *well-found* v. G.

44. *Caius Marcius Coriolanus* F. 'Martius Caius Coriolanus'. See notes on 1. 9. 65, 67; 2. 1. 162–3.

45. *We met* The construction, Mal. thinks, is 'whom to thank etc. we met or assembled here'.

47–9. *make us think...it out*=lead us to feel rather that the state lacks means to repay him fully than that we lack will to strain its means to the utmost.

49. S.D. (Camb.).

51–2. *Your...here* Your kind influence with the common people to assent to our decisions here (viz. the nomination of Cor. to the consulship).

53. *treaty* v. G.

56. *blessed* happy.

58. *off* off the point, not pertinent. Cf. Brut.'s reply.

64. S.D. (F.).

68–9. *I hope...not* Proves that Cor. has been sitting until l. 64.

69. *disbench* An Inns of Court term. v. G.

71. *soothed* flattered.

72. *weigh—* v. G. The dash (F.'s) was read by Rowe, Pope, Theob., Warb., J, Furn. But Han.+most since read 'weigh'.

73. *I had...sun* A picture of idleness. *one...head* e.g. a mistress.

74. *When...struck* When the signal for battle was sounded (Case). Cf. *R. III*, 4. 4. 149.

76. *multiplying spawn* i.e. proletarii (child-breeders) [E.K.C.].

79. *Than...it?* Supply 'let' or 'suffer'. *one on's* (F 2) F. 'on ones'. Cf. 1. 1. 16, n.

81–3. *It is held...haver* Cf. North, p. 144: 'Now in those dayes, valliantnes was honoured in Rome above all other vertues: which they called *Virtus*, by the name of vertue self, as including in that generall name, all other speciall vertues besides'.

85. *singly counterpoised* matched by any single person. *At...years* Cf. North, p. 145, 'being but a strippling'.

86. *make a head* v. G. 'head'.

87. *beyond the mark* beyond the aim. Cf. *Ant.* 3. 6. 87, 'beyond the mark of thought'.

88. *Whom...at* 'A reminiscence of the common phrase in Latin speeches *quem honoris causa nomino*' (E.K.C.).

89. *Amazonian* i.e. beardless. *chin* (F 3) F. 'shinne' —a literal.

90. *bristled* F. 'brizled'.

92–3. *Tarquin's self...knee* A Homeric incident, of which Plut. says nothing. *on...knee* = to his knees.

94. *act...scene* be a boy-actor of female parts in the theatre, i.e. his voice was not yet 'cracked within the ring' (*Ham.* 2. 2. 433).

96. *brow-bound...oak* Cf. 1. 3. 13, n. *His pupil age Man-entered thus* Having thus begun his apprenticeship as warrior in a fashion worthy of a full-grown man [after Case]. Clar. interprets 'Being thus initiated into manhood'.

97. *waxèd like a sea* Cf. *Rom.* 5. 3. 37 'savage wild | More fierce and more inexorable far | Than...the roaring sea'.

98. *seventeen battles* suggested by North, p. 159, 'seventeene yeres service at the warres' [G.G.].

99. *lurched...garland* = robbed all swords (i.e. warriors) of their glory (v. G. 'lurch', 'garland'). But Sh. prob. also had in mind the other meaning of 'lurch', viz. win an easy and sweeping victory at cards, leaving the other players 'in the lurch', as we still say today. When Jonson poked fun at the passage in *The Silent Woman*, he perh. implied that 'lurch' (= pilfer), almost thieves' cant, lacked decorum in this epical context. Cf. Introd. p. pp. ix–x.

103. *weeds* For another image of river-weeds, familiar to Sh. in Avon and Thames, v. *Ant.* 1. 4. 45 ff.

Like to a vagabond flag upon the stream, etc.

F 2 (+ most 18th c. edd.) read 'waves'—a much less vivid image.

106. *it took* Cf. G. 'stamp (ii)'. No second blow was needed.

took; from...foot (Steev. + all < Tyrwhitt conj.) F. 'tooke from...foot:'. See Furn. and Middleton Murry (*Discoveries*, 1924, pp. 281–2) for attempts to defend F. punct. by explaining 'took' as 'struck with plague' or 'infected', as it often does in Sh. (cf. *Ham.* 1. 1. 162), a metaphor carried on in 'struck... | Like a planet'. But the absolute pause at 'took', suggesting the finality of death, is to me overwhelmingly convincing and 'took' is bound up with the image of 'stamp'.

106–7. *from face...blood* Cf. *Ham.* 2. 2. 460, 'head to foot | Now is he total gules'.

107–8. *every motion...cries* 'The cries of the slaughtered regularly followed his motions, as musick and a dancer accompany each other' (J.).

109. *mortal* i.e. which it seemed death to enter.

109–10.   *painted...destiny* Usually explained 'covered with the blood of the slain'. But these epical metaphors must not be translated too explicitly. Sh. here recurs to the vague suggestion of his early plays influenced by Greene. Cf. *2 H. VI*, 5. 1. 200; *3 H. VI*, 1. 1. 168–9; 2. 1. 163–4 and Greene, *Philomela* 1592 [Grossart, XI, 187] 'with my blood to paint reuenge vpon the gates of Venice'.

111–12. *struck...like a planet* Cf. *Ham.* 1. 1. 162, 'no planets strike'; *Tim.* 4. 3. 109, and G. 'strike'.

112. *Now all's his*, (F.) Edd. 'Now all's his:' or 'his.'. But the change from past to present means 'no sooner is all his, when'.

113. *the din of war* i.e. of the battle Com. was waging.

114. *ready* 'ever quick to catch the sound of fighting' (Ver.).

117. *Run reeking* like a stream of blood swallowing up the men in his path.

118. *spoil* v. G.

120. *Worthy* heroic.

121. *He...measure* etc. 'No honour will be too great for him' (J.).

125. *misery* v. G. poss.=a miserly spirit; a sense O.E.D. 4 cites, from Elyot's *Governor* (1531), North's *Plutarch* (vol. xi 'Galba') and Holland's *Livy* (1600) —all books prob. known to Sh., though the sense does not seem to occur elsewhere in his plays.

127. *To spend...end it* J. (inheriting 'his' for 'the' from Rowe) conj. 'To spend his time to spend it', wh. secures an attractive balance; and he glossed ll. 126–7, 'To do great acts, for the sake of doing them; to spend his life for the sake of spending it'. But, as Mal. observed, 'the words (of F.) afford this meaning without any alteration'—a meaning wh. G.G. paraphrases 'Great action, to him, is its own reward, an end in itself'. Sh. is heightening one of Plut.'s asides (p. 146): 'For they [the valiant] esteeme not to receave reward for service done, but rather take it for a remembrance and encoragement, to make them doe better in time to come.'

129. S.D. F. 'Enter Coriolanus'.

131. *still* ever.

135. *naked*=here 'in civilian clothes' v. G.

139. *Put...to it*: v. G. 'put'. 'Do not press them too hard'. Men. is always trying to moderate Cor.'s absolute integrity.

142. *your form* Here 'your'='the form which custom prescribes to you' (Steev.). Han. read 'the form'.

144, 148, 149. J.D.W.'s asides and 'aloud'.

144. *Mark you that.* (F.) Rowe (+most edd.)

'Mark you that ?'. 'The admonitory form...is the more expressive' (Furn.).

148. *stand upon't*='be so obstinate, so uncompromising' (E.K.C.). The 'it' gives emphasis. Cf. 'brave it at court' (*Tit.* 4. 1. 122) and Abbott, § 226. Aside (J.D.W.)—almost whispered.

149–51. *We recommend* etc. Men. brings proceedings rapidly to an end, lest worse befall.

150. *to them* i.e. to the people. v. G. 'purpose'.

152. S.D. (J.D.W.) F. 'Flourish Cornets. | Then Exeunt. Manet Sicinius and Brutus'. For 'cornets' see 1. 10. S.D. (*init.*) and p. 137.

154. *require* v. G. Not 'demand' as in mod. Eng.

155. *what*=that what.

158. S.D. (J.D.W.).

2. 3

Plut.'s material for this important sc. is as follows:

North, p. 158: Shortely after this [the victory over the Volsces], Martius stoode for the Consulshippe: and the common people favored his sute, thinking it would be a shame to them to denie and refuse, the chiefest noble man of bloude, and most worthie persone of Rome, and specially him that had done so great service and good to the common wealth. For the custome of Rome was at that time, that suche as dyd sue for any office, should for certen dayes before be in the market place, only with a poore gowne on their backes, and without any coate underneath [ἐν ἱματίῳ...ἄνευ χιτῶνος], to praye the cittizens to remember them at the daye of election: which was thus devised, either to move the people the more by requesting them in suche meane apparell, [εἴτε μᾶλλον ἐκταπεινοῦντας ἑαυτοὺς τῷ σχήματι πρὸς τὴν δέησιν], or else bicause they might shewe them their woundes they had gotten in the warres...as manifest markes and testimonie of their valliantnes.

North, p. 159: Now Martius following this custome, shewed many woundes and cuttes upon his bodie, which

he had receyved in seventeene yeres service at the warres,
and in many sundrie battels, being ever the formost man
that dyd set out feete to fight. So that there was not a man
emong the people, but was ashamed of him selfe, to refuse
so valliant a man: and one of them sayed to another, We
must needes chuse him Consul, there is no remedie.

S.D. *Loc.* (after Cap.) *Entry* (F.) Note the per-
missive direction to the prompter. Cf. 5. 6. 8 S.D., and
Greg, *Sh.'s F.F.* p. 136.

1. *Once, if* (Theob.+most) F. 'Once if'—which
would give us 'If he do once require', etc. But 'once'
with a comma='in a word' or 'once for all', and is
more arresting.

6–7. *put...speak for them* Cf. *J. C.* 3. 1. 261;
3. 2. 229–30 'put a tongue | In every wound of
Caesar', 227 'And bid them speak for me'. Further
for 'wounds' as 'mouths' cf. *R. III*, 1. 2. 55–6;
1 H. IV, 1. 3. 96.

13. *And to make* 'etc.=it will not take much on our
part to make us thought no better than monsters, since
Cor. himself called us a many-headed one.

15. *the corn* v. 1. 1. 188; 3. 1. 43, 61, 125, etc.;
North, pp. 156–61.

many-headed Cf. 'Hydra' 3. 1. 93 and 'the beast
with many heads' 4. 1. 1–2. Sir Th. Elyot *Governour*,
Bk. 1, ii, describes democracy in ancient Athens 'a
monstre with many heades'. Cf. Tilley M 1029,
M 1308, *2 H. IV*, Prol. 18. Chief source Hor. *Ep.* 1.
i. 76 addressing the Roman people; 'Belua multorum es
capitum' (cf. Plato *Rep.* IX, 588, c. πολυκέφαλον θηρίον).

18. *abram* (F. 'Abram'). v. G. Not the same colour
as 'auburn' wh. F4 + many edd. read. Cf. Linthicum, pp. 29–30.

21–2. *their consent...way* 'their agreement to take
one straight course' (Ver.).

27. *wedged* F. 'wadg'd'.

31. *rotten* v. G.

32. *help...wife* Presumably to look after the poor creature.

34. *you may* A colloq. idiom, i.e. you may have your little joke. Cf. *Troil.* 3. 1. 109.

36. *no matter...it.* 'The vote need not be unanimous; a majority is sufficient' (G.G.). *it. I say*, (Theob.+) F. 'it, I say'.

38. S.D. (F.) For the 'gown' etc. v. G. and 2. 1. 231, n.

40. *We are not* etc. 3 Cit. directs the show acc. to the custom outlined at 2. 2. 135–42.

42. *by particulars* i.e. one by one. This 'single honour' was a privilege, no doubt, much valued by simple men. Note 'our *own* voices' and 'our *own* tongues'.

46. S.D. (J.D.W., after Cap.) F. om.

47. *you are not right* i.e. you've got it wrong.

48–9. *What...'I pray, sir—*' (Theob.+) F. 'What must I say, I pray Sir?' Poss. 'What! must I say "I pray, sir"?'

50. *to such a pace* A horsey metaphor, characteristic of the soldier man. Cf. *L.L.L.* 5. 2. 656 'Rein thy tongue', *R. II*, 1. 1. 55, and *Ado*, 3. 4. 86–7 'What pace is this that thy tongue keeps?—Not a false gallop.'

52. *roared and ran* etc. Cf. above, 1. 4. 30 ff.

55. *To think...you* 'i.e. bear you in mind', cf. North, p. 158, 'to remember them at the daye of election'. He has to act the beggar, in short. Cf. G. 'think upon', and *Mac.* 2. 3. 19–20, 'I pray you, remember the porter'. No wonder Cor. retorts 'I would they would *forget me*' [Beeching]. This *beggar* business (not found in Plut.) is of course exceedingly humiliating to Cor. and explains much of the dialogue that follows.

56. *like the virtues...'em* i.e. as they forget the virtuous advice which the preachers throw away upon them.

59. *wholesome* v. G. Cor. replies quibblingly by growling out sanitary advice sotto voce.

59. S.D. (i) (J.D.W.) F. 'Exit.' (ii) (J.D.W.) F. 'Enter three of the Citizens'. F. also heads speeches that follow 3 Cit., 2 Cit., 3 Cit., 3 Cit., 1 Cit., 2 Cit.—l. 74, 'The price...kindly', alone going to 1 Cit. Since these F. S.D.s and S.H.s do not accord with the dialogue, viz. 'a brace' (l. 60) and 'two worthy voices' (ll. 80–1), Camb. reads S.D. 'Re-enter two of the citizens' after 'clean' (l. 60) and 'Re-enter a third citizen' after 'brace' (l. 60). But this leaves 'two worthy voices' inconsistent, since there are now three citizens on the stage. Now 'brace' (l. 60) and 'two' (l. 80) seem to show that Sh. planned the dialogue for two players only and that therefore his S.D. at l. 59 was originally 'Enter two of the citizens'. On the other hand, one of the two would naturally be '3 Cit.', viz. the actor whom he could trust to speak his 'character' lines and who had been the chorus leader in ll. 1–45. He therefore, I suggest, distributed the speeches (ll. 62–83) between 3 Cit. and 2 Cit. I suggest further that someone responsible for getting the F. text into its final shape, Jaggard's reader or some other, convinced by these S.H.s that there should be three citizens, changed the two of the S.D. (l. 59) into three and gave one of '3 Cit.'s' speeches to '1 Cit.'.

61. *sir* (F.+most) Rowe (+some) 'sirs'. But 'he is to make his requests by particulars' (l. 42).

65. *desert?* (Al.) F. 'desert.'. The 'desert!' of most edd. suggests a note of indignation not, I think, intended by Sh. The simple fellows though determined to exercise their privileges are enjoying talking to the great warrior.

66. *Ay, not mine* (Rowe+many); F3 'I, not mine'; F. 'I, but mine'. In both cases I=Ay.

67. *How...desire?* As F. Edd. 'How!not...desire!'.
Cf. l. 65, n.

69. *trouble...with begging* That he should have to
play the beggar to this riff-raff! Cf. 'Misery may be the
mother when one beggar begs of another' (Heywood
Proverbs 1546, cited Tilley, M 1007).

70. *You must think* etc. 3 Cit. is puzzled and explains politely, in commercial terms, as a shopkeeper
would; and Cor. treats him as such, haughtily.

74. *The price...kindly* A gentle rebuke for Cor.'s
insulting question.

75. *Kindly, sir, I* (F 4 + Clar., Al, etc.) F. 'Kindly
sir, I' J. 'Kindly, Sir?' Cap. 'Kindly? Sir, I' Camb.
(+ C.J.S.) 'Kindly! Sir, I' With F 4 punct. Cor. com-
plies parrot-like with 3 Cit.'s suggestion. The other
readings make him express surprise or indignation.

75–6. *I have...private* This half-concession suggests
that he is hurrying to be done with the whole wretched
business. Plut. tells us he did show his wounds.

77. S.D. (J.D.W. < Clar.).

80. *A match* Done!

81. *begged...alms* Still the contemptuous beggar!
S.D. (J.D.W.) Cf. E.K.C. who suggests that Cor.,
having secured two bargains, 'turns round upon his
heel, and walks off to wait for another batch of citizens'.

83. S.D. (i) (J.D.W.). F. 'Exeunt'. (ii) (F.).

84–6. *if...gown* i.e. 'if you want me for consul
I've got the right suit on'.

87. '4 Citizen' is of the chop-logic type, popular
with Sh.'s public.

90–2. *You...people* 'the sole effort of the citizens
to put in practice the "lessoning" of the Tribunes
(v. ll. 176 ff. below). And it is more than enough to
stir the resentment of Cor.' (Ver.).

94. *not been common...love* v. G. 'common'.

94 ff. *I will, sir*, etc. Bitterly ironical—which the simpletons take to be a genuine offer of friendship. v. G. 'sworn brother', 'condition', 'gentle', 'insinuating'.

99. *be off* i.e. raise my hat. Cf. *R. II*, 1. 4. 31, 'Off goes his bonnet', and 2. 2. 25, n. (above).

100. *popular man* demagogue v. G. 'popular'.

105. *many wounds* A hint he refuses to take: no half-promise (as in l. 76) to *this* nasty fellow!

108. *make much of* v. G. 'much'. Still sarcasm, accepted as genuine.

112 ff. The heroic couplets are here 'used to express the excited overstrained condition of Cor. The citizens have got upon his nerves' (E.K.C.).

113. *hire* (F2) F. 'higher'—prob. due, as Clar. suggests, to the comp. carrying several words in his head and 'spelling as he pronounced them to himself'.

114. *woolvish toge* Gen. explained 'i.e. he feels like a wolf in sheep's clothing'—which is surely the wrong way about. But F. 'Wooluish' might be a misreading of 'wooliish' (=woolyish), and if so Cor. is referring to the fact that his gown of humility is a coarse woollen coat like those worn by the 'woollen vassals' (3. 2. 9.) he detests. Cf. O.E.D. 'Woollish'.

toge (Steev. conj.; Mal.+most) F. 'tongue'. Cf. *Oth.* 1. 1. 25 'toged consuls' F. 'Tongued Consuls'.

115. *do* (F4) F. 'does'.

116. *needless* Since the Senate has already appointed him (2. 2. 131).

117. *What...do't*=If we do all that custom commands.

118. *antique time* old-fashioned institutions and customs; v. G. 'time', and cf. 'the antique world' *A.Y.L.* 2. 3. 57.

123. S.D. (F.).

125–30. *Your voices!* etc. He whines this sarcastic rigmarole like a beggar. The charge 'ungravely' (l. 224) prob. refers to this.

125, 129. *voices!* F. 'Voyces?'. 125. *Watched* v. G.

128. *and heard of* Obvious foolery.

135. S.D. (J.D.W.) F. has no 'exeunt'.

136. S.D. (F.).

137. *limitation* v. G. Cf. *Mac.* 2. 3. 51, 'limited service'.

147. *to th'* F. 'toth''.

149. S.D. <F. 'Exeunt Coriol. and Mene.'.

152. S.D. (J.D.W.) F. 'Enter the Plebeians'.

173. *ignorant to see't* 'failing to notice it' (E.K.C.) or 'too stupid to see it' (Ver.); v. G. 'ignorant'.

183. *plebeii* Elsewhere 'plebeians'; but here thought of as an estate of the realm.

187. *think upon* v. l. 55, n. and G.

188. *Translate* v. G.

190. *touched* v. G.

193. *As...up* v. G. 'call up'.

194. *galled* rubbed up the wrong way.

195. *article* v. G.

199. *free* undisguised.

202–3. *had your bodies...you?* Was there no wisdom among the whole lot of you? For 'heart' as the seat of· wisdom see 1. 1. 115, n.

204. *Against the rectorship of judgement* 'Against what your reason determined' (E.K.C.). As Reason was the highest of human faculties, to cry against it was rebellion.

204–7. *Have you...tongues?* Have you before now refused your votes to a candidate who asked properly, and now granted them to one who did not ask but mocked?

206. *Of him* (F.) Theob. conj. 'On him', which would be much more readily understood today. But

'bestow of' is a common Eliz. idiom. Cf. Abbott, § 178.

208. *not confirmed* Cf. l. 143.

216. *therefore*='in order that they may bark' (Ver.).

217. *safer* v. G.

218. *Enforce* v. G.

224. *gibingly* (J.D.W.<Pope) F. 'most gibingly' Hudson (<Lettsom conj.) 'gibing, most'.

227. *No...between* i.e. provided nothing cropped up to prevent you meanwhile.

234. *read lectures to you* instructed you specially.

237–44. *The noble house...ancestor* A paraphrase of the opening sentences of Plut.'s *Life* (v. North, p. 143). 'This highly uninspired passage' (G.G.), is none the less a rather neat way of tucking in a piece of relevant history. We had not previously learnt of what noble lineage Cor. comes.

242–4. *And Censorinus...ancestor* (Delius+Craig, E.K.C., etc.) F. om. l. 242 and reads 'nam'd, so'. Camb.+most edd. read:

> And [Censorinus] nobly named so
> Twice being [by the people chosen] censor,
> Was his great ancestor.

Among other reconstructions is C.J.S.'s (*N.R.* ii. 126) wh. runs:

> And [Censorinus] nobly named so,
> Twice being censor, was his great ancestor.

The only evidence we possess as to what is lacking is Plut. who gives us 'Censorinus also came of that familie [i.e. the Marcii], that was so surnamed, bicause the people had chosen him Censor twise'. Apart from the name 'Censorinus', the omission of which is obvious, Camb. insists that the fact that he had been chosen by the people wd be specially apt in Sic.'s mouth, and explains the lacuna by a stain or rent in the copy. Though conceivable this seems less plausible than the omission of a single line, wh. is all Delius' text involves; and when it is noted that ll. 242, 243 both begin with 'And' such an omission wd. be readily explained by the comp.'s eye catching the wrong 'And'. Moreover North's 'that was so surnamed' supplies the right words in the right order to fill the gap.

248. *Scaling* weighing.

250. *sudden* hasty.

251. *putting on* v. G.

252. *presently* at once. *drawn your number* collected your crowd. Cf. ll. 210–16.

254. S.D. (J.D.W.) F. 'Exeunt Plebeians'.

255. *mutiny* v. G. *put in hazard* ventured.

256. *Than...greater* Than wait on the chance of one greater and more certain.

258–9. *both...anger* 'mark, catch, and improve the opportunity which his hasty anger will afford us' (J.).

262. S.D. F. 'Exeunt'.

3. 1

Loc. (Rowe+Theob.) *Entry* (F.; with 'Latius' for 'Lartius'.

1. *made...head* v. G. 'make'.

3. *Our...composition* = us to come to terms with them more quickly than otherwise.

5. *make road* v. G. 'road'.

7. *ages* v. G. For the pl. v. 2. 1. 30, n.

9. *On safeguard* Under safe-conduct.

16. *To hopeless* = Beyond all hope of.

19. *I wish...fully* Dramatic irony.

20. S.D. (F. with 'Scicinius' for Sicinius').

23. *prank* v. G. Cf. *Meas.* 2. 2. 119, 'Drest in a little brief authority'.

24. *Against…sufferance* = Beyond anything a nobleman can endure.

25. *Ha?* F. 'Hah?' Commonly = 'eh?' and so not necessarily indignant.

26. *on—* (F.).

33. *herd* Cf. 1. 4. 31; 2. 1. 92.

36. *why rule…teeth* = why don't you keep them from biting. 'The metaphor is from setting a bull-dog or mastiff upon anyone' (Warb.)—I think rather from the bating of a bear or a bull. Note 'set them on' (l.37).

40–1. *such as…ruled* Cf. Sh.'s Add. to *Sir Thos. More*, ll. 51–6 (mod. spelling): v. *Sh.'s Hand.* ad fin.

> *More* You that have voice and credit with the number
> Command them to a stilness.
> *Lincoln* A plague on them; they will not hold their peace.
> The Devil cannot rule them.
> *More* Then what a rough and riotous charge have you
> To lead those that the Devil cannot rule.

48. *You are like…business* Assigned to *Cor.* by Theob., J., Mal., Craig, E.K.C., etc.; to *Com.* by F. (+Camb., G.G., Al., C.J.S., etc.). Little graphical diff. between these abbrev. names. N.B. Brut.'s reply is clearly addressed to Cor.; and Cor. replies in turn.

48–9. *Not unlike…yours* 'Likely to provide better for the security of the commonwealth than you (whose *business* it is) will do. To which the reply is pertinent' (Warb.). N.B. 'inform' (l. 47) is an insult; it implies that Brut. is a 'common informer'. Cf. *Ven.* 655, *Son.* 125, 13.

52. *that* i.e. that insolence.

53–4. *pass…bound* proceed where you intend to go, i.e. to the consulship, via the election in the market-place.

55. *out of* = straying from.

58. *abused* v. G. *palt'ring* v. G., 'playing fast and loose' (cf. *Mac.* 5.8.20; *Ant.* 4.12.28) exactly describes the tribunes' conduct.

60. *dishonoured* dishonourable. Cf. Abbott, § 374 ('-ed' for '-ing').

60–1. *rub* v. G. *laid falsely* = treacherously placed. *plain way* = level or open track. Bowling terms.

64–8. *Now, as I...again* (Arr. J.C.M.) F. divides 'Now, as I live I will. | My Nobler...pardons: | For... Meynie, | Let...flatter, | And therein...againe.' Cap. (+most) 'Now, as...nobler friends, | I crave...pardons: | For...let them | Regard...flatter, and | Therein... again.' J.C.M.'s arr. regularises l. 66 'The...them'.

66. *meiny* (F. 'Meynie') F4 (+most exc. Sch., Case, Al., and C.J.S.) 'Many'. But 'meiny' wh. can = the 'common herd' (O.E.D. 6) as well as 'household retinue' (*Lr.* 2.4.34) fits the context. O.E.D. cites Day, *Festivals* (1619), Ep. Ded., 'the *Meyny* or Multitude'.

67–8. *Regard...themselves* 'Regard this in me, that I am no flatterer, and *in this*, in my plain speaking, behold themselves' (Whitelaw, *ap.* Furn.).

69–71. *we nourish...scattered* Cf. North, p. 161: 'Moreover he sayed they nourrished against them selves the naughty seed and cockle of insolence and sedition, which had bene sowed and scattered abroade emongest the people'.

71–2. *ploughed...sowed...scattered...mingling* North's use of 'cockle' (v. last n.) recalled the parables of the wheat and the tares (Matt. xiii. 24–30) and Sh. goes on with it. N.B. it is 'tares' in Genevan and A.V. but 'cockle' in the Rheims N.T. Noble (p. 241) cites Hosea x. 13.

72. *By mingling* etc. Alludes to the appointment of tribunes to office (1.1.214 ff.). *the honoured number* the aristocratic class. For 'honoured' = honourable v. l. 60, n.

78. *till...decay* i.e. till death. *measles*=scabs (cf. 1.
1. 165) or lepers v. G. F. 'Meazels'.

79. *tetter* v. G. Carries on the 'measles' metaphor.
Cf. *Ham.* 1. 5. 71 'tetter...lazar-like'.

82. *a man...infirmity* Cf. Acts. xiv. 15, 'man of
like passions with you'.

85. *patient* devoid of agitation.

86. *be my mind* fill my thoughts.

88. *this Triton* i.e. this petty Neptune's trumpeter.
Cf. 'the horn and noise of the monster's' (l. 95).

90. *from the canon*=quite unconstitutional. Cf. G.
'from' and 'canon'. A tribune had no authority to lay
down the law, only to voice the will of the people. An
important point wh. Cor. enlarges upon in ll. 90 ff, and
in his prophecy at 1.1. 218–20, now come true.

91. *O good* (Pope ed. ii < Theob. conj., +) F. 'O
God!'

96. *in*=into.

96–7. *turn...channel this* 'make your intentions
give way to his own mean ends' (E.K.C.).

97–8. *If he have power...ignorance* 'If this man has
power let the ignorance that gave it him vail or bow
down before him' (J.). v. G. 'ignorant'.

99. *learned* wise.

101. *have cushions by you* sit as senators. For
'cushions', v. 2. 2. S.D., n. (init.).

102. *and they no* (J.D.W. < J. conj.). F. 'they are no'.

103–4. *When...theirs* 'When the voices of the
senate and the people being blended together, the pre-
dominant taste of the compound smacks more of the
populace than the senate' (Mal.). J.'s conj. 'Must
palate' for 'Most palates' is attractive.

106. *popular* vulgar, plebeian.

106–7. *a graver bench...Greece* This hint that
Greece was less aristocratic than Rome Sh. took from
the passage in Plut. cited at ll. 114–16, n.

108. *my soul aches* How deeply he feels it!

110. *confusion*=chaos—the political nightmare of Sh.'s age.

111–12. *take...other*=destroy each other. Cf. *Troil.* 1. 3. 83 ff. (on Degree or the principle of sub-ordination) which concludes with a picture of chaos in which the human race will 'last eat up' itself; or the like picture in Sh.'s Addition to *More* ll. 80–7, ending 'and men like ravenous fishes | Would feed on one another' (*Sh.'s Hand*, ad fin.).

114–16. *The corn...power* Cf. ll. 106–7 and North, p. 161, where Cor. denounces those who propose that 'corne should be geven out to the common people *gratis*, as they used to doe in citties of Graece, where the people had more absolute power'.

117. *they* i.e. 'Whoever', etc. (l. 113).

118. *Why shall* (F.+Al.) Cap. (+most) 'Why, shall'.

121. *our recompense* i.e. something paid *by* us for services rendered.

122. *Being pressed* And when they were con-scripted.

123. *the navel*=the vital centre. *touched*=threatened. v. G.

124. *They...thread the gates* They would not 'file through them one by one...much less would they throng to the service' (Clar.). Reff. to *R. II*, 5. 5. 16 and Matt. xix. 24 are misleading.

126. *Their* (F 3) F. 'There'.

129. *native* =origin. Carries on the figure of 'cause unborn'. Cf. O.E.D. 'native' *a* 3 b='original, parent'.

131. *bosom multiplied*=at once 'fickle' and 'many bosomed' (v. G. 'bosom', 'digest'). Schmidt cites *Lr.* 5. 3. 50 'the common bosom' = the heart of the common people, and *2 H. IV*, 1. 3. 98, where the Archb. thus

upbraids 'the fond many' for the fickle loyalty of their 'vulgar heart':

> So, so, thou common dog, didst thou disgorge
> Thy glutton bosom of the royal Richard.

Dyce +many edd. read 'bisson multitude'—now gen. rejected.

132. *deeds* sc. their actions.

134. *poll* (Rowe) F. 'pole' v. G.

137. *our cares* sc. for the whole body corporate. Cf. 1. 1. 64–5, 76 ff.

139. *The crows to peck* etc. For the like figure v. *3 H. VI*, 1. 4. 41, 'doves do peck', etc.; 2. 2. 18; *Ant.* 3. 13. 197, and *Mac.* 4. 2. 9–11, 'the poor wren... will fight...against the owl'.

enough (F.) Han. 'enough, enough'. The duplication wd add point to Brut.'s reply.

142. *double worship* i.e. the 'two authorities' (l. 109).

143. *Where one* (Rowe) F. 'Whereon'—'on' for 'one', cf. 1. 1. 16, n.

144. *without all reason* beyond all reason. *gentry* v. G.

145. *conclude* come to a decision.

146. *it*='this double worship' (l. 142). *omit* v. G.

154. *To jump...physic*=to risk a dangerous treatment on a body. Cf. G. 'jump', 'physic'. N.B. 'jump' ='hazard' seems almost confined to Sh. (*Ant.* 3. 8. 6; *Mac.* 1. 7. 7; *Cym.* 5. 4. 182). O.E.D. cites no one else except Philemon Holland but gives two exx. from his translations (i) Livy (1600) 'They put it to the verie iump and finall triall what should become of those lawes'; and (ii) Pliny (1601) 'It [hellebore] putteth the Patient to a iumpe or great hazzard'—both apt to the present context. P. Holland was M.D. and perh. the term is a medical one. Cf. Introd. p. xiii.

156. *The multitudinous tongue* those who speak for the multitude, i.e. the tribunate.

157. *The sweet* sc. of power.

158. *Mangles true judgement* The degradation ('dishonour') of the Senate has disturbed Degree in the State, has destroyed its unity ('integrity') and done cruel injury to its administration of justice ('judgement'), since 'right and wrong, | Between whose endless jar justice resides', have lost 'their names'—(cf. *Troil.* 1. 3. 109 ff.).

160–1. *Not having* etc. Illustrates the Senate's loss of integrity.

162. *answer* v. G. Cf. ll. 176–79.

164. *bald*=paltry; but with quibble.

166. *th' greater bench* the higher court (the Senate).

166–8. *In a rebellion...chosen* See. 1. 1. 183–220.

167. *When...law* when we were forced to legislate by painful necessity.

169–70. *Let what...dust* 'Let it be said by you that what is *meet* to be done, *must* be meet, i.e. *shall be done*; and put an end at once to the tribunitian power' (Mal.).

172. *aediles* v. G. and North, p. 162. North calls them 'sergeantes' (=police officers) at one place and that no doubt is how Sh. and his audience imagined them. S.D. (F.).

173. S.D. (after Collier).

174. *innovator* v. G.

176. *to thine answer* to answer the charge. *old goat* cf. 2. 1. 13, n. Furn. suggests he wore a long grey beard; cf. 2. 1. 85. The age and 'rottenness' of the tribunes wd add much to this incident on the stage.

177. S.H. (Camb.) F. 'All'.

178. *rotten...shake* Cf. *K. J.* 2.1. 455–57 [Steev.]

179. S.D. (F.).

183. S.H. (after Cap.) F. 'All'.

184. S.D. (F.).

185. S.H. (J.D.W. after Camb. n. vii).

189. *Confusion's near* Anarchy is at hand. *speak* i.e. make a speech (to pacify them).

189–90. *You...people!* 'Speak, you, to the people!' He is out of breath.

203. *That is the way* etc. Pope (+some) gives this to Cor. because of 'This deserves death' follows. But Com. is trying to calm the people and Sic. refers not to this speech but to Cor.'s determination to abolish the tribunate.

205. *distinctly ranges* 'stand one storey above another' (G. C. Moore Smith, private). Cf. Matt. xxiv. 2, 'Verily I say unto you, there shall not be left here one stone upon another that shall not be cast down'. Case glosses 'extends in lines of separate houses' and cites *Ant.* 1. 1. 33–4, 'Let Rome in Tiber melt, and the wide arch | Of the ranged empire fall'. The words might comprise both.

214. S.H. (Cap. 'Cit.') F. '*All Ple.*'.

217. S.D. (Camb.).   222. S.D. (F.).

226. *Help Marcius* etc. Cf. North, p. 164, 'The noble men...beganne to crie alowde, Helpe Martius'.

228. S.D. < F. 'Exeunt. In...in'.

229. *your* (Rowe) F. 'our'.

230. *naught* v. G.

230. *Stand fast* etc. F. assigns to *Com.*; Warb. (+most) to *Cor.* N.B. (i) 1 Sen.'s shocked reply is addressed to Cor. (ii) Com. *later* urges him to go. (iii) And this urging—'Come, sir, along with us' (l. 236)—is given to '*Corio.*' by F.

234. *cause* v. G. *upon us* Pope omits, perh. rightly.

236–41. *Come sir...another* (arr. Steev.) F. assigns l. 236 to *Corio.* and ll. 237–41 to *Mene.* As it runs to the foot of a column, the incorrect assigning looks as if caused by 'crowding' in the MS.

238–9. *littered...calved* Like swine and bullocks.

240. *worthy rage* anger which does you credit.

241. *One...another* 'Time...will *owe* us a good turn for our present disgrace' (Mal.).

243. *Take up* v. G.

244. *'tis...arithmetic* i.e. their numbers are incalculably larger than ours. This crowd scene must have taken some rehearsing on Sh.'s stage.

247. *rend* tear asunder.

248–9. *o'erbear...bear* overwhelm what they usually endure. 'O'erbear' carries on Sh.'s favourite image of a river or flood breaking its bounds in spate. Cf. G.

252. S.D. (J.D.W.) F. 'Exeunt Coriolanus and Cominius'. Cor. would not have tamely gone off without some polite compulsion from Com.

259. S.D. (J.D.W.) F. 'A Noise within'.

262. S.D. (F.). *viper* Typical of unnatural treachery; cf. 'viperous traitor' l. 285; and (i) *1 H. VI*, 3. 1. 72, 'a viperous worm | That gnaws the bowels of the commonwealth'—alluding to the 'very ancient tradition affirmed by Herodotus, Nicander, Pliny, Plutarch' that young vipers force their way through the bowels of their dam (Browne, *Vulgar Errors*, Bk. III, ch. 16); (ii) *2 H. VI*, 3. 1. 343, 'I fear me you but warm the starved snake, | Who, cherished in your breasts, will sting your hearts'—alluding to the treacherous ingratitude of the frozen snake or viper of Aesop's Fable, which stung the breast that warmed it. See Tilley V 68, 'To nourish a viper in one's bosom'; O.E.D.P. 'snake', p. 600.

273–4. *Do not...warrant* i.e. the quarry you are handing over for merciless slaughter to your dogs is not rightly yours. Sh. elsewhere uses 'havoc' in connexion with the chase, and it may have been a hunting term. Cf. *Ham.* 5. 2. 362, 'This quarry cries on havoc'=This

heap of slain proclaims a great day's hunting for Death.
In *K. J.* 2. 1. 352–7, Death is again the huntsman, and
in *J. C.* 3. 1. 273 it is Caesar's spirit that cries 'Havoc'
and lets slip the dogs of war.

275. *make...rescue* An illegal act in English law;
v. G. 'rescue'.

286. *our danger* (Theob.+Moore Smith+C.J.S.)
F. (+most) 'one danger'. The context points a 'contrast between "our danger" and "our death"' (C.J.S.,
N.R. ii. 127). A graphical confusion of 'our' and 'one'
or 'on' (v. 1. 1. 16, n.) is poss.

290. *deservéd*=deserving. Cf. 'dishonoured' **3.**
1. 60.

295. *Mortal* i.e. 'certain death' (Case).

302. *clean kam* all wrong. v. G. 'kam'.

303. *Merely awry* Absolutely beside the point.

304–6. *The service...was* Han. (<Warb. conj.),
J.+a few 19th and 20th c. edd. (e.g. E.K.C., Al.)
assign to *Sic.*; F. (+Mal.+most) assign to *Men.*; Mal.
paraphrasing F., 'You alledge, says Men., that being
diseased, he must be cut away. Acc. then to your
argument, the foot, being once gangrened, is not to be
respected for what it was before it was gangrened—"Is
this just?" Men. would have added, if the tribune had
not interrupted him.'

But this overlooks the force of 'gangrened'—a point
no one seems to have noticed. At l. 294–5 Men. claims
that the limb, though diseased, can be cured: gangrene
(=mortification) cannot be cured, except by the knife.
It follows that had Men. been speaking here he must
have mentioned a less fatal disease. Sic. on the other
hand is clinching his argument of l. 293 by naming the
disease he has in mind. Cor., he says, despite all his
war services for Rome, has become a mortal danger to
the country from which it can only be cured by cutting
him off. A foot gives excellent and essential service to

the body, but the surgeon cannot take that into consideration when mortification sets in.

311. *unscanned swiftness* thoughtless haste.

312. *Tie...heels* sc. to hobble them. Cf. *Wint.* 4. 4. 674 'with his clog at his heels'. *by process* sc. of law.

313. *parties* v. G.

315. *What* = Why.

319. *a'* (Al. < F. 'a') Rowe (+most) 'he'.

320. *bolted* v. G. The figure is continued in 'meal' and 'bran'.

322. *bring him* (Pope+) F. 'bring him in peace'. The words, Mal. conj., were prob. 'caught by the eye' of the comp. or transcriber from below.

323–4. *answer...to his utmost peril* = stand his trial at whatever peril to his life.

325. *human* (Moore Smith < Rowe, Pope) F. (+most) 'humane'. Both senses sp. 'humane' in Sh., but the mod. 'humane' is not here comprehensive enough.

326. *too* F. 'to'.

330. *attend* v. G.

333. S.D. (Han.).

334. S.H. F. 'Sena.' Rowe+ 'First Sen.' S.D. (J.D.W.) F. 'Exeunt Omnes'.

3. 2

S.D. *Loc.* (Pope) *Entry* (F.+Al.) Cap. (+) reads 'Patricians' for 'Nobles'.

2. *Death...heels* Mal. notes that neither punishment has class. authority. Case cites Dekker, *Old Fortunatus* (1600), 5. 2. 238–9 (ed. Fredson Bowers):

> Thou shalt be torturd on a wheele to death,
> Thou with wild horses shalt be quartered.

which is perh. Sh.'s source.

4–5. *That...sight* 'So that no man, standing at the

top, however keen-eyed, could see the bottom' (Case).
Cf. *Lr.* 4. 6. 50 ff. See G. 'precipitation' for its two
senses, this one irregular.

9. *woollen vassals* Ref. prob. to the coarse cloth
from Kendal, worn by the lower classes. Cf. Linthicum, p. 79; 2. 3. 114, n. (above); and *1 H. IV*, 2. 4.
219 (v. G.). 'Kersey' (*Shr.* 3. 2. 65) 'linsey-woolsey'
(*All's*, 4. 1. 11) were also cloths spoken of in contempt.
For 'vassal' v. G.

10. *buy...groats* Petty trading (G.G.). One of the
hints that Sh. had London shopkeepers in mind.

11. *to yawn* (F.). Pope omits 'to'—prob. correctly.

13. S.D. (F.). Transferred from l. 6 by Dyce
(< Coll.).

18. *Let go* Enough! Theob.'s 'Let it go' (=Never
mind!) is attractive. 'Let't go' is poss.

21. *thwartings* (Theob. +) F. 'things' C.J.S. conj.
'taxings'. But cf. 'cross you' (l. 23). Perhaps copy-sp.
'thwarthings', with the comp.'s eye skipping from 'th'
to 'th'.

24. *Ay...too* Clar. conj. an 'aside', since she is
urging moderation; G.G. concurs.

26. S.H. Senator (F. 'Sen.').

29. *as little apt* as stubborn. Cf. 'apt' in G. of *J.C.*
Stanton's conj. 'of mettle apt' is accepted by Craig and
G.G.

30–1. *leads...vantage* teaches me to make better
use of my anger.

32. *herd* (Theob. +) F. 'heart'. Prob. sp. 'heard'
(influenced by 'heart' in l. 29).

34. *I would* (F.) Pope 'I'd'.

41. *But...speak* = 'but that ...physic' (ll. 32–3).

52–7. *Because...truth* (arr. Mal.) F. 'Because, that
| Now...people: | Not...matter | Which...words |
That...Tongue; | Though...Syllables | Of...truth.'—
an extra line needed for the column.

52. *lies you on* Cf. *R. II*, 2. 3. 138, 'It stands your Grace upon', etc.

55. *roted* (Mal.+Camb.) F. 'roated'. Cf. 'con'd by roate' (*J. C.* 4. 3. 97, F.) J.+Cap., Craig, etc. 'rooted'—which (even with 'but') is too strong for the context, whereas 'roted' i.e. 'repeated mechanically' fits it.

64. *I am in this* I am involved in this (at stake in). See G. 'be (i)'.

68–9. *and...ruin*=and for safeguarding that which without such fawning might be ruined.

71. *Not*=not only. Cf. 3. 3. 97; *Meas.* 4. 1. 66. [Clar.].

73–4. *with this...with them* She points at his bonnet and curtseys.

77–80. *Waving...say to them* (J. conj.+Han.) F. reads (ll. 73 ff.):

> Goe to them, with this Bonnet in thy hand;
> And thus farre hauing stretcht it (here be with them)
> Thy Knee bussing the stones: for in such businesse
> Action is eloquence, and the eyes of th'ignorant
> More learned then the eares, wauing thy head,
> Which often thus correcting thy stout heart,
> Now humble as the ripest Mulberry,
> That will not hold the handling: or say to them,

One of the two most difficult passages in the play. As F. stands 'Which' must refer to 'head', and 'humble' must be imperative. But the text, as most agree, is prob. corrupt, and J. conj. 'With' for 'Which', while Han. omitted 'or'. This Moore Smith approved; and E.K.C. notes 'In any case the grammar of Vol.'s speech is loose, but if *or* is retained the sense is wrong. She is not suggesting two alternative modes of procedure but one only. *Which* (written *w^{ch}*) and *with* are easily confused in MS.' Clearly she suggests posture and gesture first, *and then* what he ought to say.

77. *Waving* Not side to side, but bowing up and down in token of sorrowful repentance.

87. *Even...yours* To fill out the line, Cap. read 'speaks it' for 'speaks'; Pope, 'why, all their' for 'why, their'.

88–9. *For they...purpose* Sh. 'has no respect for the plainer and simpler kind of people as politicians, but he has great respect and regard for their hearts' (Bradley, *Sh. Trag.* p. 326 n.). See also R.W.C. pp. 210 ff.

92. S.D. (F.).

97–8. *He must...about it* She becomes peremptory.

99–100. *Must I...noble heart* (J.D.W.) F. reads:

> Must I goe shew them my vnbarb'd Sconce?
> Must I with my base tongue giue to my Noble Heart

Cap. (+Camb. etc.) arr.

> Must I go show them my unbarbéd sconce? must I
> With my base tongue give to my noble heart

Pope, Theob. J. read 'unbarbéd' and omit 'I with'; this wd. imply that the comp. first repeated the 'must' of l. 99 and then the reader added 'with' to make sense. My reading implies the comp. has simply repeated 'Must I'.

99. *show...sconce* Cf. l. 73. To bare one's head in Sh.'s time betokened the utmost respect. *unbarbéd* (Rowe) F. 'unbarb'd'.

100. *noble* i.e. belonging to one of the noblest families in Rome; cf. 2. 3. 237.

102. *plot* i.e. piece of earth, viz. his body. Cf. *Son.* 137. 9.

113. *choiréd* (J.D.W.) Most edd. 'quired' (<F. 'quier'd'); I modernise. See G. and cf. *M.V.* 5. 1. 63 (ed. ii.).

115. *lulls* (Rowe) F. 'lull'.

123–30. *At thy choice...pride thyself* A prelude to 5. 3. 22 ff.

137. *Do your will* A pretty touch. She maintains her coolness. 'His will!' (Ver.).

142. *word*=watchword. Cf. *Ham*. 1. 5. 110.

145. *mildly* (Al.) F. ', Mildely.' Camb. '. Mildly!' He repeats it lest he should forget it, but has just said that if they tell lies about him he will defend his honour.

145. S.D. F. 'Exeunt.'.

3. 3

S.D. *Loc*. 'The Forum' (Pope) *Entry* (F.).

1. *charge him home* press home your accusations.

3. *envy* v. G.

5. S.D. (F.).

8–10. *Have you...by th' poll?* North (p. 166) relates that when Cor. agrees to submit to be tried the tribunes arranged 'that the people would proceede to geve their voyces by Tribes, and not by hundreds: for by this meanes the multitude of the poore needy people...came to be of greater force (bicause their voyces were numbred by the polle) then the noble honest cittizens'. The clause in brackets is North's trans. of Amyot's '(à cause que les voix se contoyent par teste)'; but there is nothing in the Greek to correspond. On the contrary, Plut.'s point is not that the rabble out-numbered the patricians but that voting by centuries wd. give the patricians the undoubted predominance, since (as the Loeb translator points out, p. 167) 'out of the 193 centuries the richest class alone had 98 against 95 of all the other five classes put together'.

And what Amyot had misrepresented, Sh. in turn put to his own use by implying that the Tribunes were organising a claque, 'voices' (l. 9) meaning, not votes, but cries in chorus (ll. 15–16).

17. *Insisting...prerogative* This is Sh.'s addition, a characteristically English one, followed in l. 18 with

a piece of demagogic hypocrisy; cf. 'seasoned office' (l. 64) and 'ancient strength' (4. 2. 7).

18. *th' truth...cause* the justice of our case.

21. *present execution* immediate carrying into effect.

24. S.D. (<Pope) F. om.

26. *have his worth of contradiction* Mal. explains 'to have his pennyworth; his full quota or proportion' (of answering back) so 'give as good as he gets' (White-law). Cf. *Rom.* 4. 5. 4, 'your pennyworths' (of sleep). But Schmidt, rightly I think, interprets 'worth' as reputation or merit, which wd give us 'he is wont to acquire fame or win glory through conflict' or 'to flourish in opposition', and this is surely what Brut. means. Cf. North, p. 160: Marcus thought "that to overcome allwayes, and to have the upper hande in all matters, was a token of magnanimitie."

29-30. *looks...to break* looks like breaking.

30. S.D. (<F.) but reading 'Senators and Patricians' (Cap.) for 'others' (F.).

32. The aside, conj. by E.K.C., is certainly right. *for th'* (F2) F. 'fourth'. *piece·* sc. of money.

33. *bear...volume* endure being called 'knave' to any extent. Anon (*ap.* Camb.) conj. 'thou knave' for 'the knave'.

36. *Throng* (Theob.+) F. 'Through'.

38. S.D. (F.).

55. *accents* (Theob.+) F. 'Actions'. The comp. perh. misread 'accents' as 'accõns'=actions [C.J.S., *N.R.* p. 128].

57. *envy you* Keightley conj. 'envy to you'.

64. *seasoned* v. G. Refers to the recently instituted 'tribunate' which Cor. wished to abolish (cf. 1. 1. 208-14), and Sic. now claims as delectable and time-honoured. Cf. l. 17, n.

69. *their traitor* traitor to them. *injurious* v. G.

70-1. *sat...clutched* Conditional mood.

75, 106, 119, 137, 142. S.H. *Citizens* (Cap.+most). F. 'All.'

80. *whose great power must try him* Cf. above 2. 1. 43, n.

85. *You!* (Al.) F. 'You?' 'The tribunes are no soldiers' says Auf. (4. 7. 31).

92. *courage* spirit. Cf. *3 H. VI*, 2. 2. 57.

97. *not*=not only. Cf. 3. 2. 71, n.

99. *do* (F 2 'doe'). F. 'doth'.

110. *for* (Theob.+) F. 'from'.

120. *cry*=pack.

120–1. *breath...fen* Cf. above 1. 1. 59, n.

123. *I banish you* The 'you' is emphatic. Cf. *R. II*, 1. 3. 279–80.

127. *Fan...despair* sc. 'into the chill of despair'. Cf. *Mac.* 1. 2. 50–1, 'the Norweyan banners...fan our people cold'.

129. *finds not* perceives no danger.

130–1. *Making...foes* Leaving none in the city but yourselves who are always your own worst enemies (after J.). Camb. (<Cap.) reads 'Making not' for 'Making but'—the effect being 'to spoil both lines' (G.G.).

135. S.D. (J.D.W.) F. 'Exit Coriolanus, Cominius, Cumalijs'. This last 'seems to have been mistaken for a personal name' (Greg, *Sh.'s F.F.*, p. 406).

137. *Hoo-oo!* (Al.). F. 'Hoo, oo'. Most edd. 'Hoo! hoo!' <F 3 'Hoo, hoo'. S.D. (F. following 135 S.D.).

140. *vexation* v. G.

143. S.D. F. 'Exeunt'.

4. 1

S.D. *Loc.* (Mal.) *Entry* (F.).

1–2. *the beast...heads* cf. 2. 3. 15, n.

4. *extremity was* (<F 2+most), F. (+Al., C.J.S.) 'extremities was', Mal. 'extremities were'.

5. *chances common* (F4) F. 'chances. Common'—
prob. due to Sh.'s trick of using a majuscule instead of
a minuscule 'c' initially. Cf. 1. 9. 46, n., and *Sh.'s
Hand* p. 115.

7–9. *fortune's...cunning* The syntax has broken
down, but the sense is clear: to take one's wounds like
a gentleman when fate strikes her hardest blows
demands noble, i.e. gentleman's, philosophy.

13. *red pestilence* Perhaps typhus. Cf. *Temp.* 1. 2.
365.

14. *What* etc.=Come, come, come!

15. *loved...lacked* Clar. cites *Ado*, 4. 1. 216–21;
Ant. 1. 4. 41–4.

22. *tears...man's* Note Sh.'s interest in physiology.
Cf. *Troil.* 5. 3. 54–5; *Ham.* 1. 2. 154–5.

24. *thee* (F3) F. 'the'.

27. *Mother* (C.B.Y. priv.<Pope) F. 'My Mother'.
The 'my' is extra-metrical and lets the style down
also.

29. *Believe...lightly* Be confident of this (Case).

30. *a lonely dragon* Perh. Sh. had in mind the Hydra
of the Lernaean marsh (cf. 3. 1. 93) which Spenser
likens to Orgoglio's 'monstrous beast ybredd in filthy
fen' (*F.Q.* 1. vii. 16).

32–3. *Will...practice* The irony here is that both
futures await him.

33. *My first son*=(*a*) first-born, (*b*) noblest of sons.
She is 'fond of no second brood' (5. 3. 162).

35–7. *some course...before thee* J.C.M. (priv.) notes
a striking parallel with *Wint.* 4. 4. 562–5 'A course...
enough'.

36. *exposure* (Rowe) F. 'exposture'. 'Exposure'
was a new word in 1600, prob. invented by Sh. (cf.
Troil. 1. 3. 195; *Mac.* 2. 3. 127). It is more likely that
the comp., not recognising it, assimilated it to a form
he knew like 'posture', 'imposture', than that Sh.

invented a second form, not related, as the first was, to 'expose'.

37. *O the gods!* (Keightley + Al. assign to *Vir.*;) F. to *Corio.* The cry, similar to that in l. 12, is a natural comment by Virg. upon Vol.'s picture of the dangers that beset her banished husband's path. If the initials of the S.H.'s were minuscules, as often in the Three Sh. Pages of *Sir T. More*, 'vir' and 'cor' wd. not be unlike.

49. *of noble touch* i.e. tested and found pure gold. See G. 'touch', 'noble'.

52-3. *never...formerly* Another stroke of irony. N.B. The plan of going over to Auf. is not yet in mind.

58. S.D. F. 'Exeunt'.

4. 2

S.D. *Loc.* (Camb.) *Entry* (F.).

2. There have been varied attempts to mend the metre of this line; e.g. Pope read 'Vexed are the nobles', etc. For the confusion of two constructions in 'whom' see Abbott § 410.

7. S.D. (J.D.W. < Cap. 'Exit Aedile'). F. om.

8. S.D. (F.).

11. *you're* (Cap.) F. 'y'are'. *the hoarded plague.* Cf. *R. III*, 1. 3. 219-24 [Clar.].

16. *mankind* He means 'mad', but Vol. takes it in its ord. sense of 'the human race'. See G. 'mankind'.

17. *this, fool* (Staun.; Al.) F. (+Camb. and most) 'this Foole'.

18. *foxship* 'mean cunning' (J.). Her retort to 'mankind'.

32. *The noble knot* sc. the ties of gratitude.

34. *Cats* A term of contempt. Cf. *Tp.* 2. 2. 86; *All's* 4. 3. 271; *M.N.D.* 3. 2. 260.

36. *let's* (F.+Al., C. J.S.) Pope (+most) 'Let us'.
44. S.D.<F. 'Exit Tribunes'.
53–4. S.D.<F. 'Exeunt. | Exit.'

4. 3

S.D. *Loc.* (Mal.) *Entry* (F.)+ 'meeting' (Cap.).
C.J.S., who follows Mal. for *Loc.*, inconsistently gives
as *Entry* 'Enter Nicanor and Adrian at several doors'.

2. *Adrian* Perh. an unconscious memory of Pope
Adrian in Camden (cf. Introd. p. xi).

4–5. *my services are* etc. i.e. he is in the pay of the
Volsces.

9. *approved* (Steev.) F. 'appear'd'. 'Appear' is not
elsewh. found in this trans. sense—a poor sense at that,
whereas 'approved'=confirmed. Cf. *Ham.* 1. 1. 28,
'That if again this apparition come, He may approve
our eyes and speak to it'.

44–5. *their charges* i.e. the men under them.
billeted v. G. *in th' entertainment* mobilised.

53. S.D.<F. 'Exeunt'.

4. 4

S.D. *Loc.* (Cap.) *Entry* (F.). Cf. North, p. 169, 'ill
favoredly muffled and disguised', but there the disguise
is assumed, while Sh. leaves us to imagine a state of
destitution.

3–4. *'fore...drop*=have I heard groan and fall in
face of my onslaughts.

6. S.D. (F.).

11. S.D.<F. 'Exit Citizen.'.

12. *slippery turns* fickle changes. Cf. *Wint.* 1. 2.
273, 'My wife is slippery'. These 'reflections on the
mutability of friendship and amity are designed to
diminish the shock and unnaturalness of his own

defection' (Ver.). But reflection of any kind is not in Cor.'s character, though Beeching's comment is more like him, viz. that he 'treats his alliance with Auf. as nothing but a private concern: he has left old friends for new, that is all: the state is but his birthplace'.

13–16. *Whose…Unseparable* Mal. compares the similar picture of girlhood friendship in *M.N.D.* 3. 2. 198 ff., in which 'So, with two seeming bodies, but one heart' resembles l. 13, while 'hours' (l. 14), for which Dyce and others would read 'house' is supported by 'the hours that we have spent' (*M.N.D.* 3. 2. 199).

17. *a dissension of a doit* 'a dispute about the merest trifle' (Clar.).

19–20. *whose plots…other* who have lain sleepless at nights planning how one might destroy the other.

22. *interjoin…issues* 'throw in their lot with each other' (G.G.).

23. *hate* (Cap.+) F. 'haue'. Rome is not his country, merely his birthplace.

25. *give…way* v. G. 'give (iv)'.

26. S.D. F. 'Exit'.

4. 5

S.D. *Loc.* (J.D.W.)<Rowe+ 'A hall in Aufidius's house'. There is of course no change of Loc. on Sh.'s stage. At the end of 4. 4. Cor. exits by one side-door to enter at 4. 5. 4. by the other. Meanwhile 1 Serv. enters from the inner stage. *Entry* (F.)+ 'from the chamber'. The S.H.s for the Servants in this sc. after a few '*1 Ser*' and '*2 Ser*' are marked 1, 2, 2 simply.

2. *fellows*=fellow-servants. S.D. (i) (J.D.W.); (ii) (F.)+ 'from the chamber'.

3. *Cotus* A name app. not known in the Classics except as that of Thracian princes. Where did Sh. find it?

4. S.D. (i) (J.D.W.<F. 'Exit'), (ii) (F.)+'from without'.

6. *Appear…guest* Alludes to his 'mean apparel'. S.D. (J.D.W.). F. 'Enter the first Seruing man'.

8. *go to the door* Go out! S.D. (J.D.W.) F. 'Exit'.

10. S.D. (J.D.W.). F. 'Enter second Seruant'.

13. *companions* rascals v. G.

16. *thou'rt* (Camb.) F. th'art'.

17. *brave* v. G.

18. S.D. (J.D.W.). F. 'Enter 3 Seruingman, the 1 meets him'. F. is not quite consistent with the 'exit' it gives *1 Serv.* at l. 8.

34. *Follow your function* Attend to your duties.

35. S.D. (F.).

38. S.D. (J.D.W.). F. 'Exit second Seruingman'.

40. *the canopy* Cf. *Ham.* 2. 2. 303–4, 'this most excellent canopy, the air'. In both ironical, since kings dwelt under a canopy (above the throne, or carried over them, as they walked).

46. *daws* Proverbially stupid birds.

48, 50. *meddle* v. G. for the quibble.

52. S.D. (i) (J.D.W.). F. 'Beats him away', (ii) (Camb.) F. 'Enter Aufidius with the Seruingman'.

55. S.D. (Camb.) F. gives no re-entry.

56. *wouldst thou* (F 3) F. 'woldst ẙ'.

57. S.D. (Cap.<North).

64–5. *though thy tackle's torn…vessel.* Here 'vessel' = (*a*) ship, (*b*) 'the body as receptacle of the soul' (O.E.D. 3 b; cf. 1 Thess. iv. 4; 1 Pet. iii. 7). Sh. has the same word-play at *All's* 2. 3. 209; *Cym.* 4. 2. 319.

68–104. *My name is…thee service* This follows very closely, at times verbatim, what North labels 'Coriolanus oration to Tullus Aufidius' (pp. 169–70).

74. *memory* memorial. The word is North's.

78. *dastard nobles* Again North's words. But what a change is here from 4. 1. 49, 'friends of noble touch'!

Sh. does nothing to reconcile the two. Did the specific 'with the young nobility' in 4. 1. S.D. (init.) register an intention to do so which was not carried through? Cf. G.-B. pp. 115, 117, nn.

86. *To be full quit of* to settle my account with.

88. *of wreak* disposed for vengeance. Cf. North, p. 170, 'if thou hast any harte to be wrecked of the injuries', etc.

that wilt (F.+Camb.) Han.+others 'that will'. But the sense is 2nd pers.

89–90. *maims Of shame* disgraceful mutilations, e.g. the annexation of Corioli.

95. *under fiends* infernal fiends.

96. *prove* try.

106–8. *If... 'Tis true'* Root cites Matt. xvii. 5.

111. *grainèd ash* 'tough ashen lance. "Grained" means close-grained' (G.G.). This seems the most likely interpretation, though it has no support in O.E.D. Schmidt explains 'showing the grain of the wood, rough, furrowed' and cites *Err.* 5. 1. 311, 'this grained face of mine'. But 'tough' is clearly needed to go with 'broke' and 'splinters'.

112. *scarred* (F.). Rowe ii 'scared'. Mal. restored F. 'scarr'd'. Steev. rejects this notion of 'scarefying the moon' and points out that 'scared' might' be spelt 'scarred' and is so spelt in *Wint.* (F.) 3.3. 65. Either notion seems tenable. Cf. (for 'scared') *R. III*, 5. 3. 341, 'Amaze the welkin with your broken staves'; and (for 'scarred') *Wint.* 3. 3. 89–90, 'the ship boring the moon with her main-mast', while Case cites *2 Tamb.* 2. 4. 104, 'And with the cannon break the frame of heaven', etc.

clip (Pope) F. 'cleep'.

113. *the anvil...sword* 'upon which my sword has struck as a hammer' (Clar.). Cf. *Ham.* 2. 2. 493–96, 'And never did the Cyclops' hammers fall', etc.

[Steev.]; Aeschylus, *Persians*, 5, λόγχης ἄκμονες
[L. Roussel, *T.L.S.* 2 Feb. 1946]..

118. *Sighed…breath* Cf. *Ven.* 189 and *Two Noble
Kins.* 5. 1. 131–2, 'Lover never yet made sigh | Truer
than I' [Mal.].

127. *down together* Cf. *H. V.* 4. 7. 151–2, 'when
Alençon and myself were down together' [Case].

133. *Into the bowels* etc. Cf. *R. III*, 5. 2. 3. [Case].

134. *o'erbear't* (R.G.W.<Z. Jackson conj.) F.
(+Mal., Camb., etc.) 'o're-beate', Rowe (+many)
'o'er-bear'. Misprints *t* :*r* are v. common in F. and
'o'erbear' is Sh.'s usual word for an overwhelming
flood. Cf. above 3. 1. 248; *Per.* 5. 1. 197; *Oth.* 1. 3.
56; *M.N.D.* 2. 1. 92; *Cym.* 5. 3. 48. The ''t' supplies
the object the context needs, and 'overbear' is always
trans. elsewhere in Sh. or in O.E.D.

150. S.D. (i) (J.D.W.<F. 'Exeunt') (ii) (F.).

156–7. *set up* v. G.

166–7. *a greater…wot one* (F.)=you wot a greater
soldier than he [servant's grammar]. Dyce's 'than he
you wot on' is better grammar, and Sh. spelt 'one' and
'on' alike (v. nn. 1. 2. 4; 2. 2. 79; 3. 1. 143); the 'but'
however rules it out. 1 Serv. wishes to defend Auf.
though preferring not to be too positive, as 2 Serv. is
at first; until 3 Serv.'s outspokenness (ll. 182–7) forces
them all to admit what they know all along is the truth.

170. *him*=Coriolanus.

171. *him*=Aufidius.

175. S.D. (F.).

178. S.H. F. '*Both*'.

191–2. *him directly. To say the troth on't, before
Corioli he* (F. but reading 'directly, to' and omitting
comma after 'on't'). With this punctuation 'directly'
would mean 'face to face' or 'hand to hand'. Cf. 1. 6.
58. But 'directly' can also mean 'without ambiguity'
and J.C.M. finding this attractive, and citing *Oth.* 2. 1.

216 'Desd. is directly in love with him', conj. 'him, directly to say the truth on't: before Corioli', wh. Moore Smith also conj. Camb. (+Al.) punct. 'him directly, to...on't: before Corioli'.

195. *broiled* (Pope+most) F. 'boyld'. A boiled carbonado wd. be a contradiction in terms since 'carbonado' meant 'a rasher on the coles' (Minsheu). C.J.S. (*N.R.* ii. 129) defends F. on the plea that 'two servants are speaking'; but servants shd. know all about what goes on in the kitchen. v. G. 'Carbonado'.

196. *news?* (Cap.+Camb.). F. 'Newes.'.

198. *at upper end* at the head (presum. next to Auf.).

199–200. *no...bald* Here 'but'=unless, except. Any senator who wished to speak to him had to come and stand hat in hand before him. N.B. Eliz. gentle-men wore hats indoors even at meals; v. the frontis-piece to *Timon* (N.S.). *bald*=showing their bald heads (O.E.D. 4 d 'bare-headed' quotes no other ex. and is prob. contextual).

201. *sanctifies...hand* 'considers the touch of his hand as holy; clasps it with the same reverence as a lover would clasp the hand of his mistress' (Mal.). Cf. *Rom.* 1. 5. 93, 'If I profane with my unworthiest hand | This holy shrine' and *A.Y.L.* 3. 4. 13–14, 'And his kissing is as full of sanctity as the touch of holy bread'.

202. *turns up...eye* 'as an expression of piety' (E.K.C.).

206. *sowl* (Rowe) F. 'sole' v. G.

207–8. *leave...polled* leave a shorn (i.e. a desert) track behind him. See G. *polled* (<Rowe) F. 'Poul'd'.

214, 215 *dejectitude* (Coll. ii) F. (+most) 'Directi-tude'. Mal. conj. 'discreditude'—noting that Sh. clearly intended a grand word 'which had some re-semblance to sense', but not 'absolute nonsense'. Coll.'s conj. is graphically much nearer F. than Mal.'s, more idiomatic, and a good contrast to 'crest up again'

(l. 216). Cf. *Lr.* 4. 1. 3, 'The lowest and most dejected thing of fortune'; *Per.* 2. 2. 46, 'From the dejected state wherein he is He hopes by you his fortunes yet may flourish'.

217. *in blood* v. G. 'blood'.

228. *waking* (Pope+) F. 'walking'.

229. *audible* alert for any sound (the opp. of 'deaf' l. 230). *full of vent* Much discussed; many taking 'vent' as the hunting term for 'the scent given off by a hunted animal' (O.E.D. 13a) so that 'full of vent' might mean full of sport or excitement. But, as Clar. notes, the epithets for peace correspond in an inverted order with those for war, so that 'mulled' and 'full of vent' sh. be opposites; and since 'mulled' refers to drink, 'vent' should also do so. Now 'mulled' means—(of persons) 'dulled' or 'stupefied' (O.E.D. v²) and (of ale, sack, etc.) made 'into a hot drink with the addition of sugar and spices, beaten yoke of egg, etc.' (O.E.D. v³) i.e. the kind of drink topers would despise, as Falstaff evidently does, when he refuses 'pullet-sperm in his brewage' (v. *Wives* 3. 5. 31). On the other hand, 'vent' (sb.²) meant the emission or discharge of something, generally pent up, so that 'full of vent' wd mean 'bursting with life' (like strong wine), 'bubbling over' (G.G.) or, for man, 'full of spunk'—the opposite of 'mulled' which Han. glosses 'softened and dispirited', as wine is when it is burnt and sweetened.'

230. *sleepy* (F3) F. 'sleepe'.

240. S.D. (J.D.W.) F. 'Exeunt'.

4. 6

S.D. *Loc.* (Rowe: Theob.) *Entry* (F.).

2. *remedies* 'means of redress' (Schmidt). *tame* ineffectual.

2–4. *tame. The...hurry, here do make* (R.G.W.+Al.)
F. 'tame, the...hurry. Here do we make'. Han. anticipated R.G.W., but read 'hurry here, do make'. The
F. 'we' makes l. 4 'redundant in verse and paralogical',
since it is not the Tribunes, but the peace and quietness
of the people that 'make the Patricians ashamed of
having predicted popular commotions' (Hudson).
C.J.S. (*N.R.* ii. 130) defends F. by explaining 'his
remedies' as 'remedies against Coriolanus, antidotes to'.
But if so, why does Sic. call them 'tame'?

10. *stood to 't* v. G. 'stand'. S.D. (F.).

19. S.D. (F.).

26. S.D. (J.D.W.) F. 'Exeunt Citizens'.

33. *assistance* F. 'assistāce'. Han., 'assistants' is
attractive, since after 'sole throne' a personal rather than
an abstract noun was to be expected, and 'nce' is not
an improb. misreading of 'nts'.

37. S.D. (F.).

43–6. *Thrusts...peep out* Cf. Nashe *1 Pasquil*
(McK. 1. 131) [Case] 'I wonder how these seelie
snayles...dare thrust out theyr feeble hornes against so
tough and mighty adversaries'.

46. *what*=why.　　　　　　52. *reason* v. G.

57. S.D. (F.).

59. *come* (Rowe+) F. 'comming'—which C.J.S.
(*N.R.* ii. 130) defends and interprets 'coming in'. But
'coming' seems an impossible jingle after 'going' at the end
of l. 58 and is easily explained as a comp.'s echo of the same.

61. *raising* v. G. 'raise'.

68. *as spacious as between* 'so comprehensive as to
include' (Ver.).

74. *contrarieties* (Han.) F. 'Contrariety'—'atone'
requires a plur. S.D. (Camb.) F. 'Enter Messenger'.

79. *O'erborne their way* overwhelmed everything in
their path. Cf. 3. 1. 248–49, n.

80. S.D. (F.).　　　　　　83. *leads* roofs. Cf. G.

86. *in their cement* lit. into their mortar; i.e. to the ground. Accent 'cément'.

88. *Into an auger's bore* Cf. G. 'auger' and *Mac.* 2. 3. 122.

90. *wi'th'* (Al.) F. 'with'.

94. *brats* Implies insignificance as well as contempt (v. O.E.D.).

95. *boys* etc. Cf. 1. 3. 58–62.

96. *flies* Prob. caught from l. 95. Cap. conj. "Sheep".

97. *apron-men* Cf. *J. C.* 1. 1. 7.; *Ant.* 5. 2. 208, 'mechanic slaves | With greasy aprons, rules, and hammers'.

98–9. *voice, breath* Both=vote. See G. 'occupation'. 'App. the lower class Londoner ate more garlic than he does today' (E.K.C.). Cf. Bottom's advice to his fellow actors, *M.N.D.* 4. 2. 38.

99–101. *He will...work!* Divided as Steev. (+O.S.). F. divides 'Hee'l shake...eares. | As Hercules ...Fruite: | You...worke'. *He will* (Steev.+O.S.). Most edd. (<F.) 'He'll'.

shake...fruit i.e. in the garden of the Hesperides.

104. *resist* (Han.+Camb.,etc.) F.(+many) 'resists'.

105. *valiant ignorance* Again at *Troil.* 3. 3. 312.

107. *something* Sarcastic.

113–15. *they charged...And therein showed* i.e. 'they would charge...And therein show' (Mal.). Cf. 2. 2. 16 'he waved'. For 'charged' v. G.

118. *made fair hands* made a great success of it. See G. 'make' (iii). Cf. *H. VIII*, 5. 4. 69 'made a fine hand' and Tilley H 99 'Used ironically; to make a mess of a thing.'

121. *S'incapable* F. (+Al.) Rowe (+most) 'So incapable'.

122. *Was't* (F.+Rowe, Al., C.J.S.) Pope (+most) 'Was it'.

125. *roar* i.e. for mercy. v. G.

129. S.D. (F.).

147. *You're* (Cap.) F. (+Al., C.J.S.) 'Y'are'. Most 'Ye 're'.

148. *Cry* v. G.

149. S.D. (J.D.W.)<F. 'Exeunt both'.

157. S.D. F. 'Exit Cit.'.

161. *let us* (Pope) F. (+most) 'let's'. S.D. F. 'Exeunt Tribunes'.

4.7

S.D. *Loc.* (Theob.) *Entry* (F.).

5. *dark'ned* obscured.

6. *your own* sc. people; or poss. 'by your action'.

11. *changeling* See G.

13. *particular* See G.

14. *Joined in commission* 'Thus he [Cor.] was joyned in commission with Tullus as general of the Volsces' (North, p. 174).

15. *Had borne* (Mal.+most) F. 'haue borne'. C.J.S. (*N.R.* II, 131), defending F., writes: 'Shifting of construction is a characteristic of Sh.'s later style'. But, as this shifts back again in 'had left', two shifts so quickly are too many, and it is safe to give F. 'haue' to the comp.

28–57. *All places...thou mine* Coleridge (1, 91) found the speech out of keeping with Auf.'s mood in this scene and E.K.C. agrees, writing: 'Perhaps the explanation is that it is not wholly dramatic; for once the dramatist and not the puppet speaks. On the eve of the catastrophe Sh. pauses, to sum up his hero's career so far.' Certainly some discussion of Cor.'s character was needed here to ease for an audience the sudden and unexpected change at 4.4, and the almost as remarkable revolution to come in 5.3.

28. *yield* (F2) F. 'yeelds'.

29–30. *the nobility...him too* Many have remarked on this app. distinction between nobles and patricians and G.G. suggests Sh. was led astray by North's reference to 'the Nobility and the Patricians' (e.g. p. 147), a phrase originating in Amyot, but not found in Plut.

34. *the osprey* See G. Sometimes trained by falconers for the catching of fish, which it was supposed so to fascinate that they turned up their white underbellies to its eye, as it flew over the water. Cf. Peele, *Alcazar* (M.S.R. ll. 602–5):

> I will prouide thee of a princely ospraie,
> That as she flyeth ouer fish in pooles,
> The fish shall turne their glistering bellies vp,
> And thou shalt take thy liberall choice of all.

osprey (Theob.) F. 'Aspray'.

36–7. *he could not...even* Cf. Sic. at 2. 1. 221 'He cannot temp'rately transport his honours'. *even* = and keep his balance.

38. *daily fortune* 'uninterrupted success' (E.K.C.).

39. *defect* (F2) F. 'detect'.

41–5. *nature...the war* This, I suspect, was Sh.'s own view of Cor.

43. *cushion* i.e. the magistrate's seat. See 2. 2. S.D. (init.).

44. *austerity and garb* Hendiadys, = rigid discipline. See G. 'garb'.

45–7. *but one...feared* the 'all, not all' is awkward, but the text, I think, is sound and not difficult if one remembers the natural inconsequence of an extempore speaker. Re-arranged the sense runs: 'he has touches—I will not say more—of all these faults and for one he grew feared', etc.

48–9. *but...utterance* The 'merit' is of course courage and skill in war; and 'it' is the one fault, whichever it was, that caused his banishment. Moore

Smith's conj. 'be it' for 'but' wd bring out Auf.'s meanness; cf. *Shr.* 2. 1. 124, 'be it that she survive me'. *choke...utterance*=choke any mention of the fault before one could get it out. J.'s 'He has a merit for no other purpose than to destroy it by boasting it' goes surprisingly astray.

49–50. *So...time* Thus our very virtues lie at the mercy of contemporary interpretation. Cf. Falstaff on Honour—'Detraction will not suffer it' (*1 H. IV*, 5. 1. 138–9). *virtues* (F2) F. 'Vertue'.

51–3. *And power...done* This has baffled many, but the meaning seems clear, once the general drift is grasped which is that if virtue or honour is subject to detraction; success, which is the public recognition of virtue or honour, is still more so. To paraphrase: Power, which seems a worthy object enough to those who have succeeded, receives its death-blow from the first public speeches proclaiming the deeds by which it was acquired. [*chair*=pulpit, rostrum; *evident*=inevitable.] The Forum speeches in *J. C.* provide a classical example. And the couplet that follows gives the reason why this is so: 'power falls by stirring up inevitably another power to oppose it' (G.G.); other 'virtuous' or ambitious men are pressing on behind. 'O, let not virtue seek | Remuneration for the thing it *was*' says Ulysses in the great speech which is but an expansion of ll. 49–55 here (*Troil.* 3. 3. 145–79).

55. *falter* (Dyce+O.S., Al., etc.) F. 'fouler'; Mal. (<J. conj.) 'founder'; Clar. defends F. by taking 'fouler' as an adj. and 'fail' as predicate of both clauses. But this upsets the double antithesis, evidently intended in ll. 54–5, which Mal. and Dyce preserve. 'Falter,' sp. 'faulter' or 'foulter' after 16th and 17th c. fashion, might easily be misread 'fouler'. Mason+ C.J.S. (*N.R.* ii. 131) conj. 'Right's by rights fouler'.

57. S.D.<F. 'exeunt'.

5. 1

S.D. *Loc*. Rowe ('Rome')+Theob. ('A public place') *Entry* (F.).

3. *In...particular* With great personal affection [Quibbling on 'general'].

5–6. *knee...mercy* Sh. has in mind the practice of penitents approaching shrines. Cf. his Addition to *Sir Thomas More* ll. 110–11, 'and your unreverent knees | Make them your feet to kneel to be forgiven' (*Sh.'s Hand*, p. 237). He was fond of making noun-verbs like 'knee'; cf. 'nose' (l. 28), 'lip' (*Oth*. 4. 1. 71), 'arm him'=take him in your arms (*Cym*. 4. 2. 402). As G.G. remarks, 'they hit the mind'.

6–7. *coyed To hear* listened scornfully (as Com. spoke). Clar. cites *Ven*. 112, 'my coy disdain' and *Gent*. 1. 1. 29–30, 'To be in love, where scorn is bought with groans; Coy looks with heart-felt sighs'. That Cor. did not disdain to hear altogether is clear from what follows.

12. *to* (F2) F. 'too'.

13–15. *He was...Rome* A report of what Cor. said. Note the vision of Rome burning; cf. Introd. p. xxxvi.

14. *i' th'* (J.+Mal.+Al.) F. 'a' th'' F4 'o' th'' <Cap. 'o' the' (read by Camb.+most). But 'forge' requires '*in* the fire'.

16. *wrecked fair* (Williams conj.+Dyce ii, Deighton, Neils., etc.) F. (+Al.) 'wrack'd for'. Other emendations include 'racked for' (Pope, J., Mal., Camb.+most) and 'recked for' (Theob. conj.+Warb.). 'Racked' (explained by Steev. 'harassed by exactions' or 'acted good stewards', and in Clar. etc. 'strained every effort, exerted yourselves to the utmost'; cf. *M.V.* 1. 1. 181) is never intrans. elsewh. in Sh., nor so cited, before 19th c., in O.E.D. except in Scots; nor is it coupled with 'for' elsewh. 'Recked' conj. by

Theob. and explained by him 'been careful, provident' is more attractive, since it implies sarcasm. But Men. is clearly alluding to 'burning Rome' and is composing an epitaph or memorial ['memory'] for the tribunes. Williams's reading fits this exactly—a pair of hucksters who have brought down the price of coal by offering the ruins of fair Rome as fuel.

19. *When it was less* = the less it was.

20. *state* A retort to 'royal'. On the contrary, he implies, I am no king but an expelled criminal; it is the ruling power of Rome that now makes this barefaced request of one they had punished, and refused to pardon.

21. *very well* i.e. that's well said.

23. *offered* tried, ventured.

25–8. *He could...offence* Sh. is fond of images from winnowing, but here he seems to have specially in mind Matt. iii. 12, 'Whose fan is in his hand, and he will throughly purge his floor, and gather the wheat into his garner; but he will burn up the chaff with unquenchable fire'. *leave unburnt* and *nose* both govern *th'*. P. A. Daniel proposed 'leave't unburnt'.

32. *Above the moon* Cf. *Ham.* 3. 3. 36, 'my offence... smells to heaven'; *Ado* 2. 1. 232, 'she would infect to the north-star'.

34. *In...help* = 'In this time when help was never so much needed'. Phrase-compounds are common in Sh. (v. Abbott, § 434), but this one is more than usually contorted. Yet the sense is clear enough to the ear and only becomes puzzling when one begins to think about it.

37. *the instant...make* i.e. any army we can levy at the moment. On. glosses 'instant' as existing, now present. But, if so, why 'can make'?

44. *But as* etc. Understand 'returned' again before this.

46–7. *that thanks...well* 'such thanks as are proportionate to your good intentions' (Clar.).

49. *hum at* See G. and 5. 4. 21.

50. *taken well* tackled at the right moment. Cf.
M.N.D. 3. 2. 16; *Ham.* 3. 3. 80.

51–5. *the veins...With wine and feeding* Cf.
Introd. p. xvi and 1. 1. 134, n.

52. *pout upon* Cf. *Rom.* 3. 3. 144.

56. *watch* No reference to 'watching' (=keeping
awake) a falcon, as some suppose.

57. *dieted* Here used in the obvious sense of 'fed'
but 'dieted to' might also mean 'habituated to', or
'disciplined (to accede) by a prescribed course of
feeding'. See G.

60. *prove* try.

61–2. *I shall...success* 'I shall not be kept long in
suspense as to the result of my embassy' (Steev.). But
for 'I' Theob. conj. 'Ye', Han. (+others) 'You', and
that seems apter as a parting assurance from the ebul-
lient Men. v. G. 'success'.

S.D. F. 'Exit'.

63. *in gold* Cf. North, p. 177, 'he was set in his
chayer of state, with a marvelous, and an unspeakable
majestie'. Moore Smith conj. (<Blackstone) 'en-
galled' (sp. 'ingald') wh., as giving us a glimpse of Cor.'s
face, is attractive and more in accordance with the
context. O.E.D. ('*en-* 1 b) cites Florio (*Queen Anna's
new world of wordes,* 1611) '*Affielire...to* engall or
enbitter'—only instance given. See 5. 4. 21–2, wh.
might suit either reading.

64. *Red* Cf. *K. J.* 4. 2. 162, 'With eyes as red as
new-enkindled fire', and *2 H. VI,* 3. 1. 154 [Case].

64–5. *his injury...pity* To parody *J. C.* 3. 1. 270;
his pity choked with memories of his wrongs.

67–9. *What he would do...conditions* Prob. an in-
soluble crux. It seems clear that the comp. has missed
out a line after l. 68, since 'what he would not' is left
in the air; or perh., as Mal. suggests, two half lines;

'Bound with an oath' being the beginning of one line and 'to yield to his conditions' the conclusion of the other. Further, since we learn from 5. 2. 48–9 that Cor. has sworn not to grant the Romans reprieve and pardon, l. 69 must be corrupt and ought to run either 'Bound with an oath to hold to his conditions' (conj. Solly: 'hold' being easily misread 'yeld') or 'Bound with an oath to yield no new conditions' (conj. J.).

71. *Unless* = 'If it were not for'. Cf. *All's* 4. 1. 6; *R. II*, 5. 3. 32; *R. III*, 4. 4. 475–6.

74. S.D. < F. 'Exeunt'.

5. 2

S.D. *Loc.* (Camb. < Rowe + Theob.). *Entry* (Al. < F., but reading 'on' for F. 'or').

1. S.H.s < F (+ Rowe, Pope, J.) '1 Wat.; 2 Wat.' (with '1' and '2' later). Cap. + Mal. read '1 G.', '2 G.'; Camb. + most mod. edd. 'First Sen.', 'Sec. Sen.'. Al. restores F. rightly, since 'watch' is Sh.'s usual word for a military guard of any kind, though 'sentinel' is common with him also.

10. *lots to blanks* i.e. a thousand to one. v. G. 'lot'.

13. *passable* See G. for quibble.

14. *lover* v. G.

15. *The book* The recorder. Cf. *Lucr.* 615–16.

17. *varnishèd* (J.D.W.; Edwards conj. c. 1750) F. 'verified'. F. is explained 'borne witness to' (J.), 'spoken the truth of' (Mal.), 'maintained the credit of' (Schmidt). But Aldis Wright (Clar.) comments, 'These are all forced explanations of a word which is most likely corrupt, and they none of them fit in with "size" in the next line'; while G.G. roundly declares that F. 'satisfies nobody'. The general sense is not in doubt, viz. 'I have done my best to cherish or keep

bright my friends' reputations' and is attested by emendations like 'magnified', 'amplified', 'rarified', 'deified', 'certified', 'notified', 'glorified', all however ruled out on stylistic grounds, since Sh. is unlikely to have used two p.pl. adjs., both ending ''ified' in consecutive lines. Word-play being often the clue to his meaning, 'size' (l. 18), which means both magnitude and a sticky wash used by artists or upon walls, suggests 'varnished', which Sh. generally uses in the transf. sense of 'embellish, trick out, cover or overlay with a specious appearance' (O.E.D.), a sense exactly suited to the context. Cf. *Ham*. 4. 7. 131, 'Set a double varnish on the fame | The Frenchman gave you' and *Tim*. 5. 1. 63–5, 'I...cannot cover | The monstrous bulk of this ingratitude | With any size of words'. Again if 'vernished' was the copy-sp. it might have been misread 'verrifyed', esp. with 'verity' (l. 18) to mislead the compositor. After working all this out, I found the conj. reading anticipated by Th. Edwards (*Canons of Criticism* (3rd ed.) 1750, p. 98, cited Furn.), who translated the passage: 'I have laid on as much praise as would stick', explained it as 'an allusion either to painting or white-washing', pointed out its agreement with the following metaphor of 'size', and noted the spelling 'vernish'.

19. *lapsing* slipping. Cf. *M. V.* 3. 1. 11 'true, without any slips of prolixity'.

21. *tumbled...throw* inadvertently gone too far. See G. 'tumble', 'throw'.

22. *stamped the leasing* given falsehood currency. See G. 'stamp', 'leasing'.

34. *dined* Dinner was served between 11 and 12 in Sh.'s time (*Sh.'s Eng.* ii, 134).

43. *palms* uplifted hands.

44. *dotant* Not found elsewhere. Poss. misp. for 'dotard'.

54–5. *Back, I say; go,* (Al.)　F. (+most) 'Back I say, go:'.

55. *your half-pint* etc. Cf. *Mac.* 5. 1. 38 'Who would have thought the old man to have had so much blood in him?'

56. *the...having* all you can get.

57. S.D. (F.).

59.　*companion* Insulting; see G.

59–60. *say...for you* deliver the message for you. The point, I take it, is that Men. will tell the general about the Watch before they can tell about him. *errand* (Pope+ most) F. 'arrant'.

61. *a Jack guardant* a rascally watch. See G. 'Jack'.

office A verb suggested prob. by Jack-in-office, which almost certainly suggested Jack guardant. (Cf. *1 H. VI*, 1. 1. 175, 'Jack out of office'.)

62. *but by my* (Mal.+most)　F. 'but my'.

62–5. *Guess...suffering; behold* (Mal.+most)　F. 'guesse but my entertainment with him: if thou... suffering, behold'.

66. S.D. (J.D.W.).　Otherwise the reader might be puzzled for a moment.

72. *your gates* i.e. the gates of your native city [Case].

76. *block* For the quibble see G.

80–1. *I owe...properly* i.e. it belongs personally to me. *remission* v. G.

82–4. *That we...how much* Much debated, but 'ingrate forgetfulness' can I think only refer to that of Rome or of the 'dastard nobles' including Men. I paraphrase: I had rather the memory of our old friendship should be poisoned by thoughts of your ungrateful forgetfulness of my services to Rome, than that pity for you should record or call to mind how great the friendship was.

83. *Ingrate forgetfulness* Cf. *Troil.* 3. 3. 146–7, 'oblivion, A great-sized monster of ingratitude'.

83–4. *poison rather Than pity note* Punct. (Theob.+) F. 'poison rather Then pitty: Note'. But for 'poison' Theob. (+Han. and Cap.) reads 'prison', citing *1 H. VI*, 5. 4. 121, *L.L.L.* 4. 3. 301 in which he makes a similar change, more plausibly than here, where it gives the forced meaning of 'keep secret'.

88. S.D. (Pope+).

89. S.D. (J.D.W.).

91. *You...temper* 'Concealed irony' (E.K.C.). S.D. (after Cap.) F. 'Exeunt. | Manet the Guard and Menenius.'.

100. *by himself* 'by his own hands' (Mal.).

102. *long* He cannot think of a worse fate than that they should long live their miserable lives.

103. S.D. < F. 'Exit'.

106. S.D. < F. 'Exit Watch'.

5. 3

S.D. *Loc.* (< Cap.) *Entry* (J.D.W. < Plut., cited ll. 40–2, n.). F. 'Enter Coriolanus and Auffidius'.

3. *plainly* 'openly' (J.).

11. *latest refuge* last resources.

14. *The first conditions* i.e. those sent to Com. (5. 1. 67–8).

15–17. *accept; to...more, a very...to* (J. but I read 'accept;' for his 'accept,') F. 'accept,...onely, That... more: A very ...too'. The 'very little' is to offer 'the first conditions' over again. *embassies* (F4) F. 'Embasses'.

19. S.D. (< F. 'Shout within').

21. S.D. (F.) and 'in mourning habits' (Cap.)—

which most edd. accept, though without any clear warrant in text or North. Cf. ll. 94f n.

22. *My wife foremost* Sh. gives Virg. a more prominent part than Plut., who makes Valeria the moving spirit, at whose request Vol. and Virg. visit Cor. at the Volscian camp. The 'aside' is J.D.W.'s.

22-3. *mould...framed* Cf. G. 'mould' and Nashe (McK. ii. 74. 31 ff.) 'the Mould wherein thou wert cast' (a mother speaks to her child) [J.C.M.].

24-37. *But out...no other kin* The soliloquy is a spiritual tussle to and fro, ending with the greatest of blasphemies against Nature (or natural affection), expressed in other words by Crookback, 'I am myself alone' (*3 H. VI*, 5. 6. 83). Cf. Introd. p. xxxv.

25. *bond and privilege of nature* the reciprocal ties of human affection (here between husband and wife).

26. *obstinate* v. G. and Sir T. Browne *Rel. Med.* i, § 25 (Gold. Treas. ed.) 'Obstinacy in a bad cause is but constancy in a good'.

27. *doves' eyes* Cf. Song of Solomon i. 15; iv. 1; v. 12.

28. *Which...forsworn* A foretaste of what is coming. His oath would seem far more solemn and binding in Sh.'s day than in ours.

30. *Olympus to a molehill* An implicit recognition of how much stronger her character is than his.

32. *aspect of intercession* pleading look. Accent aspéct' like 'instínct' l. 35.

35. *stand* i.e. stand fast (as in Eph. vi. 13, 14).

38. *These eyes* etc. i.e. they see things differently.

40-2. *Like...disgrace* Aside and S.D.s (J.D.W.). Cor. cannot have meant Auf. and the Volsces, or indeed Virg., to hear 'Even to a full disgrace', for though on the surface it alludes to an actor forgetting his part being hissed from the stage, the ominous second meaning is obvious. And the S.D.s are based on North, p. 183 already cited in the Introd. p. xviii):

Nowe was Martius set then in his chayer of state, with all the honours of a generall, and when he had spied the women comming a farre of, he marveled what the matter ment: but afterwardes knowing his wife which came formest, he determined at the first to persist in his obstinate and in-flexible rancker. But overcomen in the ende with naturall affection, and being altogether altered to see them: his harte would not serve him to tarie their comming to his chayer, but comming downe in hast, he went to meete them, and first he kissed his mother, and imbraced her a pretie while, then his wife and little children. And nature so wrought with him, that the teares fell from his eyes, and he coulde not keepe him selfe from making much of them, but yeelded to the affection of his bloode, as if he had bene violently caried with the furie of a most swift running streame.

41. *out* For this sense cf. *Son* 23.1; *L.L.L.* 5.2.149–52, 165, 173.

42. *Best of my flesh* Cf. Matt. xix. 5, 'they twain shall be one flesh'.

46. *the jealous queen* 'Juno, the guardian of marriage, and consequently the avenger of connubial perfidy' (J.).

48. *prate* (Pope < Theob. conj. +)F. 'pray'.

50. *Sink...earth* Cf. 2. 1. 167, S.D. n. for this customary kneeling to ask a parent's blessing—which she refuses to give. S.D. (F.).

51. *deep duty* profound obeisance. *impression* in the earth.

52–6. *O, stand...parent* The whole speech is deeply ironical. *blest* = not blessed by her; but lucky, favoured by fortune. *unproperly* = against propriety.

55–6. *as...parent* I have 'been "all this while" mistaken in thinking that the duty is from children to parents' (G.G.).

56. S.D. (Rowe) F. om.

57. S.D. (J.D.W.) Cap. 'preventing her'. *corrected* i.e. rebuked.

58. *hungry* Usually explained 'sterile' (Steev.). Mal.'s 'hungry for wrecks' (cf. *Tw. N.* 2. 4. 100, 'as hungry as the sea') is better, but his 'idle conjecture', 'angry', has much to commend it from the context and is, I suspect, the right reading. The image is that of a beach in a violent storm, boiling with rage (cf. *R. II*, 2. 1. 62–3; *Oth.* 2. 1. 11 ff.). And Case well asks, 'Is there any connection between the hunger of the beach and its attack on the stars?'.

61. *Murd'ring impossibility* making anything or everything possible.

62. *slight work* an easy task.

63. *holp* (Pope+) F. 'hope'.

64–7. *The noble...Valeria* All Plut. says of Valeria is that she was Publicola's sister, that she 'did so modestlie and wiselie behave her selfe, that she did not shame nor dishonour the house she came of'; and that, while praying with other ladies in the temple of Jupiter Capitoline, she was inspired 'by some god as I thinke' to get Volumnia and Virgilia to go and intercede with Coriolanus (pp. 181–2).

65. *chaste* etc. Chaucer (*Frankelyns Tale*, l. 728, Ox. ed.) mentions a Valeria as an ex. of 'wyfly chastitee' [Case].

66. *curdied* Not found elsewhere. Poss. 'curdled', or 'curded'. Cf. 'candied', *Tp.* 2. 1. 276; *Tim.* 4. 3. 227. The vb. is 'curd' in *Ham.* 1. 5. 69; *All's* 1. 3. 146.

68. S.D. (Pope).

68–9. *epitome...interpretation* The image seems one of Time as a preacher or orator expounding or developing the headings of a sermon or speech.

70. *god of soldiers* Mars.

73. *stick* stand out. Case cites *Ham.* 5. 2. 255, 'stick fiery off' =stand out brilliantly (Dowden).

74. *sea-mark* Cf. G. and *Son.* 116. 5–6 'an ever-fixed mark | That looks on tempests and is never shaken'. *standing* withstanding. *flaw*=gust.

75. *those that eye thee* i.e. that use thee as their guide (like the ships at sea).

77–8. *Even he* etc. Vol. is a good strategist: she waits till the boy is on his knees and his father's heart overflowing with the sight of him to begin her direct attack.

78. *peace!* (Al.) F. 'peace:'. Cor.'s angry start needs an exclamation.

80. *thing* F. (+Camb., Al., etc.) Cap.+Mal. etc. 'things'. *forsworn to grant* sworn not to grant. Cf. *Rom.* 1.1.222 'forsworn to love'; *Tw. N.* 3.4.252–3 [Clar.].

81. *Be...denials* Be taken as a refusal to grant your requests.

denials Plur. because he is addressing them all; cf. 'comforts' (l. 99).

82. *capitulate.* v. G.

85–6. *T' allay...colder reasons* Cf. *M.V.* 2.2.183; *Troil.* 4.4.8, etc. [Case].

93. S.D. (J.D.W.). Cf. l. 131. Thus laying aside the son, husband, and father.

94–5. *our raiment...bodies* i.e. rags and emaciation.

103. *to poor we* Loose grammar, natural enough in speech.

106. *For how can we* etc. Cf. Blanche's dilemma in *K.J.* 3.1.326–36 [Deighton].

112. *evident* v. G.

114. *a foreign recreant* traitorous deserter to a foreign country.

115. *thorough* (J.+most) F.(+Al.; C.J.S.) 'through.'

120. *determine* conclude. Cf. 3.3.43.

124. *thou shalt not* i.e. thou shalt not march without treading, etc.

127–8. *A' shall not...fight.* The boy's only speech.

129–30. *Not...see* i.e. If I'm not to become woman-ish I must stop looking at them. G.G. thinks the rhyme denotes a softening on Cor.'s part; I suppose rather that as usual it intimates a rounding-off, here his inten-tion to end the business which grows too uncomfortable by far. Prob. an aside.

131. *sat* S.D. (Cap.). But no previous S.D. for the sitting though Plut. says he sat. See l. 40, S.D. n.

139. *the all-hail* universal acclamation. Cf. *Mac.* 1. 5. 54.

141. *The end...uncertain* Anders (p. 47) cites 'Belli excitus incertus' from Culmann's *Sententiae Pueriles* wh. Sh. is supposed to have used at school. But Furn. cites from Vol.'s speech in North (p. 185), 'though the ende of warre be uncertain'.

146. *it* i.e. his nobility.

149–53. *Thou hast affected...oak* i.e. he 'has brought Rome to her knees to save his honour, never meaning really to injure her, just as Jove when he thunders injures nothing more important than a tree' (E.K.C.).

151. *To tear...air* Cf. *R. II*, 3. 3. 54–7. The winds in the old maps were shown issuing from the swollen cheeks of cherubs. [Tucker Brooke.]

152. *charge* (Theob.+) F. 'change'.

155. *Still*=for ever.

155–6. *Daughter...weeping* Cf. 4. 2. 52.

159. *lets me prate* Perhaps intended to recall his words to her ll. 48–50. *Like one i' th' stocks* 'as a worthless vagabond to whose compliments...no one pays heed' (Clar.). See Introd. pp. xxii–iii.

160–64. *Thou hast...honour* 'She falls back on a woman's last resource, the pathetic. Perhaps a tear comes, which Cor. has never seen on her cheek before' (E.K.C.). Auf. notes it (v. 5. 6. 46, 97).

162. *fond of* desirous of, wishing for. Cf. *Cym.* 1. 1. 37.

163. *clucked* (F 2) F. 'clock'd'—still a dial. form. (See E.D.D. 'clock' vb. 2. 1.) Case cites Nashe *Christes Teures* (McK. ii. 42–3) 'The Henne clocketh her Chickins'.

166–8. *Thou art…belongs* = 'You can't deceive your-self; and your conscience will plague you later that you withheld from your mother the obedience you owe her.' Her trump card, though she doesn't know it, and Cor. turns away so that she may not see it.

167. *restrain'st* v. G.

168. *To a* E.K.C. 'T' a'—which gives the elided pronunciation.

169. *him with* (F 2) F. 'him with him with'.

173. *Nay behold's!* She tugs at his tunic.

176. *reason* argue for.

177. *Come, let us go* She rises as he still keeps an averted face.

180. *Yet…dispatch* This, her last attempt to force him to say something, makes him turn to look at her, and the victory is hers.

181. S.D. (J.D.W.).

181–2. *I am…little* Spoken, I think, looking straight at him. He then comes to her.

181. *hushed* F. 'husht'—actually an adj., (=silent) not a p.pl.; the vb. being orig. derived from it. [Case citing O.E.D.] Cf. *Tp.* 4. 1. 207; *Ven.* 458.

182. S.D. (<F.) A famous S.D. and certainly Sh.'s. Cf. North, p. 186.

Martius…could refrane no lenger, but went straight and lifte her up, crying out: Oh mother, what have you done to me? And holding her hand by the right hande, oh mother, sayed he, you have wonne a happy victorie for your countrie, but mortall and unhappy for your sonne: for I see my self vanquished by you alone. These wordes being spoken openly, he spake a litle a parte with his mother and wife, and then let them returne again to Rome, for so they dyd request him.

184–5. *The gods...laugh at* Cf. the Christian version
(*Meas.* 2. 2. 118, ff.), 'But man, proud man...Plays such
fantastic tricks before high heaven | As make the angels
weep'. Sh. prob. gets the laughter of the gods from the
proverb 'Jove laughs at lovers' perjuries' (cf. *Rom.* 2.
2. 92–3).

184. *unnatural* 'The whole situation is unnatural:
a Roman making war on Rome; a mother pleading with
her son for mercy; a conqueror melted by a woman'
(E.K.C.).

189. *mortal* An adverb.

190. *make true wars* keep my promise to you in this
campaign (see Introd. p. xxxi). Plur. for sing.

191. *convenient* proper, decent. Cf. l. 197.
Aufidius The repetition of the name adds a touch of
pleading to the question.

192. *stead* (F4) F. 'steed'.

194. *I...withal* Ominously reserved.

196. *Mine eyes...compassion* Cf. Auf.'s words
5. 6. 97–8.

199. S.D. (Neils.) F. om. Cf. North quoted l. 182
S.D. n. Most edd. read, after 'fortune' in l. 202, the
S.D. (J.) 'The Ladies make signs to Cor.'.

200. The aside (Rowe+).

201–2. *I'll work...fortune* 'I'll continue to raise my
fortunes to their former height' (Case).

202. S.D. (J.D.W.) F. om. Rowe (+) 'To
Volumnia, Virgilia,' etc.
Ay, by and by 'Prob. they urge him to return to
Rome' (E.K.C.).

203. *drink together* Steev. cites *2 H. IV*, 4. 2. 63,
'Let's drink together firmly and embrace, | That all
their eyes may bear those tokens home | Of our restored
love and amity', and Schmidt *J. C.* 4. 3. 156–7, 'Give
me a bowl of wine. In this I bury all unkindness,
Cassius'. R.G.W. and Hudson found Sh. here a little

lacking in 'female delicacy' and Furn. agrees. The ladies of James I's court would not.

203–5. *you shall bear...counter-sealed* i.e. you shall carry back a copy of a treaty between Romans and Volscians duly sealed and countersealed.

207. *a temple built* This reflects Plut. who relates that the Senate having ordained that the magistrates should grant 'the ladies' all they would require they built a temple of Fortune they had asked for (North, p. 186).

209. S.D.<F. 'Exeunt.'

5.4

S.D. *Loc.* (J.D.W.) after Dyce in 5.5; see S.D. there. *Entry* (F.).

1. *coign o' th' Capitol* Takes us back to Rome at once. Cf. also Plut.'s account of Calpurnius's dream of the pinnacle on the house that fell and killed Caesar (North, v, p. 68). *coign* (Cap.) F. 'coin'. See G.

19. *like an engine* e.g. a battering-ram.

22. *as...Alexander* like an image of Alexander. The neuter 'thing' adds the touch of rigidity required. *state*=chair of state.

26. *in the character*=as he is. Men. resents 'if you report him *truly*' (Ver.).

29. *'long* (Cap.) F. 'long'.

34. S.D. (F.).

39. *death by inches* Cf. *Cym.* 5.5.52; *Tp.* 2.2.3. S.D. (F.).

41. *dislodged* Cf. North, p. 186, 'the next morning he [Cor.] dislodged'.

47. *Ne'er...tide* Cf. *Lucr.* 1667, 'As through an arch the violent roaring tide'. See Spurgeon, pp. 97–8 (and frontispiece) for the current under Clopton bridge. But the image would also appeal to those familiar with the 'tide' roaring through the arches of London Bridge.

blown=either 'swollen' (cf. *Lr.* 4. 4. 27 'blown ambition'; *1 H. IV*, 4. 2. 47 'blown Jack [Falstaff]'), or 'helped by the wind'. A high tide with a strong easterly wind may raise the Thames to a dangerous level.

48. S.D. F. 'Trumpets, Hoboyes, Drums beate, altogether.'

51. *Make...dance* Cf. *Tw. N.* 2. 3. 60, 'make the welkin dance', and the old belief that the sun dances on Easter Day. S.D. (<F.) 'A shout within'.

57. S.D. (J.D.W.) F. 'Sound still with the Shouts' —a command to the instrumentalists, trumpeters and servitors in the tiring-house. Camb. (+most) 'Music still, with shouts'.

59. *Accept* etc. Sic. affects the regal air.

60. *city*! (J.D.W.) F. 'city.' F 3 (+) 'city?'.

62. S.D. (J.D.W.<Cap. 'going') F. 'Exeunt'.

5.5

Entry (Cap.) F. 'Enter two Senators, with Ladies, passing over the Stage, with other Lords'. Dyce and Camb. mark a change of place here and head 'The same. A street near the gate'. But Sic. said 'We will meet them', and they do!

8. S.D. (J.D.W.+F.) No 'exeunt' in F.

5.6

S.D. *Loc.* 'Corioli' (Singer, O.S., G.G., Al.) 'A public place' (Theob.). Rowe (+most) 'Antium', as it is in Plut. and is implied in Auf.'s opening speech and in ll. 50, 73, 80 (see notes); but cf. the explicit

statement in l. 90. Clearly Sh. changes his mind. G.G.
suggests 'Sh....wrote with Antium in his mind until
he came to Auf.'s speech in l. 88. Here he was carried
away by the magnificent opportunity of placing Coriolanus in Corioli' (l. 90), 'and for the rest of the scene
thought rather of Corioli than of Antium'. What
matter? Antium had not been *mentioned* and nothing
had been said to set even the most judicious of spectators thinking of it though Sh.'s edd. do. *Entry* (F.).

1–8. *Go...words* The 'city' here must be the
Volscian capital.

5. *accuse* (F4+) F. 'accuse:' *Him* For 'he' by
attraction with 'whom' understood (Abbott, § 208).

8. S.D. (i) (J.D.W.) F. om. (ii) (F.).

11. *by his...empoisoned* i.e. by bread and wine given
in charity. Cf. O.E.D. 'alms-bread', 'alms-drink'.

20. *pretext* Accented 'pretéxt'.

22–6 *who...free* Auf. is lying and 3 Consp. is about
to express surprise, when he rapidly takes him up by
changing the course of his thoughts. *free*=outspoken.

37. *did end all this* finally harvested all himself. See
G. 'end', and E.D.D. 'end'.

40–1. *waged...mercenary* i.e. was generously pleased
to smile upon me, as if I had been one of his mer-
cenaries. Clar. cites a passage in Plut. which, account-
ing for Auf.'s envy of Cor., runs (North. p. 178): 'This
fell out the more, bicause every man honoured Martius,
and thought he only could doe all, and that all other
governours and captaines must be content with suche
credit and authoritie, as he would please to countenaunce them with.' Here 'countenance with'=grant;
but Sh. gives it a different turn by relating it to the
treatment of mercenary soldiers, who in his day were
usually kept waiting for their wages and had to be
content with the favour of their royal employers
instead of hard cash.

waged (<F3) F. 'wadg'd'.

42. *in the last* Cf. 'in the best' *Ham.* 1. 5. 27; 'in the least' *Lr.* 1. 1. 190 [Clar.].

43. *had carried* might have taken.

44–5. *There...upon him* Cf. *Mac.* 1. 7. 79–80, 'bend up | Each corporal agent'. *upon*=against.

49. S.D. (<F.)—but reading 'sound' for 'sounds'.

50. *Your native town* i.e., by implication, Antium.

a post a mere messenger (bringing news of the surrender of Rome).

54. *at your vantage* when you see your opportunity.

57–8. *second. When...way his* (Theob.+) F. 'second, when...way. His'.

58–9. *After...body* you can tell his tale your own way and so his cause (any defence he may put up) goes to the grave with him.

60. S.D. (F.).

64. *made* committed.

65. *fines* v. G.

66–8. *give...charge* throw away the whole cost and trouble of raising an army (v. G. 'levy') and repaying us by merely handing back the money and office we entrusted to him at the beginning. That this was all lies appears from Cor.'s statement (ll. 77–9) that the spoils exceed the costs by more than a third.

70. S.D. (F.).

73. *hence* sc. from Antium; cf. 4. 4. 1, 8–11.

80. *Antiates* Cf. previous note and 5. 6. S.D. (head-note).

85. *traitor...degree* Cf. *R. III*, 5. 3. 196, 'perjury in the high'st degree', and *Tw. N.* 1. 5. 53, 'misprision in the highest degree'.

traitor (F.). Theob. (+many) 'traitor,'—incorrect.

87. *Traitor!* Cf. Introd. p. xxxii.

90. *Coriolanus in Corioli* Cf. head-note S.D.

93. *drops of salt* i.e. the tears, not of Cor. himself

(cf. 5. 3. 196), but of Vol. and Virg. And if Vol. does not actually weep it suits Auf. to say she does (cf. 'his nurse's tears', l. 97). For 'salt', cf. *Ham.* 1. 2. 154.

95. *oath and resolution* Hendiadys: what he swore was his fixed purpose.

96–7. *never...war* 'never consulting his fellow officers'. Cor. asks Auf. to advise him on the terms of the peace (5. 3. 196–7), but not whether to make peace or no.

98. *whined and roared* Cf. 5. 3. 182–5, 'O mother... mother! O!'

102. *No more* i.e. just a blubbering boy.

107. *his own notion* his own consciousness of the truth.

116. *Fluttered* (F 3) F. 'Flatter'd'.

120. S.H. The Conspirators (J.D.W.) F. 'All Consp.'.

121. S.H. The People (J.D.W.) F. 'All People'. Punct. (<Camb.).

125–6. *folds in...earth* 'overspreads the world' (J.). Cf. 3. 3. 68 'The fires...fold in the people'.

127. *judicious* judicial. *stand* v. G.

129. *his tribe* the whole race of Aufidius.

131. S.D. (Camb.) F. 'Draw both the Conspirators, and kils Martius, who falles, Auffidius stands on him.' No warrant in Plut. for this last indignity, which Sh. prob. derives from the Bible, e.g. Ps. lx. 12.

134. *upon...quiet* (punct.<Cap.+) F. 'vpon him Masters, all be quiet'.

147. *My rage is gone* Cf. Introd. *Oth.*, p. lv.

149. *one* i.e. the fourth. It usually took four men to carry corpses from the stage. Cf. *Ham.* 5. 2. 393.

155. S.D. (F.).

GLOSSARY

Note. Where pun or word-play is intended, meanings are distinguished as (*a*) and (*b*). Conjectural readings by J. D. W. are starred.

A', he; 2. 1. 121; 5. 3. 127

ABATED, humbled, abject; 3. 3. 132

ABRAM, dark brown; 2. 3. 18

ABSOLUTE, (i) positive, unqualified; 3. 1. 90; 3. 2. 39; (ii) incomparable, perfect; 4. 5. 139

ABUSE, (i) deceive, mislead; 3. 1. 58; (ii) misuse; 5. 6. 86

ACHIEVE, (i) win; 1. 9. 33; (ii) (abs.) accomplish a purpose; 4. 7. 23

ACTION, military action, campaign; 1. 1. 278; 2. 1. 134; 4. 7. 5, 15; 5. 6. 48; 'out of act.' = in inactivity, abstaining from military action; 1. 3. 25

ADDITION, title (added to a name); 1. 9. 66, 72

ADMIRE, wonder, marvel; 1. 9. 5

ADMIT, (i) accept ('receive into any office'); 2. 3. 142; (ii) allow; 5. 6. 96

ADVANCE, raise; 1. 6. 61; 2. 1. 159

ADVANTAGE, opportunity; 2. 3. 197; 4. 1. 43

ADVERSELY, contrary to taste, disagreeably; 2. 1. 55

AEDILE. When instituted, the Tribunes were allowed two aediles, to arrest at their bidding and to hurl from the Tarpeian rock those they condemned to death, with other police duties; 3. 1. 172, etc.

AFFECT, (i) aim at, desire; 2. 2. 20; 3. 3. 1; 4. 6. 32; (ii) display (cf. *Lr.* 2. 2. 94) or sense (i); 5. 3. 149

AFFECTION, inclination, bent 1. 1. 103, 176; 2. 3. 230

AFRIC, Africa (4 times Sh.; only 1 'Africa'); 1. 8. 3

AFTER, according to, in accordance with; 2. 3. 225, 229

AGAINST, 'when exposed to' (Clar.); 1. 9. 30

AGE, lifetime; 3. 1. 7; 4. 6. 52

AGUED, trembling, like a person with a shivering fit in malaria; 1. 4. 38

ALARUM or 'LARUM, lit. summons with drum and trumpet to arms, or sound of such a summons to an army in battle, but often (as here) 'noise of battle' (cf. 1. 4. 20), or simply the 'battle' itself; 1. 4. 9, 19, S.D., 29 S.D., etc.; 2. 2. 74

ALLAYING, diluting; 2. 1. 48

ALLOW, acknowledge; 3. 3. 45

ALLOWANCE, admission; 3. 2. 57

ALMOST, even. Emphatic use (cf. *Tp.* 3. 3. 34); 1. 2. 24

ALMS, i.e. bread and wine given in charity. Cf. O.E.D. 'alms-bread', 'alms-wine'; 5. 6. 11

GLOSSARY

246

ALONG, prostrate on the ground, at full length; 5. 6. 57

AMAZONIAN, as beardless as those of the Amazons (women warriors of Greek legend); 2. 2. 89

AN, if; 2. 1. 128, etc.

ANCUS MARCIUS, legendary king of Rome, the third after Romulus; 2. 3. 238

AN-HUNGRY, hungry (here only Sh.); 1. 1. 204

ANON, in a short while; 2. 3. 140, 143, etc.

ANSWER (sb.), reply to, or defence in, a charge; 3. 1. 176

ANSWER (vb.), (i) meet in combat; 1. 2. 19; 1. 4. 53; (ii) act in conformity with, 'play up to' (E. K. Chambers); 2. 3. 258; (iii) suffer the consequences, pay the penalty; 3. 1. 162; (iv) stand on one's defence; 3. 1. 323; (v) repay, requite; 5. 6. 67

ANTIATES, people of Antium (3. 1. 11), a town in Latium, chief city of the Volsces; 1. 6. 53, etc.

ANTIQUE, old-fashioned (cf. *M.N.D.* 5. 1. 3), out of date; 2. 3. 118

ANVIL, fig., body (upon which the sword of an enemy strikes); 4. 5. 113

APPREHENSION, perception; 2. 3. 223

APPROBATION, (i) 'prosperous approbation' = 'confirmed success'; 2. 1. 102; (ii) approval, ratification; 2. 3. 143, 250

APPROVE, approve of; 3. 2. 8

APRON-MAN, mechanic (wearing a leather apron); 4. 6. 97

APT, impressionable, yielding; 3. 2. 29

APTNESS, readiness; 4. 3. 23

ARMS, army, armed forces; 5. 3. 208

ARRIVE, reach, arrive at; 2. 3. 180

ARTICLE, stipulation; 2. 3. 195

ARTICULATE, come to terms; 1. 9. 77

AS, as if; 1. 1. 212; 5. 1. 64

ASH, spear of ash wood; 4. 5. 111

ASPECT, look, appearance; 5. 3. 32

ATONE, become reconciled; 4. 6. 73

ATTACH, arrest; 3. 1. 174

ATTEND, (i) ('attend upon'), accompany; 1. 1. 236; (ii) await, wait for; 1. 1. 75, 244; 1. 10. 30; 2. 2. 158; 3. 1. 330; 3. 2. 138; (iii) listen; 1. 9. 4

AUDIBLE, quick of hearing (O.E.D. 2); 4. 5. 229

AUDIENCE, (i) attention, silence; 3. 3. 40; (ii) formal interview; 2. 1. 71

AUDIT, statement of accounts; 1. 1. 143

AUGER, tool for boring small holes (cf. *Mac.* 2. 3. 122); 4. 6. 88

AUGURER, augur, member of Roman priestly college whose business was to study auguries and decide whether favourable or unfavourable to an undertaking; 2. 1. 1

AVOID, quit; 4. 5. 24, 33

BALD, (i) (*a*) mod. sense, (*b*) paltry; 3. 1. 164; (ii) bare-headed; 4. 5. 200

BALE, injury; 'have b.', get the worst of it; 1. 1. 162

BARE, mere, with no word of restitution; 5. 1. 20

BASTARD, i.e. spurious; 3. 2. 56

BAT, stick, club; 1. 1. 55, 160

BATTEN, grow fat; 4. 5. 34

BATTLE, army; 1. 6. 51

BE, (i) 'be in', be involved in (cf. *L.L.L.* 4. 3. 17 'if the other three were in'; O.E.D. 'in' adv. 6*b*); 3. 2. 64; (ii) 'be off', doff the cap; 2. 3. 99; (iii) 'be with', comply with (their wish), lit. 'go along' with (cf. O.E.D. 'with' 20, 21*a*); 3. 2. 74

BEAM, lit. ray of light; here, fig.=range of vision; 3. 2. 5

BEAR, (i) conduct, manage, carry on; 1. 1. 269; 1. 6. 82; 4. 7. 21; 5. 3. 4; (ii) be endowed with; 2. 3. 179; (iii) carry; 3. 1. 212; (iv) endure; 1. 1. 99; 3. 1. 249; 3. 2. 35; 3. 3. 33

BEASTLY, like cattle; 2. 1. 93

*BEGNAW, gnaw, rot; 2. 1. 183

BELONGING. Either (sb.) accessory; hence, here=trappings, caparison. Or (adj.) appertaining; 1. 9. 62

BENCH, seat of authority, court, government (cf. *Tim.* 4. 1. 5); 3. 1. 106, 166

BENCHER, member of the senate, senator; 2. 1. 80

BEWITCHMENT, enchanting manner; 2. 3. 100

BEWRAY, reveal; 5. 3. 95

BILLET (vb.), enroll; enter on a list; 4. 3. 45

BISSON, purblind; 2. 1. 63

BLANK, a blank ticket in a lottery; 5. 2. 10

BLEEDING, fig. unhealed, unsettled; 2. 1. 75

BLESS, guard, protect; 1. 3. 46

BLESSED, 'blessed to do', mod. 'happy to do'; 2. 2. 56

BLOCK, lit. a lump of wood or stone; here (*a*) blockhead, (*b*) 'a lump of wood...that obstructs one's way; fig. an obstacle or obstruction' (O.E.D. 11); 5. 2. 76

BLOOD, 'in bl.' (fig. from the chase, of a hound) in full vigour; 4. 5. 217; hence, 'worst in bl.'=in worst condition for running; 1. 1. 158

BLOODY, blood-red, 'bl. flag', a sign of warfare; 2. 1. 74

BLOWN=either 'swollen' or 'wind-driven'; 5. 4. 47

BODY OF THE WEAL, commonwealth, body corporate; 2. 3. 180

BOLTED, lit. (of flour) passed through a sieve or bolting-cloth so as to separate the flour from the bran, i.e. to rid it of its coarser elements, thus fig. refined, carefully sifted; 3. 1. 320

BONNET (vb.), take off bonnet or cap as a sign of respect (cf. Cotgrave, 1611, '*bon-neter*, to put off one's cap unto'; and the mod. coll. 'to cap someone'); 2. 2. 25–6

BORE, small hole; 4. 6 88

BOSOM, (i) (a) 'the seat of emotions, desires, etc.' (O.E.D. 6b), the 'heart' (cf. *Mac.* 5. 3. 44), (b) *phys.* 'the cavity of the stomach' (O.E.D. 4b); 3. 1. 131; (ii) sense (i) (a) 3. 2. 57

BOTCHER, cobbler, or mender of old clothes; 2. 1. 86

BOTTOM, essence (O.E.D. 12); 4. 5. 203

BOUND (ppl. of obs. 'boun'=to prepare, set out, to go), 'bound to'=setting out for; 3. 1. 54

BOUND (ppl. of 'bind'), under an obligation; 5. 3. 108, 109, 159

BOUNTIFUL, bountifully; 2. 3. 101

BRAND, (i) stigma; 3. 1. 302; (ii) torch; 4. 6. 116

BRAVE, (i) fine; 2. 2. 5; (ii) (of conduct) insolent; 4. 5. 17

BRAWN, arm; 4. 5. 123

BREAK, fall out, quarrel; 4. 6. 49

BREATH, voice, speech (O.E.D. 9); 2. 2. 148

BREATHE, pause, 'rest from action' (Schmidt). Cf. *1 H. IV*, 1. 3. 102, 'three times they breathed'; 1. 6. 1

BRIEFLY, 'within a short time, measured either backwards or forwards' (O.E.D. 2); 1. 6. 16

BROIL, uproarious strife; 3. 1. 33

BRUISING, fig. damaging, injurious; 2. 3. 201

BUDGE, flinch; 1. 6. 44

BUDGER, one who flinches; 1. 8. 5

BULK, flat projecting framework in front of shop (cf.

Oth. 5. 1. 1). 'Butchers and fishmongers displayed their goods on them; tailors and cobblers sat and worked on them' (G.G.); 2. 1. 207

BUSS, kiss; 3. 2. 75

CALL UP, rouse in any way; 2. 3. 193

CANKERED, depraved, corrupt; 4. 5. 94

CANON, law (properly, Church law); 3. 1. 90

CANOPY, fig. firmament; 4. 5. 40

CAP, doffing of the cap; fig. bow; 2. 1. 67

CAPITAL, deadly, fatal; 5. 3. 104

CAPITOL, senate-house (cf. *Titus* and *J. C.*), properly the Capitoline Hill N.W. of the Forum, near which in the Curia Hostilia the Senate generally met; 1. 1. 47, 191, etc.

CAPITULATE, 'arrange or propose terms, bargain, parley'; 5. 3. 82

CARBONADO (<Sp. *carbonada*, 'a Carbonado on the coles' (Minshen)), meat scored or 'scotched' across and broiled; 4. 5. 193

CARES, solicitude for others; 3. 1. 137

CARRY, (i) win; 2. 1. 235; 4. 7. 27; 5. 6. 43; (ii) 'c. it', win; 2. 2. 4; 2. 3. 36

CASQUE, helmet (as symbol of the warrior's life); 4. 7. 43

CAST, (i) 'cast upon', confer on; 2. 1. 199; (ii) throw up; 4. 6. 131

CAT. A term of contempt (cf. *All's*, 4. 3. 234); 4. 2. 34

GLOSSARY

CATO, the elder Cato, 234–
149 B.C., famous after the
3rd Punic War for his
'delenda est Carthago'; 1. 4.
58

CAUSE, (i) case to be tried in a
court of law; 3. 3. 18;
(ii) disease, ailment (<late
Lat. 'causa'); 3. 1. 234

CAUTELOUS, crafty (cf. *J.C.*
2. 1. 129); 4. 1. 33

CENSORINUS, Martius C., of
the same family as Corio-
lanus, but not ancestor,
censor *c.* 265 B.C.; 2. 3. 242

CENSURE (sb.), (i) opinion;
1. 1. 267; (ii) condemna-
tion; 3. 3. 46

CENSURE (vb.), judge, estimate;
2. 1. 22, 24

CENTURION, commander of a
century (*q.v.*); 4. 3. 44

CENTURY, a division of the
Roman army, originally of
100 men; 1. 7. 3

CHANGE OF HONOURS (sb.), a
new or fresh set (gen. of
clothes); 2. 1. 195

CHANGELING, a fickle person
(cf. *1 H. IV*, 5. 1. 76);
4. 7. 11

CHARGE (sb.), body of troops
under command; 4. 3. 45

CHARGE (vb.), (i) blame, accuse; 3. 3. 42; (ii) adjure,
entreat earnestly (cf.
Schmidt); 4. 6. 113

CHARM, magic spell; 1. 5. 22

CHARTER, lit. a document in
which a king grants a privilege; and so, privilege,
conceded right; 1. 9. 14;
2. 3. 179

CHAT (vb.), gossip about; 2. 1.
205

CHOIR (vb.), make music
(with); 3. 2. 113

CIRCUMVENTION, means or
power to circumvent; 1. 2. 6

CLAP TO, shut (a door)
smartly; 1. 4. 52

CLIP, embrace; 1. 6. 29; 4. 5.
112

CLUSTER, mob; 4. 6. 123, 129

COBBLED, (of shoes) patched,
clumsily or ill-mended; 1. 1.
195

COCKLE, darnel, tares, *Lolium
temulentum*. At Matth.
xiii. 25, Rheims New Test.
(1582) reads 'cockle' for
'tares' (A.V.). The mod.
'corn-cockle' is a different
plant; 3. 1. 70

COG, wheedle; 3. 2. 133

COIGN, corner-stone, (in mod.
sp.) quoin; 5. 4. 1

COLD, (i) cool, unimpassioned;
3. 1. 219; (ii) without power
to influence (cf. *M. V.* 2. 7.
73); 5. 3. 86

COME, (i) interj. expressing
mild rebuke; 1. 1. 271; (ii)
'c. off'=get clear, with-
draw successfully (from a
battle) (cf. *H. V*, 3. 6. 71);
1. 6. 1; 2. 2. 110

COMELY, becoming, decorous;
4. 6. 27

COMFORT, happiness, cheerfulness; 5. 3. 99

COMFORTABLE, cheerful; 1. 3. 2

COMMAND, (i) body of troops
under command of officer;
1. 6. 84; (ii) air of command,
of authority; 4. 5. 64

COMMANDED (mil.), to be c.
under=to be under the
command of (cf. O.E.D.
'commanded'); 1. 1. 261

COMMISSION, (i) military warrant for an officer; 1. 2. 26; 4. 7. 14; (ii) troops assigned to an officer by warrant, military command; 4. 7. 14

COMMON (adj.), (i) of the common people; 2. 2. 51; 3. 1. 22; (ii) 'be common', make oneself cheap or not sufficiently exclusive (cf. *Son.* 69. 14); 2. 3. 94

COMMON (sb.) (i) common people; 1. 1. 150; 3. 1. 29; (ii) what is usual; 4. 1. 32

COMMONALTY, common people; 1. 1. 28

COMMONERS, common people, plebians; 2. 1. 224

COMPANION, term of contempt, 'fellow'; 4. 5. 13; 5. 2. 59

COMPLEXION, lit. blend of humours which determined mental and bodily temperament; hence, temperament, disposition, 'nature'; 2. 1. 209

COMPOSITION, agreement or 'compromise'; 3. 1. 3

COMPOUND, agree, come to terms, settle by concession; 5. 6. 84

CON, get to know, commit to memory, learn by heart; 4. 1. 11

CONCLUDE, come to a decision, decide; 3. 1. 145

CONDEMNED, damnable; 1. 8. 15

CONDITION, (i) terms of agreement; 1. 10. 2, 3; (ii) (*a*) terms, (*b*) character, quality; 1. 10. 5, 6; 5. 4. 10; (iii) behaviour, manner; 2. 3. 96

CONFIRMED, (i) resolute, determined; 1. 3. 60–61; (ii) confirmed in office; 2. 3. 208

CONFOUND, waste, consume; 1. 6. 17

CONFUSION, anarchy, destruction (civil); 3. 1. 110, 189; 4. 6. 29

CONJURE, adjure, beseech, implore; 5. 2. 73

CONSPECTUITY, power of sight ('app. a humorous or random formation from "conspectus"', O.E.D.); 2. 1. 63

CONSTANT, unshaken in purpose or promise (cf. *J. C.* 3. 1. 60); 1. 1. 238; 5. 2. 91

CONTENT, agreed, 'all right'; 2. 3. 46

CONTRIVE, plot; 3. 3. 63

CONVENIENT, appropriate, suitable; 1. 5. 12; 5. 3. 191

CONVENT (vb.), convene; 2. 2. 52

CONVERSE (with), be conversant with, associate (freq.); 2. 1. 50

CONVERSATION, intercourse, society; 2. 1. 92

CONVEYANCE, channel (for conveying a liquid); 5. 1. 54

CONY, rabbit; 4. 5. 218

CORMORANT (adj.), insatiably greedy; 1. 1. 120

COUNTENANCE, favour, patronage; 5. 6. 40

COUNTERFEITLY, feigningly; 2. 3. 99

COUNTERPOISE (vb.), balance in quality, equal in value; 2. 2. 85

COUNTER-SEALED, sealed by both parties; 5. 3. 205

COURAGE, spirit, disposition; 3. 3. 92

COURSE, one of a succession or series; 1. 5. 16

COVERTURE, covering for the body, apparel, clothing; 1. 9. 46

COXCOMB, head (ludicrous or jeering); 4. 6. 135

COY (vb.), disdain; 5. 1. 6

CRACK, pert little boy, little imp (cf. *2 H. IV*, 3. 2. 32); 1. 3. 69

CRAFT (vb.), (*a*) carry out a job, (*b*) act craftily; 4. 6. 119

CRANK (sb.), winding passage; 1. 1. 136

CROOKED, wry; 2. 1. 55

CRY (sb.), pack (of hounds); 3. 3. 120; 4. 6. 148

CRY HAVOC, *v.* Havoc; 3. 1. 273

CUNNING, knowledge (of life), skill (in living), i.e. philosophy; 4. 1. 9

CUPBOARD (vb.), hoard up; 1. 1. 99

CURDIED, congealed; poss. 'curdled' misprinted; 5. 3. 66

CUSHION, (i) seat (in Senate); 3. 1. 101; (ii) seat (as symbol of peaceful life of ease and civil authority); 4. 7. 43

DAMASK, orig. colour of Damascus rose, here, red; 2. 1. 213

DARKEN, deprive of lustre (cf. *Ant.* 3. 1. 24), or eclipse; 4. 7. 5

DAW, jackdaw, type of extreme stupidity; 4. 5. 46

DEADLY, mod. slang 'like sin'; 2. 1. 60

DEAR, valuable, precious; 1. 1. 19; 1. 6. 72

DEARTH, famine; lit. dearness, scarcity (e.g. of corn); 1. 1. 66

DEBILE, weak, feeble; 1. 9. 48

DECLINE (vb.), fall; 2. 1. 159

DEED-ACHIEVING, achieved by deeds; 2. 1. 171

DEGREE, step; 2. 2. 24

*DEJECTITUDE. A coined word < 'dejected', downcast, crest-fallen; 4. 5. 214

DELIVER, (i) release (mod. sense); 5. 6. 14; (ii) intr., speak, tell one's tale; 1. 1. 94; (iii) tr. report; 2. 1. 56; 4. 6. 64; (iv) present (cf. *Tw. Nt.* 1. 2. 41); 5. 3. 39; 5. 6. 140

DEMERIT, merit, desert (the orig. sense; cf. *Oth.* 1. 2. 22); 1. 1. 271

DENIAL, refusal; 5. 3. 81

DENY, refuse, reject; 1. 6. 65; 2. 3. 2, 205, 208, 209; 5. 2. 76; 5. 3. 33, 89, 177

DESERVED, deserving (cf. *All's*, 2. 1. 189); 3. 1. 290

DESIGNMENT, undertaking, enterprise (cf. *Oth.* 2. 1. 22); 5. 6. 35

DESPITE, contempt; 3. 1. 163; 3. 3. 139

DETERMINE, (i) decide; 2. 2. 35; 4. 1. 35; (ii) come to an end, terminate; 3. 3. 43; 5. 3. 120

DEUCALION, Prometheus' son, who, warned by his father, escaped with his wife Pyrrha the world-wide deluge, like the biblical Noah, by building a boat wh. landed on Parnassus, as Noah's ark on Ararat, when the flood subsided; 2. 1. 89

DIAN, Diana, goddess of chastity; 5. 3. 67

DIET, lit. prescribe a diet, hence (i) fatten, inflate;

1. 9. 52; (ii) bring into condition, i.e. render amiable by
a good dinner; 5. 1. 57

DIFFERENCE, (i) variance; 5. 3.
201; (ii) disagreement; 5. 6.
18

DIFFERENCY, difference (in
mod. sense); 5. 4. 11

DIGEST, (a) mod. sense, (b)
interpret, understand; 1. 1.
149; 3. 1. 131

DIRECTLY, face to fàce; 1. 6.
58; 4. 5. 191 (or plainly,
unambiguously)

DISBENCH, cause to leave seat,
unseat (usu. of Inn's of
Court membership; only
inst. in O.E.D. of general
sense); 2. 2. 69

DISCIPLINE (vb.), punish by
thrashing; 2. 1. 124

DISCOVER, reveal; 2. 2. 19

DISEASE (vb.), disturb, make
uneasy; 1. 3. 106

DISGRACE, misfortune, lit. the
disfavour of Fortune (v.
O.E.D. 2); 1. 1. 93

DISHONOURED, dishonourable;
3. 1. 60

DISLODGE. A tech. mil. term
='leave a place of encamp-
ment' (O.E.D.); 5. 4. 41

DISPATCH (sb.), (i) execution of
a matter; 1. 1. 276; (ii) dis-
missal, leave to go; 5. 3. 180

DISPATCH (vb.), hasten; 5. 6. 8

DISPOSE OF, make the best of;
4. 7. 40

DISPOSED, inclined; 3. 2. 22

DISPOSITION, inclination, humour; 1. 6. 74; 2. 1. 30;
3. 2. 21

DISPROPERTY (vb.), 'alienate',
'dispossess' (O.E.D.; On.)
Better, I think, 'deprive of

its essential property', 're-
duce to a farce'; 2. 1. 245

DISSEMBLE WITH, disguise, act
or speak in contradiction of;
3. 2. 62

DISSOLVED, dispersed; 1. 1.
203

DISTINCTLY, separately; 4. 3.
45

DISTRIBUTE, administer; 3. 3.
99

DIVIDE, share; 1. 6. 87

DOIT, old Dutch coin, worth a
½d. or ¼d.; 1. 5. 6; 4. 4. 17;
5. 4. 57

DOTANT, dotard (only known
inst.); 5. 2. 44

DOUBLED, redoubled; 2. 2.
114

DOUBT (vb.), fear; 3. 1. 152

DOWNRIGHT (adv.), absolutely;
2. 3. 158

DRACHMA, ancient Greek silver
coin, worth c. 9¾d. in pre-
war money; 1. 5. 5

DRAW, gather, assemble; 2. 3.
252

DRAW OUT. Mil.='detach
from the main body'
(O.E.D.), pick out; 1. 6. 84

DRENCH (orig.=drink),
'draught or dose of medicine
administered to an animal'
(O.E.D.); 2. 1. 116

DULL, stupid (or 'gloomy');
1. 9. 6

DUTY, reverence; 5. 3. 51, 55,
167

EACH, every; 3. 1. 49

EARTH, substance of which
man is made, the human
body (cf. Gen. ii. 7; *Rom.*
2. 1. 2, 'turn back, dull
earth'); 5. 3. 29

EASY, requiring little effort; 5. 2. 42

EDGE, sword; 1. 4. 29; 5. 6. 113

EFFECT (vb.), give effect to (*Troil.* 5. 10. 6); 1. 9. 18

ELDER, senator; 1. 1. 225; 2. 2. 40

ELECTION, choice; 2. 3. 218, 228, 254

ELEMENTS, the powers of the air, e.g. 'rain, wind, thunder, fire' (*Lr.* 3. 1. 4); 1. 10. 10

EMBARQUEMENT (of), lit. placing of embargo on ships in port (O.E.D.; cf. also Cotgrave, 1611 'embarquement'), stoppage, bottling up; 1. 10. 22

EMPIRICUTIC (adj.), lit. empirical, (hence) quackery. A 'nonce-word', perh. Sh. coinage; 2. 1. 115

EMULATION, rivalry (or perhaps 'malicious triumph'); 1. 1. 213; 1. 10. 12

END, 'for an end'=in conclusion, to cut the matter short; 2. 1. 241

END (vb.), gather in a crop. 'A dial. variant or corruption [not here textual] of *inn*' (O.E.D.); cf. *All's Well*, 1. 3. 44, 'to in the crop', and *L'Allegro*, 109, 'the corn That ten day labourers could not end'; 5. 6. 37

ENDUE, endow; 2. 3. 138

ENFORCE, (i) lay stress on; 2. 3. 218; so, (ii) 'enforce him with', ply him hard with; 3. 3. 3; (iii) press for, demand; 3. 3. 21

ENGINE, war machine; 5. 4. 19

ENORMITY, irregular conduct, 'deviation from moral rectitude'; 2. 1. 16

ENTERED (in), let in to the secret of; 1. 2. 2

ENTERTAINMENT, (i) 'in the entertainment'=being paid; 4. 3. 45; (ii) welcome, reception; 4. 5. 9; 5. 2. 62–3

ENVY (sb.), enmity, hate; 1. 8. 4 (or perh. vb. here); 3. 3. 3; 4. 5. 77, 106

ENVY (vb.), feel ill will to; 3. 3. 57; 'envy against'=show malice towards (On.); 3. 3. 95

EPITOME, (*a*) representation in miniature, (*b*) summary or abstract of a speech to be spoken; 5. 3. 68

ESTATE, property, fortune; 2. 1. 112

ESTIMATE, repute, reputation; 3. 3. 114

ESTIMATION, (i) estimate, valuation; 2. 1. 88; (ii) esteem; 2. 2. 27; 2. 3. 96; 5. 2. 51, 60

EVEN (adv.), steadily, without losing one's balance; 4. 7. 37

EVENT, outcome; 2. 1. 267

EVIDENT, indubitable, certain; 4. 7. 52; 5. 3. 112

EXTREMITY, the utmost point (of danger); 3. 2. 41; 4. 1. 4

FABRIC, (i) building; 3. 1. 246; (ii) frame, body; 1. 1. 118

FACTIONARY, active as a partisan (O.E.D.); 5. 2. 29

FAIR (adj.), (i) clean; 1. 9. 69; (ii) even, smooth (mod.

slang 'decent'); 3. 1. 241;
(iii) civil, courteous; 3. 2.
96; (iv) fine (iron.); 4. 6.
89

FAIR (adv.), civilly, cour-
teously; 3. 1. 262; 3. 2.
70

FAIRNESS, 'to the fairness of
my power'=as becomingly
as I can (cf. 'fairly', *M. V.*
1. 1. 128); 1. 9. 73

FAITH. Ellipt. for 'in faith',
truly; 2. 2. 7, etc.

FAMILIAR (adj.), intimate;
5. 2. 82

FAMOUSLY, splendidly, excel-
lently, so as to become
renowned; 1. 1. 35

FANE, temple; 1. 10. 20

FATIGATE, fatigued ('not post-
Sh.', On.); 2. 2. 115

FAUCET, tap for drawing liquor
from a barrel; 2. 1. 69

FAVOUR, countenance; 4. 3. 9

FEAR, (i) (*a*) fear for (w. 'person', (*b*) 'be afraid of' (w.
'ill report'); 1. 6. 69; (ii)
fear for, distrust; 1. 7. 5

FEEBLE (vb.), disparage, de-
preciate; 1. 1. 194

FELLOWSHIP, 'for fellowship'=
for company; 5. 3. 175

FETCH OFF, rescue; 1. 4. 63

FEVEROUS, afflicted with ague;
1. 4. 62

FIDIUS (vb.). Humorous coinage from 'Aufidius' (cf.
'fer', *H. V*, 4. 4. 29); 2. 1.
129

FIELD (sb.), (i) battle-field,
campaign; 1. 2. 17; 'i' th'
field', 'engaged in military
operations'; 1. 9. 43; (ii)
battle; 1. 7. 4; 1. 9. 33;
2. 2. 119

FIELDED, engaged in battle (of.
FIELD); 1. 4. 12

FILE, lit. '*Mil.* the number of
men constituting the depth
from front to rear of a formation in line' (O.E.D. 7),
hence (i) rank; 5. 6. 34; (ii)
'the right-hand file'=those
in the place of honour in the
ranks (cf. *Sh. Eng.* 1, 114),
the best men, the patricians;
2. 1. 23; (iii) 'the common
file'=the common herd;
1. 6. 43

FIND, (i) experience, feel; 5. 3.
111; (ii) understand, discover
the truth; 3. 3. 129

FINE, punishment; 5. 6. 65

FIRE, 'fires of heaven'=stars
(including sun and moon);
1. 4. 39

FIST (vb.), seize with the fist,
i.e. try to throttle; 4. 5.
128

FIT (adj.), ready, prepared;
1. 3. 45

FIT (sb.), paroxysm of lunacy
(app. Sh.'s special use;
O.E.D. cites *Tit.* 4. 1. 17;
Err. 4. 3. 88, and not again
till Dryden, *Aeneid*, 1697);
3. 2. 33

FITLY, reasonably (iron.); 1. 1.
111

FIXED, unchanging; 2. 3. 249

FLAG, 'the bloody flag' was
raised upon a declaration of
war; 2. 1. 74

FLAMEN, ancient Roman
priest, devoted to the service
of a particular god; 2. 1. 210

FLAW, squall or gust of wind;
5. 3. 74

FLOURISH, a fanfare of trumpets, etc. to signalise the

approach or entrance of a great or victorious person; 1. 9. 40 S.D., 66 S.D.; 2. 1. 154 S.D., 164 S.D., 202 S.D.; 2. 2. 152 S.D.; 5. 5. 7 S.D.

FLY OUT OF (itself), break out from its natural limits; 'depart from its own natural generosity' (J.); 1. 10. 19

FOB OFF (with), set aside by a trick (of); 1. 1. 93

FOIL (vb.), overcome, defeat; 1. 9. 48

FOLD IN, extend around, envelop; 3. 3. 68; 5. 6. 125

FOND, foolish; 4. 1. 26; 'fond of' wishing for; 5. 3. 162

FOOLERY, foolishness, foolhardiness; 3. 1. 245

FORCE, press, urge; 3. 2. 51

'FORE ME, mod. 'upon my soul'; 1. 1. 119

FORM, (i) formality; 2. 2. 142; (ii) formal, regular, procedure; 3. 1. 323

FOXSHIP. A coined variant of 'worship' = worthiness; the fox being the type of cunning and ingratitude; 4. 2. 18

FRAGMENT, sc. of a man (cf. *Troil.* 5. 1. 8); 1. 1. 221

FRANK, liberal; 3. 1. 130

FREE, (i) frank, unrestrained, undisguised; 2. 3. 199; 3. 3. 73; 5. 6. 26; (ii) generous; 3. 2. 88

FREE (vb.), absolve (cf. *Lucr.* 1208; *Wint.* 3. 2. 111); 4. 7. 47

FRIENDLY (adv.), in a friendly, peaceable way; 4. 6. 9

FROM, contrary to, divergent from; 3. 1. 90

FRONT (vb.), meet, confront, oppose; 5. 2. 41

FUNCTION, occupation, job; 4. 5. 34

FUSTY, (*a*) musty, mouldy, (*b*) smelly, ill-smelling; 1. 9. 7

GALEN, famous Greek physician, *c.* 130–199 A.D. (here an anachronism, like Cato, *q.v.*); 2. 1. 114

GALL (vb.), orig. 'make sore by chafing', hence, irritate, annoy; 2. 3. 194

'GAN, past tense of ''gin'= begin; 2. 2. 113

GARB, manner, behaviour; 4. 7. 44

GARLAND, fig. chief ornament, 'glory' (O.E.D. cites Spenser, *Ruins of Time*, 1591); 1. 1. 183; 1. 9. 60; 2. 2. 99

GENERAL, (i) common, collective; 1. 1. 130; 3. 1. 146; 5. 3. 6; (ii) belonging to the common people; 3. 2. 66

GENEROSITY, the nobility (<Lat. *generosus*, of noble birth); 1. 1. 210

GENTLE, (i) gentleman-like; 2. 3. 96; (ii) 'being gentle wounded' = bearing oneself like a gentleman when wounded; 4. 1. 8

GENTRY, (i) men of high birth; 2. 1. 235; 3. 1. S.D. init.; (ii) high birth; 3. 1. 144

GET, (i) beget; 1. 3. 34; (ii) 'g. off', escape; 2. 1. 126

GETTER, begetter; 4. 5. 230

GIDDY, empty-headed, frivolous; 1. 1. 267

GILDED, golden coloured (cf. *Ant.* 1. 4. 62); 1. 3. 61

GIRD, sneer or scoff at; 1. 1. 255

GIVE, (i) 'g. out', announce, proclaim; 1. 1. 192; (ii) report, represent; 1. 9. 55; (iii) (of the mind) misgive, make to suspect; 4. 5. 153; (iv) 'give way'=give one scope, fall in with one's plan; 4. 4. 25; 5. 6. 32

GLASS, eye-ball; 3. 2. 117

GOD-DEN, good evening or good afternoon (as parting greeting); 2. 1. 91; (as welcome); 4. 6. 20, 21

GOOD, well-to-do (cf. *M. V.* 1. 3. 12); here a quibble; 1. 1. 16

GOWN, long garment, open in front, gen. worn over the coat; cf. mod. academic g.; 2. 3. 38, S.D.

GRACE (sb.), (i) favour; 5. 3. 121; (ii) charm, elegance; 5. 3. 150

GRACE (vb.), (i) (*a*) show favour to, (*b*) embellish, adorn (cf. *L.L.L.* 5. 2. 72); 1. 1. 263; (ii) show favour to; 5. 3. 15

GRACIOUS, lovely; 2. 1. 173

GRAFT, fix graft on (a stock); 2. 1. 187

GRAINED, close-grained, tough, or showing the grain, rough; 4. 5. 111

GRATIFY, reward; 2. 2. 38

GRIEF-SHOT, sorrow-stricken; 5. 1. 44

GROAT, four-penny piece; 3. 2. 10

GUARD, custody or protection; 1. 10. 25

GUARDANT, 'Jack guardant'; *v.* JACK; 5. 2. 61

GUESS, think (cf. mod. American Eng.); 1. 1. 18

GUIDER, guide; 1. 7. 7

GULF, whirlpool (cf. *Ham.* 3. 3. 16) or bottomless pit (e.g. hell) that sucks down everything nearby (cf. 'sink', 1. 1. 121); 1. 1. 97; 3. 2. 91

HA. Excl. of surprise, joy, indignation, etc. (or simply interrog.=eh?); 2. 1. 100; 3. 1. 25; 5. 3. 19

HABITS, clothes, dress; 5. 3. 21 S.D.

HAND, 'in someone's hand'= led by someone; 5. 3. 23

HANDKERCHER, handkerchief (sp. 6 times, but 'handkerchief' a commoner Sh. sp.); 2. 1. 261

HAP (vb.), happen; 3. 3. 24

HASTY, rash, quick-acting (cf. *Rom.* 5. 1. 64; *K. J.*, 4. 3. 97, 'thy hasty spleen'); 2. 1. 49

HAUTBOY, oboe, 'a wooden double-reed wind instrument of high pitch' (*Sh. Eng.*); 5. 4. 48 S.D.

HAVE, 'h. with you'=mod. coll. 'I'm with you!'. Common in Sh.; 2. 1. 267

HAVER, possessor; 2. 2. 83

HAVOC, merciless slaughter; 'cry "havoc"'=cry 'no quarter'. Orig.=give an army the signal for pillaging. But also a hunting-term; 3. 1. 273

HAZARD, game of dice with highly complicated chances; 'put in h.'=take the risk of; 2. 3. 255

HEAD, 'make a head'=gather together an army, raise an armed force; 2. 2. 86; 3. 1. 1

HEART. Regarded as the seat of wisdom as well as courage; 1. 1. 115, 135, etc.; 'h. of hope' here=person on whom all one's hopes are centred or depend; 1. 6. 55

HEAVY, heavy at heart, sad; 2. 1. 182; 4. 2. 48

HECTOR, chief Trojan hero in the *Iliad*; 1. 3. 42

HECUBA, Hector's mother, wife of Priam, King of Troy; 1. 3. 41

HELM, steersman, here fig., one who guides the affairs of the state; 1. 1. 76

HELP, remedy; 3. 1. 220

HOB, by-form of 'Rob', used generically for a rustic; 2. 3. 115

HOLD, keep, preserve; 2. 1. 237

HOLD! stop! (as an excl.); 5. 6. 131

HOLLOA (vb.), chase and holloa after; 1. 8. 7

HOLP, helped; 3. 1. 275; 4. 6. 82; 5. 3. 63; 5. 6. 36

HOME (adv.), (i) to the goal aimed at; so here, right into the enemy forces; 1. 4. 38; (ii) fully, plainly, thoroughly, effectively; 2. 2. 101; 3. 3. 1; 4. 1. 8, etc.

HONEST, upright, honourable; 1. 1. 52, 61; 2. 3. 132; 5. 3. 166

HOO! excl. of joy; 2. 1. 104; 3. 3. 137

HORSE (vb.), sit as on a horse, bestride; 2. 1. 208

HORSE-DRENCH, *v.* DRENCH; 2. 1. 116

HOSTILIUS, legendary king of Rome, second after Romulus, 2. 3. 239

HOUSEKEEPER, (*a*) one who stays at home, (*b*) woman engaged in domestic occupations; 1. 3. 52

HOW! what! 3. 1. 47, 75; 3. 3. 67; 4. 6. 122; 5. 2. 78

HUM. An interj. expressing dissent or dissatisfaction (cf. O.E.D. vb. 2); 5. 4. 21

HUM (vb.), 'h. at,' greet with a 'hum' (*q.v.*); 5. 1. 49

HUMANELY, out of kindness of heart; 1. 1. 19

HUMOROUS, capricious, whimsical; 2. 1. 46

HUNGRY, unfertile, barren (O.E.D. 6), or 'eager for shipwrecks' (Mal.; cf. *Tw. Nt.* 2. 4. 100); 5. 3. 58

HUSBANDRY, careful, profitable management; 4. 7. 22

HUSWIFE, housewife; 1. 3. 71

HYDRA, many-headed monster slain by Hercules; as soon as he struck off one head two new ones grew; 3. 1. 93

IGNORANT. Either (i) unconscious (cf. *Tp.* 5. 1. 67) or (ii) stupid, simple (cf. *Meas.* 2. 4. 74, etc.); 2. 3. 173

IN, into; 2. 3. 257; 3. 1. 33, 96; 'to be in' (*v.* BE); 3. 2. 64

INCH, 'death by inches'=a lingering death; 5. 4. 39

INCLINE (to), side (with); 2. 3. 37

INDIFFERENTLY, neutrally; 2. 2. 16

INFECT, taint, deprave; 2. 1. 92

INFECTION, moral contamination (O.E.D. 6); 3. 1. 308

INFORM (trans. vb.), (i) make known, tell; 1. 6. 42; (ii) inspire, animate; 5. 3. 71

INGRATE, ungrateful; 5. 2. 83

INGRATEFUL, ungrateful; 2. 2. 30; 2. 3. 10

INHERENT, permanently fixed; 3. 2. 123

INHERIT, enjoy the possession of (cf. *Rom.* 1. 2. 30); 2. 1. 196

INHERITANCE, gaining possession of; 3. 2. 68

INJURIOUS, insulting; 3. 3. 69

INNOVATOR, revolutionary. 'Innovation' = 'revolution' elsw. in Sh.; change in civil affairs being in that age considered an evil; 3. 1. 174

INSINUATING, ingratiating; 2. 3. 98

INSTANT, immediate, here=got together at a moment's notice; 5. 1. 37

INSTRUMENT, organ (of the body); 1. 1. 100

INTEGRITY, organic unity; 3. 1. 159

INTERIM, 'by interims'=at intervals; 1. 6. 5

INTERJOIN, join reciprocally, unite; 4. 4. 22

INTERPRETATION, development (of a theme); 5. 3. 69

INVENTORY, a priced list of goods (cf. O.E.D. 1); 1. 1. 21

IRON, sword or dagger; 1. 5. 6

ISSUE, action (O.E.D. 8b, 'rare', citing *J.C.* 3. 1. 295; *Cym.* 2. 1. 44; cf. also *Meas.* 1. 1. 36); or poss. offspring (Rolfe); 4. 4. 22

ITHACA, island in the Aegean Sea, the domain of Ulysses; 1. 3. 85

JACK. Contemptuous term; 'Jack guardant'=fellow on guard; 5. 2. 61

JUDGEMENT, the administration of justice; 3. 1. 158

JUDICIOUS, ?judicial (or) just (cf. *Lear*, 3.4.73); 'meaning doubtful' in these two exx. (O.E.D.); 5. 6. 127. (N.B. 'judicial' non-Sh.)

JUMP, take risks for, i.e. 'by extension, apply a desperate remedy to' (On.); 3. 1. 154

JUNO, wife of Jupiter, given to anger; 2. 1. 99; 4. 2. 53

KAM (<Welsh *cam*), askew, awry (not again Sh.); 3. 1. 302

KNEE, walk kneeling; 5. 1. 5

LA. Excl. to call attention to, or emphasize, a statement; 1. 3. 68, 90

LAPSE, (*a*) glide, drop (of liquid), (*b*) fall into sin; 5. 2. 19

LEAD, flat lead-covered roof; 2. 1. 208; 4. 6. 83

LEASING, falsehood, lie; 5. 2. 22

LEG, fig. obeisance by drawing back one leg, and bending the other; 2. 1. 68

LESSON (vb.), teach, instruct, admonish; 2. 3. 176

LET GO, let it be, say no more; 3. 2. 18

LETTERS, letter (pl. for sing.); 2. 1. 132

LEVY, 'the action for enrolling ...men for war' (O.E.D. 1*b*); 5. 6. 67

LIBERTY, right, privilege; 2. 3. 179, 214

LICTOR, Roman functionary, who walked before the magistrates carrying the *fasces*, a bundle of rods fastened with a strap round an axe; 2. 2. 34 S.D.

LIE, (i) 'lie in', i.e. for childbirth; 1. 3. 78; (ii) 'lie on', be incumbent on; 3. 2. 52

LIGHT, light-hearted, cheerful, merry; 2. 1. 182

LIGHTLY, thoughtlessly; 4. 1. 29

LIKE, likely; 1. 1. 191; 1. 3. 13; 2. 1. 238, etc.

LIKING, 'in their liking'=in favour with them; 1. 1. 194

LIMITATION, appointed time; 2. 3. 137

LIP, 'make a lip at'=despise (cf. *Wint.* 1. 2. 373, 'falling a lip of much contempt'); 2. 1. 113

LIST (vb.[1]), please, wish; 3. 2. 128

LIST (vb.[2]), hearken; 1. 4. 20; 3. 3. 40

LITTER (vb.), bring forth young (of animals); 3. 1. 238

LOCKRAM, 'a loosely woven fabric of hemp...used by lower-class persons for ruffs', coifs, etc. (Linthicum, 99—100); 2. 1. 206

'LONG, belong; 5. 3. 170

'LONG OF, because of; 5. 4. 29

LOOK, promise, look likely. The only ex. in O.E.D. (8*b*), an extension of 'tend, point (in a particular direction)' (8*a*); 3. 3. 29

LOSE BY, throw away on (Schmidt.); 2. 3. 57

LOT, prize ticket in a lottery, 'lots to blanks'=a thousand to one; 5. 2. 10

LOVER, dear friend; 5. 2. 14

LURCH (vb.), (*a*) cheat, rob (O.E.D. vb.[1] 2); (*b*) to gain an easy and sweeping victory at cards, etc. (*v.* O.E.D. sb.[1] 2); 2. 2. 99

LYCURGUS, legendary wise lawgiver of Sparta; 2. 1. 54

MAGISTRATE, public functionary; 2. 1. 43; 3. 1. 104; 3. 1. 201

MAIM, 'mutilation or loss of some essential part' (O.E.D.); 4. 5. 89

MAKE, (i) represent as, make out to be; 1. 1. 174; (ii) 'make good'=secure, make sure of (mil. *v.* O.E.D. 'good', 22*d*); 1. 5. 12; (iii) 'make a hand'=make a success (of); 4. 6. 118; (iv) (with 'head' or 'the army'), muster, raise; 2. 2. 86; 3. 1. 1; 5. 1. 37

MALICE, malicious act; 2. 2. 31

MALKIN, untidy female, esp. servant, slut (dimin. of Malde=Matilda, Maud); 2. 1. 205

MAMMOCK, tear into fragments (cf. E.D.D. 'mammock' (sb.), scrap, broken piece—esp. of food); 1. 3. 66

MAN-ENTERED, initiated into manhood (O.E.D. 'man' 20; only ex.); 2. 2. 97

MANGLE, fig. mutilate, impair cf. O.E.D. 3); 3. 1. 158

Manhood, courage; 3. 1. 245

Mankind (adj.), (*a*) mad, frenzied (of diff. origin from (*b*), cf. O.E.D. *a²*); (*b*) human; 4. 2. 16

Map, 'fig. A detailed representation in epitome. Very common in the 17th c.' (O.E.D. 2); 2. 1. 61

Mark, limit aimed at; 2. 2. 87

Mars, Roman god of war; 1. 4. 10; 4. 5. 121, 198

Mastership, masterly skill; 4. 1. 7

Match, bargain; 2. 3. 80

Matter, 'no m. for that', that doesn't matter; 4. 5. 169

Mature, ripe, ready, fully developed; 4. 3. 25

May, *v.* You may; 2. 3. 34

Mean (vb. trans.), purpose, design; 1. 9. 57

Measle, scab, 'scurvy wretch' (On.). The word looks back both to O.F. *mesel*=leper, and to M.E. meseles=mod. 'measles'; the expr. 'why the meazils' (=pox! why, etc.) occurs in Jonson, *Barth. Fair*, (3. 4. 29); 3. 1. 78

Measure, 'with m.', commensurately, adequately; 2. 2. 121

Meddle, (i) busy oneself interferingly (with); 4. 5. 48; (ii) have sexual intercourse (with); 4. 5. 50

Meiny (orig.=household staff: cf. *Lr.* 2. 4. 34), 'the common herd' (O.E.D.); 3. 1. 66

Memory, memorial; 4. 5. 74; 5. 1. 17

Mercenary, earning pay like a mere hired soldier; 5. 6. 41

Mercy, 'at mercy'='(that has surrendered) at discretion; absolutely in the power of the victor' (O.E.D. 5*b*); 1. 10. 7

Merely, utterly; 3. 1. 303

Merit (abs.), deserve well; 1. 1. 275

Microcosm, individual man (considered as a world or universe ('macrocosm') in miniature); 2. 1. 61

Mind, remind (cf. *H. V.* 4. 3. 13); 5. 1. 18

Minnow, type of extreme insignificance (cf. *L.L.L.* 1. 1. 245); 3. 1. 89

Misery, wretchedness (usual gloss), but poss.=avarice (Warb.); 2. 2. 125

Modest, (i) chaste; 1. 1. 256; (ii) moderate, 'modest warrant'=authority to act with moderation; 3. 1. 274

Moe, more; 2. 3. 124; 4. 2. 21

Monster (vb.), declare wonderful, beyond the bounds of nature; 2. 2. 75

Monstrous, unnatural; 2. 3. 9, 12

Morrow, morning (in 'good morrow'); 3. 3. 93

Mortal, fatal; 2. 2. 109

Moth, (*a*) mod. sense, (*b*) fig. parasite, idle person living at another's expense; 1. 3. 85

Motion, (i) impulse, excitement, or (perhaps) motive; 2. 1. 50; (ii) prompting, influence; 2. 2. 51

Mould, (i) bodily form (with quibble on 'mould'=earth); 3. 2. 103; (ii) matrix; 5. 3. 22

Mountebank (vb.), win, like a quack at a fair, by tricking simpletons; 3. 2. 132

Move, make angry; 1. 1. 255

Mover, person full of life and activity (cf. *Ven.* l. 368). Here ironical; 1. 5. 4

Much, 'make much of'=hold dear; 2. 3. 108

Mulled (from 'm. ale', sweetened and spiced ale), fig., dispirited, dull (On., Schmidt.); 4. 5. 230

Multitudinous, 'of or pertaining to a multitude' (O.E.D. cites no other ex.); 3. 1. 156

Mummer, actor in a dumb-show; 2. 1. 73

Muniments, lit. fortifications; hence, 'furnishings' (O.E.D.) or 'defences' (O.E.D.); 1. 1. 117

Murrain, lit. a cattle plague (cf. *M.N.D.* 2. 1. 97); so, plague in general; 1. 5. 3

Muse (vb.), wonder; 3. 2. 7

Musty, lit. 'mouldy'; here, fig., lethargic through want of practice (cf. O.E.D. 2*b*); 1. 1. 225

Mutineer, rioter, rebel; 1. 1. 249

Mutinous, riotous, insurrectionary; 1. 1. 110, 148

Mutiny, popular rising; 2. 3. 255; 3. 1. 126, 228 S.D.

Mutually, in common (now regarded as incorrect); 1. 1. 102

Naked, unarmed; 1. 10. 20; 2. 2. 135

Name, (i) honour, fame, repute (cf. *1 H. VI*, 4. 4. 9); 2. 1. 133; (ii) famous person; 4. 6. 126

Napless, threadbare, with the nap worn off; 2. 1. 231

Native (sb.), origin, what gives birth to; 3. 1. 129

Nature, filial affection, natural ties; 5. 3. 25, 33

Naught, lost, ruined (cf. *Ant.* 3. 10. 1); 3. 1. 230

Navel, fig. vulnerable centre; 3. 1. 123

Neptune, god of the sea; 3. 1. 255

Nerve, sinew; 1. 1. 137

Nervy, sinewy (O.E.D. 1); 2. 1. 158

Nicely, scrupulously; 2. 1. 214

Nightly, at night; 4. 5. 125

Noble (adj.), (*a*) mod. sense, (*b*) alchem. epithet for gold; 4. 1. 49

Nod, obeisance (ironical); 2. 3. 99

Noise, music; here=military music; 2. 1. 157

Nose (vb.), smell; 5. 1. 28

Nothing (adv.), not at all; 1. 3. 100

Notice, observation; 2. 3. 156

Notion, understanding; 5. 6. 107

Now, at one moment (folld. by 'straight'; cf. 'now... then', *3 H. VI*, 2. 5. 10; 'now...again', *A.Y.L.* 3. 2. 405); 3. 1. 34

Numa, first of the legendary kings of Rome after Romulus; 2. 3. 238

NUMBER, troop, class, multitude; 2. 3. 252; 3. 1. 72; 4. 6. 7.

OAK, oak-leaves. Actually the symbolic prize of a soldier who had rescued one taken prisoner in battle; but taken by Sh. as='garland', i.e. emblem of glory; 1. 3. 15; 2. 2. 96

OAKEN GARLAND (*v.* OAK); 2. 1. 123, 159 S.D.

OBJECT, spectacle (evoking pity or the opposite; cf. *Tim.* 4. 3. 123); 1. 1. 20

OBSTINATE, hard-hearted. Almost=sinful; contrasted with 'constant'; 5. 3. 26

OCCASION, opportunity; 2.1.29

OCCUPATION, (i) handicraft; 4. 1. 14; (ii) manual workers (abstr. for concr.); 4. 6. 98

O'ERBEAR, overwhelm ('particularly of waters overwhelming the land', Schmidt; cf. *M.N.D.* 2. 1. 92; *Ham.* 4. 5. 102, etc.); 3. 1. 248; 4. 5. 134; 4. 6. 79

O'ERLEAP, omit; 2. 2. 134

O'ERPEER, look over, so as to be visible behind; 2. 3. 120

O'ERPRESSED, overwhelmed; 2. 2. 91

OF, (i) by; 2. 1. 22; 2. 2. 3; (ii) about; 2. 1. 70; 2. 2. 33; 4. 4. 17

OFF, beside the mark; 2. 2. 58

OFFENCE, offensive object; 5. 1. 28

OFFEND, annoy; 2. 1. 166

OFFER, (i) attempt; 2. 2. 64 S.D.; (ii) venture, dare, presume (cf. *Shr.* 5. 1. 60; *Troil.* 2. 3. 61); 5. 1. 23

OFFICE (sb.), (i) official duty; 3. 1. 35; (ii) inferior or outlying room of a house; 1. 1. 136

OFFICE (vb.), 'drive by virtue of one's office' (O.E.D.); 5. 2. 61

OFFICIOUS, offering or giving unwelcome help (cf. *M.N.D.* 3. 2. 330); 1. 8. 14

OLYMPUS, mt. at eastern end of range separating Thessaly and Greece proper; nearly 10,000 ft. high, seat of the gods in Greek mythology; hence type of very high mountain; 5. 3. 30

OMIT, neglect, disregard; 3. 1. 146

ONCE, once for all; 2. 3. 1

OPE (adj. and vb.), open; 1. 4. 43; 3. 1. 138; 5. 3. 183

OPINION, (i) self-conceit; 1. 1. 164; (ii) popular favour; 1. 1. 270

OPPOSER, antagonist, opponent; 1. 5. 22; 2. 2. 92; 4. 3. 35

OPPOSITE (sb.), adversary, opponent; 2. 2. 19

ORDINANCE, rank, order (only ex. cited in O.E.D.); 3. 2. 12

OSPREY, or fish-hawk, large bird of prey, feeding on fish (*Pandion haliaetus*); 4. 7. 34

OSTENTATION, display, demonstration (of enthusiasm); 1. 6. 86

OTHER (adv.), otherwise; 4. 6. 103

OUT (adj.), forgetful of one's part (in acting); 5. 3. 41

OUT (adv.), outright (cf. *Tp.* 1. 2. 41); 4. 5. 124

Out (prep.), out of; 5. 2. 39

Out! (interj.), away! 5. 3. 24

Outward, merely outward (show), not inward (reality); 1. 6. 77

Overta'en, caught up with; so, fig. equalled; 1. 9. 19

Owe, (i) mod. sense; 2. 2. 131; (ii) be bound to pay for (nearly mod. sense); 3. 1. 241; (iii) possess (orig. sense); 5. 2. 80; 5. 6. 138 ('you'=for you); (iv) (a) owe (to yourself), (b) possess (as your own); 3. 2. 130

Pace, way of walking, gait; here, a term of the manage or riding-school (used fig.); 2. 3. 50

Page (fig.), attendant; 1. 5. 23

Painful, arduous; 4. 5. 71

Palate (vb.), taste, smack; 3. 1. 104

Palt'ring, playing fast and loose, trickery; 3. 1. 58

Parcel, part, portion; 1. 2. 32; 4. 5. 222

Part, (i) share; 1. 9. 39; (ii) side, party; 1. 10. 7; 5. 3. 121; so, 'upon the p.', on behalf (of); 3. 1. 209

Particular (adj.), individual, special; 5. 2. 67

Particular (sb.), (i) 'by particulars'=one by one; 2. 3. 42; (ii) 'for your particular' =as far as you are concerned; 4. 7. 13; (iii) 'in a dear particular'=very specially; 5. 1. 3

Particularise, lit. specify; and so, emphasize by contrast; 1. 1. 21

Party, (i) side, faction; 1. 1. 233; 3. 1. 313; 5. 2. 29; (ii) litigant (O.E.D. 11); 2. 1. 72; (iii) supporter, sharer; 5. 6. 14

Pass, (i) pass by, disregard; 2. 2. 137; 2. 3. 198; (ii) proceed; 3. 1. 53

Passable, current. Quibbling on 'able to pass' (cf. *Cym.* 1. 2. 8); 5. 2. 13

Passing (adv.), exceedingly; 1. 1. 202

Patience, 'by your patience' = by your leave; 1. 3. 75; 1. 9. 55

Patient (adj.), long-suffering; 5. 6. 52

Pawn, stake, risk; 3. 1. 15; 5. 6. 21

Penelope, wife of Ulysses of Ithaca, who, pestered in his absence by parasite-suitors (l. 85, 'moths'), promised to choose one when she had finished the web she spun by day (and unravelled by night); 1. 3. 83

Peremptory, determined (cf. *K.J.* 2. 1. 454); 3. 1. 284

Perfect, accomplished; 2. 1. 80

Person, personal appearance, bearing, or behaviour; 1. 3. 10; 3. 2. 86

Pester, infest; 4. 6. 7

Petitionary, suppliant; 5. 2. 74

Physic, medical treatment of any kind; 3. 1. 154

Physical, good for the health; 1. 5. 18

Pick, pitch, toss; 1. 1. 199

Piece (sb.), coin; 3. 3. 32

PIECE (vb.), lit. add pieces to, patch (shoe, garment), hence, augment, eke out (cf. *Ant.* 1. 5. 45; *H. V*, 1. Pr. 23); 2. 3. 211

PIERCING, affecting painfully, distressing; 1. 1. 82

PIKE, (*a*) lance (the chief weapon of the infantry), (*b*) pitch-fork; 1. 1. 23

PIN (vb.), fig. bolt; 1. 4. 18

PINCH (vb.), gripe, afflict with colic pains; 2. 1. 73

PLAINLY, 'without concealment or disguise' (O.E.D.); 5. 3. 3

PLANT, fix, establish firmly; 2. 2. 27

PLEBEII, plebeians; 2. 3. 183

PLOT, piece of earth; here, fig. single person (cf. MOULD); 3. 2. 102

PLUTO, god ruling Hades; 1. 4. 36

POINT, (i) 'at point to', about to; 3. 1. 193; 5. 4. 61; (ii) detail, 'obeys his points' = obeys him in every point (On.); 4. 6. 126

POLICY, stratagem (in war), political cunning (in statecraft); 3. 2. 42; 3. 2. 48

POLL (sb.), (i) number of heads; 3. 1. 134; (ii) 'by the p.', by counting of heads; 3. 3. 10

POLL (vb.), lit. shear; fig. pillage, despoil; 4. 5. 208

POPULAR. [Contemptuous in Sh.] (i) 'Studious of the favour of the common people' (O.E.D. 5*a*); 2. 3. 100; (ii) plebeian, vulgar;

2. 1. 211; 3. 1. 106; 5. 2. 40

PORCH, portico, colonnade; 3. 1. 239

PORT, gate; 1. 7. 1; 5. 6. 6

PORTANCE, bearing, behaviour; 2. 3. 223

POSSESS, inform; 2. 1. 130

POST, messenger (lit. one riding post-haste), courier; 5. 6. 50

POSTURE, attitude, bearing; 2. 1. 218

POT, 'to the pot' (sc. cut in pieces like meat for cooking) = to death, destruction; cf. mod. 'gone to pot'; 1. 4. 48

POTCH (vb.), thrust (at) (see O.E.D. 'poach') 'Survives in Warwickshire' (On.); 1. 10. 15

POTHER, turmoil; 2. 1. 215

POUND UP, shut up as in a pound (i.e. an enclosure for stray cattle); 1. 4. 17

POUT, look sullen; 5. 1. 52

POWER, (i) armed force, army; 1. 2. 9, 32; 1. 3. 99; 1. 6. 8; 4. 5. 122; 4. 6. 67; (ii) exercise of power, control; 2. 1. 243

PRACTICE, plot, trickery; 4. 1. 33

PRANK (ref. vb.), lit. dress oneself up (or 'out'), here fig.; 3. 1. 23

PRECIPITATION, (i) precipice (O.E.D. does not cite again till 1890); 3. 2. 4; (ii) being hurled down from a height (the regular meaning); 3. 3. 102

PREPARATION, force equipped for battle; 1. 2. 15

PRESENT (sb.), 'the (this) present', the present time or occasion, 'the affair in hand' (On.); 1. 6. 60; 3. 3. 42

PRESENT (adj.), immediate; 3. 1. 211; 4. 3. 48

PRESENT (vb.), prescribe; 3. 2. 1

PRESENTLY, (i) mod. sense, rare in Sh.; 2. 3. 252; (ii) immediately (usu. sense in Sh.); 3. 3. 12; 4. 5. 220; 5. 6. 121

PRESS (vb.), impress, conscript; 1. 2. 9; 3. 1. 122

PRETENCE, intention, design; 1. 2. 20

PRETTY, pleasing; 1. 1. 89; 1. 3. 59

PRIVILEGE, right, claim; 1. 10. 23; 5. 3. 25

PROBABLE, 'worthy of belief', or 'capable of proof'; 4. 6. 66

PROCESS, regular course of law; 3. 1. 312

PROFESS, declare openly, affirm; 1. 3. 21

PROGENY, race, stock; here of progenitors, ancestors, not descendants; 1. 8. 12

PROOF (adj.), lit. proved and tested (of armour), hence fig. impervious (to fear); 1. 4. 25

PROPER, one's own; 1. 9. 57

PROPERLY, personally, for oneself; 5. 2. 81

PROSPERITY, success; 2. 1. 169

PROSPEROUS, successful; 2. 1. 102

PROSPEROUSLY, successfully; 5. 6. 75

PROUD, (a) (of animals) excitable, quarrelsome, lit. high-mettled, (b) (of warriors) valiant; 1. 1. 169

PROVAND, provender (here only in Sh.); 2. 1. 248

PROVE, try, put to the test; 1. 6. 62; 5. 1. 60

PSALTERY, 'ancient and medieval stringed instrument, more or less resembling the dulcimer, but played by plucking the strings with finger or plectrum' (*Sh. Eng.*); 5. 4. 49

PURCHASING, gaining, winning; 2. 1. 138

PURPOSE (sb.), proposal; 2. 2. 150; (vb.) resolve; 5. 3. 119

PURPOSED, intentional; 3. 1. 38

PUT, (i) 'put...to 't', force one to do one's utmost, press one hard; 1. 1. 228; 2. 2. 139; (ii) 'put forth', lit. bud, burgeon (cf. *Ven.* l. 416; *H. V*, 5. 2. 44; *H. VIII*, 3. 2. 352; O.E.D. 'put', 42 g), so here, show promise, 'show fair blossom' (J.); 1. 1. 250; (iii) 'put upon, on', incite; 2. 1. 253; 2. 3. 251; (iv) 'put to that' = drive to such an extremity; 3. 1. 232

QUAKE, make tremble; 1. 9. 6

QUARRY, lit. heap of slain deer at the end of a chase; so, heap of dead men (cf. *Mac.* 4. 3. 206; *Ham.* 5. 2. 362); 1. 1. 197

QUARTERED, cut up (of a carcass); 1. 1. 198

QUESTION (vb.), doubt; 2. 1. 227

QUIT OF, 'even with by retaliation' (O.E.D.); 4. 5. 86

RAISE, originate a rumour (O.E.D. 14*b*); 4. 6. 70; 'raising' = originating a rumour; 4. 6. 61

RAKE, very lean person (quibble on the gardening tool); 1. 1. 23

RANGE (vb.), stretch out in a line (of buildings); 3. 1. 205

RANK-SCENTED, malodorous; 3. 1. 66

RAPT, transported, enraptured; 4. 5. 119

RAPTURE, fit, convulsions; 2. 1. 204

RARE, fine, splendid; 4. 5. 165

RASCAL, (*a*) one of a rabble, fellow of low birth, (*b*) lean, young, or inferior deer or other animal (here a hound); 1. 1. 158; 1. 6. 45

READ LECTURES, give instruction (or lessons), (*v.* O.E.D. 11*b*); 2. 3. 234

REASON (sb.). Ellipt. = 'that's reasonable', 'there's good r. for it'; 4. 5. 236

REASON (vb.), (i) 'reason with', talk with, question; 4. 6. 52; (ii) support by argument (cf. *Lr.* 1. 2. 108); 5. 3. 176

RECEIPT, 'his receipt' = what was received by him; 1. 1. 111

RECOMMEND, consign, commit; 2. 2. 149

RECREANT, deserter, one who breaks allegiance; 5. 3. 114

RECTORSHIP, guidance, direction; 2. 3. 204

RED PESTILENCE. Perh. typhus (cf. *Tp.* 1. 2. 365); 4. 1. 13

REECHY, 'squalid, dirty' (O.E.D.); 2. 1. 206

REFUGE, resource; 5. 3. 11

REGARD, pay heed, pay attention; 3. 1. 67

REIN, rein in, restrain; 3. 3. 28

REJOURN, adjourn, put off; 2. 1. 70

RELISH, fig. 'to your r.' = to taste as you will like; 2. 1. 187

REMAIN (sb.), stay, 'make remain' = stay, remain (cf. *Mac.* 4. 3. 148); 1. 4. 63

REMEMBER, commemorate; 2. 2. 45

REMISSION, forgiveness; here prob. = authority to pardon; 5. 2. 81

REMOVE (sb.), raising of siege; 1. 2. 28

RENDER, give in return; 1. 9. 34

REPEAL (sb.), recall; 4. 1. 41

REPEAL (vb.), recall; 5. 5. 5

REPETITION, recital, mention; 1. 1. 45; 5. 3. 144

REPINE, complain, express dissatisfaction; 3. 1. 43

REPORT, reputation, good repute; 2. 1. 116; 2. 2. 27

REPOSE (reflex.), rest; 1. 9. 74

RE-QUICKEN, reanimate (O.E.D.); 2. 2. 115

REQUIRE, (i) make request of (a person); 2. 2. 154; (ii) ask for (something); 2. 3. 1

RESCUE, 'forcible. taking of a person...out of legal custody' (O.E.D. 2); 3. 1. 275

RESPECT (sb.), regard, consideration; 3. 1. 180

RESPECT (vb.), pay heed to, (or) show respect for; 5. 3. 5

RESTRAIN, withhold, keep back; 5. 3. 167

RETIRE (sb.), retreat; 1. 6. 3

RETIRE (refl. or intrans. vb.), withdraw; 1. 3. 28; 1. 6. 50; 3. 1. 11

RETREAT (sb.), trumpet call to recall a pursuing force (O.E.D.; cf. *2 H. IV*, 4. 3. 70); 1. 9. S.D. init.

REVEREND, worthy of reverence; 2. 1. 59; 2. 2. 40

RHEUM, lit. water secreted by glands; here, contemptuous =tears; 5. 6. 46

RIDGE, 'the horizontal edge or line in which the two sloping sides of a roof meet at the top' (O.E.D.); 2. 1. 208

RIGHT, true; 2. 1. 233

ROAD, inroad, raid, incursion; 3. 1. 5

ROAR, utter loud cries of distress (cf. Schmidt); 4. 6. 125

ROTE (vb.), learn by heart; 3. 2. 55

ROTTEN, (i) mod. sense freq.; (ii) unwholesome (of fog, damp, etc.); 2. 3. 31; 3. 3. 121

RUB (sb.), check, obstacle (lit. obstruction or inequality on a bowling-green); 3. 1. 60

RUDELY, with violence; 4. 5. 145

RUTH, compassion; 1. 1. 196

SACKBUT, 'a bass trumpet, with a slide like that of a trombone for altering the pitch' (*Sh. Eng.*), now obsolete; 5. 4. 49

SAFEGUARD, guarantee of safe conduct; 3. 1. 9

SAFER, sounder; 2. 3. 217

SALT, i.e. tears; 5. 6. 93

SAUCE (vb.), spice, season; 1. 9. 53

SCAB, (a) mange, itch or other skin disease, (b) term of abuse ('scurvy' fellow); 1. 1. 165

SCALE (vb.), weigh, compare (cf. *Meas.* 3. 1. 253); 2. 3. 248

SCANDAL (vb.), slander, defame, or revile; 3. 1. 44

SCAPE (aphet. var.; freq. Sh.); escape; 1. 8. 13

SCONCE, (jocular) head; orig.= small fortification; 3. 2. 99

SCORN, (i) mock; 2. 3. 221; (ii) contemptuously refuse; 3. 1. 267

SCOTCH, gash (O.E.D. 4*b*, citing); 4. 5. 192

'SDEATH! Oath='God's (i.e. Christ's) death'; 1. 1. 216

SEAL, authenticate, confirm; 2. 3. 107

SEA-MARK. Conspicuous object for the direction of mariners set up by Trinity House, acc. to the Act of 1566 (cf. *Oth.* 5. 2. 271); 5. 3. 74

SEASONED, (a) matured, (b) made palatable; 3. 3. 64

SECOND (sb.), supporter; 1. 4. 43; 1. 8. 15

SECOND (vb.), support; 4. 6. 63

SEEKING, object sought for; 1. 1. 187

SELD-SHOWN, seldom seen; 2. 1. 210

SENNET (prob.<signet=sign), notes on a trumpet or cornet for the entrance of a procession. App. a theatrical term only; 2. 1. 159 S.D.

SENSELESS, incapable of feeling; 1. 4. 54

SENSIBLE, sensitive; 1. 3. 86

SENSIBLY, i.e. with his sensitive body; 1. 4. 54

SENTENCE (vb.) pronounce as judgment, 'decree judicially'; 3. 3. 22

SERVANT (vb.), 'put in subjection to' (O.E.D.); 5. 2. 80

SET, (i) 'set down'; (a) encamp; 1. 2. 28; 1. 3. 99; 5. 3. 2; (b) trans. put down (in a time-table of duties), appoint; 1. 7. 2; (ii) 'set up' (of a top), start spinning, lit. get something going; 4. 5. 156

SEVERAL, separate, different; 1. 1. 184; 4. 5. 125; 4. 6. 39

SHAME (vb.), be ashamed; 2. 2. 65

SHENT (ppl. of 'shend'), reproached, rebuked; 5. 2. 95

SHOP, workshop, factory; 1. 1. 132

SHOUT FORTH, acclaim; 1. 9. 50

SHOW (sb.), indication; 3. 3. 36

SHOW (vb.), appear, seem; 4. 6. 115; 5. 3. 13, 70

SHUNLESS, unshunnable; 2. 2. 110

SIDE (vb.), take sides with; 1. 1. 192

SINEWS, strength, lit. nerves; 5. 6. 45

SINGLE, (i) (a) solitary, (b) feeble (cf. *Mac.* 1. 3. 140; 1. 6. 16); 2. 1. 36; (ii) individual, separate; 2. 3. 43

SINGLY, by any other single person; 2. 2. 85

SINGULARITY, individual, distinctive character (e.g. his insolence); 'more than his s.' ='apart from his s.' (On.); 1. 1. 277

SINK, cesspool, sewer (cf. *Troil.* 5. 1. 74); 1. 1. 121

SIRRAH. Address to an inferior or to a child; 5. 2. 50; 5. 3. 75

SITHENCE, since; 3. 1. 47

SIT DOWN, begin a siege; 4. 7. 28

SLIGHT, of little worth, insignificant; 5. 2. 100

SLIGHTNESS, triviality; 3. 1. 148

SLIP, i.e. slip the leash; 1. 6. 39

SLIPPERY, uncertain, unstable; 4. 4. 12

SMOKING, reeking (with blood); 1. 4. 11

SOFT, gentle; 3. 2. 82

SOFT! (excl.), stop! 1. 1. 49

SOFT-CONSCIENCED, sloppy-minded; 1. 1. 36

SOMETHING (adv.), somewhat; 2. 1. 48; 2. 3. 82; 3. 2. 25

SOOTHE, flatter; 2. 2. 71; 3. 1. 69

SOOTHING, flattery; 1. 9. 44

SORT, (i) manner; 1. 3. 2; 4. 5. 232; (ii) class of people; 4. 6. 70

SOURLY, disagreeably; 5. 3. 13

SOUTH, i.e. S. wind, thought of as bringing fogs and pestilence; 1. 4. 30

Sovereign, excellent, paramount; 2. 1. 114

Sowl, lug by the ears; 4. 5. 206

Speak, tell of, report; 2. 2. 101

Spectatorship (in), =for spectators to enjoy; 5. 2. 64

Spend, give vent to, utter (On.); 2. 1. 52

Spice, touch or trace, tincture; 4. 7. 46

Spire, summit; 1. 9. 24

Spoil, (i) ravage; 2. 1. 214; (ii) slaughter, massacre (esp. of deer; cf. *J. C.* 3. 1. 207); 2. 2. 118; (iii) (plur.) plunder, booty; 2. 2. 122

Spot, an embroidered pattern of small flowers, fruits, etc. (cf. Linthicum, p. 148); 1. 3. 53

Sprightly, spirited, lively, brisk; 4. 5. 228

Stain (sb.), overshadowing, eclipse, disgrace; 1. 10. 18

Stale (vb.), make stale; 1. 1. 91

Stamp (sb.), (i) distinguishing mark, characteristic; 1. 6. 23; (ii) tool for stamping a mark, figure, design or the like, upon a softer material (O.E.D. 5); 2. 2. 105

Stamp (vb.), lit. coin, hence, pass into currency; 5. 2. 22

Stand, (i) stand fast (intr.); 5. 3. 35; withstand (trans.); 5. 3. 74; (ii) stop; 5. 6. 127; (iii) 'stand out', refuse to take part; 1. 1. 240; (iv) 'stand for', (*a*) defend, support; 2. 2. 39; (*b*) be a candidate for; 2. 3. 186; (v) 'stand upon' or 'on', insist on; 2. 2. 148; 4. 6. 87; (vi) 'stand up', make a stand; 2. 3. 14; (vii) 'stand with',

agree, be consistent with; 2. 3. 84; (viii) 'stand to', uphold, support; 3. 1. 207; 5. 3. 199; (ix) 'stand to 't', fight stoutly; 4. 6. 10

State, (i) government; 1. 1. 68, 76; (ii) chair of state or throne; 5. 4. 22

Stay, (i) 'stay behind', fail to take part in; 1. 1. 242; (ii) 'stay by', stand up to; 2. 1. 128; (iii) 'stay upon', wait for; 5. 4. 7–8

Stem, prow of a ship or boat; 2. 2. 105

Stick (vb.), (i) be fixed as an ornament; 1. 1. 270; (ii) hesitate; 2. 3. 15; (iii) stand out and stand fast; 5. 3. 73

Still (adj.), silent, quiet; 3. 2. 11; 4. 6. 37

Still (adv.), always, constantly; 1. 1. 99, etc.

Stir, become excited; here prob., make a commotion, rise in revolt; 3. 1. 53

Stoutness, overbearing arrogance or obstinacy; 3. 2. 127; 5. 6. 27

Strains, 'the fine strains'= the refinements; 5. 3. 149

Straight, immediately; 2. 2. 114; 2. 3. 146; 3. 1. 35; 3. 3. 25; 4. 5. 90

Stretch, stretch out, strain to the utmost; 2. 2. 49; 5. 6. 45

Strike, (i) fight, lit. wield a weapon (cf. *Ant.* 3. 8. 3; *H. V.* 2. 4. 54); 1. 6. 4; (ii) blast, destroy. 'Astrol. term: by the influence of planets in opposition'; 2. 2. 111

Strucken, struck; 4. 5. 153

SUBDUE, subject to punishment (On.); 1. 1. 174

SUBJECT, 'creature, being; that which is in existence' (Schmidt); 2. 1. 83

SUBTLE, (i) crafty; 1. 10. 17; (ii) 'tricky', 'deceptively smooth' (G.G.); 5. 2. 20

SUCCESS, (i) fortune, result of action (good or bad); 1. 1. 259; 1. 6. 7; 5. 1. 62; (ii) mod. sense; 2. 2. 42

SUDDEN, (i) 'on the sudden', very quickly (O.E.D. 'very common c. 1560–1700'); 2. 1. 218; (ii) hasty, done on the spur of the moment; 2. 3. 250

SUFFER, allow; 3. 1. 40

SUFFERANCE, suffering, distress; 1. 1. 21–2

SUFFRAGE, vote; 2. 2. 136

SUGGEST, insinuate to; 2. 1. 242; insinuate; 2. 1. 250

SUMMON, call to surrender; 1. 4. 7

SUPPLE, compliant; 2. 2. 25

SURCEASE, cease; 3. 2. 121

SURE, SURE ON'T (adv.), assuredly; 2. 3. 28; 3. 1. 271; 5. 1. 35

SURE (adj.), to be relied upon; 1. 1. 171

SURETY (vb.), stand surety for, go bail for; 3. 1. 177

SWAY (vb.), hold sway, rule; 2. 1. 201

SWORN BROTHER, most intimate friend. Lit. the 'frater juratus' of medieval chivalry, under oath to share another's fortunes (cf. Ado, 1. 1. 68; R. II, 5. 1. 20); 2. 3. 95

SYNOD, assembly; 5. 2. 67

TABLE, meal, banquet; 2. 1. 80

TABOR, 'a merry little side-drum' (G.G.); 1. 6. 25; 5. 4. 50

TACKLE, ship-rigging; 4. 5. 64

TA'EN FORTH, picked out, selected; 1. 9. 34

TAG, lit. odds and ends; here= rabble; 3. 1. 247

TAINT, sully, discredit; 4. 7. 38

TAKE, (i) lit. take an impression; here = take effect (cf. *Tp.* 1. 2. 353); 2. 2. 106; (ii) destroy; 3. 1. 111; 4. 4. 20; (iii*a*) 'take up', take on (cf. *2 H. IV*, 1.3.73); 3.1.243; (iii*b*) 'take up', fill up, obstruct (cf. *H. VIII*, 1. 1. 56); 3. 2. 116; (iv) 'take in', capture; 1. 2. 24; 3. 2. 59; (v) find, catch; 5. 1. 50

TARGET, shield, 'targe'; 4. 5. 123

TARPEIAN ROCK, rock on the Capitoline hill, from which traitors were hurled headlong; 3. 1. 212, 265; 3. 2. 3; 'Tarpeian death'=death thus brought about; 3. 3. 88

TARQUIN, Tarquinius Superbus, the younger of the two kings of this surname, expelled from Rome (Livy, Bk. I); he was the violator of Lucretia, acc. to the story in Livy, the subject of Sh.'s *Lucrece*; and was defeated at Lake Regillus, when endeavouring to recover his throne, c. 496 B.C.; 2. 1. 148; 2. 2. 92

TASK (vb.), set a task; 1. 3. 37

TASTE, (i) preference (with quibble on taste='flavour'); 'greatest taste'=the preference of the majority; 3. 1. 103; (ii) sample; 3. 1. 316

TAUNTINGLY, sneeringly, mockingly (cf. O.E.D. 'taunt', vb. 2); 1. 1. 109

TELL, 'canst thou tell?'=do you know?; 5. 2. 34

TEMPERANCE, self-control, restraint; 3. 3. 28

TENDER-BODIED, i.e. very young; 1. 3. 6

TENT (vb.¹), lit. apply a roll of lint to probe and cleanse a wound, hence, cure, heal; 1. 9. 31; 3. 1. 235

TENT (vb.²), lodge; 3. 2. 116

TETTER (vb.), affect with tetter (=a gen. term for skin eruption, cf. *Ham.* 1. 5. 71); 3. 1. 79

THEME, subject, discussion; 1. 1. 219; 2. 2. 55

THINK UPON, think kindly of (cf. *Ant.* 1. 5. 27), 'remember with compassion' (Beeching, citing Jonah i. 6); 2. 3. 55, 187

THOROUGH, through; 5. 3. 115

THREAD, pass through one after another; 3. 1. 124

THROAT, voice (cf. *Oth.* 3. 3. 357); 3. 2. 112

THRONE (vb.), be enthroned; 5. 4. 24

THROW, distance to which anything should be thrown; here a term in bowling; 5. 2. 21

TICKLE, gratify (cf. *K. J.* 2. 1. 573); 1. 1. 259

TIGER-FOOTED, 'fierce and swift' (On.); 3. 1. 310

TIME, (i) the present; 2. 1. 266; (ii) state of affairs; 2. 3. 118; 4. 1. 40; 4. 6. 27; (iii) one's contemporaries; 4. 7. 50; (iv) future ages (cf. *Son.* 18. 12); 5. 3. 127

TIME-PLEASER, time-server; 3. 1. 45

TINDER-LIKE, flaring up quickly; 2. 1. 49

To, (i) compared with, 'even to the altitude of his virtue', even when you take into account his exalted valour; 1. 1. 39; 2. 1. 115; (ii) in addition to; 2. 1. 162; (iii) '(pawn) to'=(stake) upon; 3. 1. 16

TOGE, toga; 2. 3. 114

TOP (vb.), surpass; 2. 1. 20

TOUCH (sb.), lit. the test for gold by a touchstone; hence, fig., stamp, quality ('of noble t.'; *v.* NOBLE); 4. 1. 49

TOUCH (vb.), (i) affect; 2. 1. 55; (ii) threaten (a fencing term); 3. 1. 123; 2. 1. 252; (iii) test; 2. 3. 190

TOUCHING, concerning; 1. 1. 150

TOWARDS, with, in dealing with; 5. 1. 41

TRADE, handicraft; so, workers; 3. 2. 134; 4. 1. 13

TRADUCEMENT, calumny; 1. 9. 22

TRANSLATE, transform; 2. 3. 188

TRANSPORT, (i) carry away by violent passion; 1. 1. 74; (ii) 'temperately transport'=control himself while he carries; 2. 1. 221

TREATY, proposal requiring ratification, negotiation; 2. 2. 53; 5. 6. 68

TRIBE, (i) Lat. *tribus.* The citizens were divided into political divisions called tribes; three for the patricians and thirty for the plebs; 3. 3. 11; (ii) race, perh. contemptuous, 'pack'; 4. 2. 24; 5. 6. 129

TRIER, tester; 4. 1. 4

TRIM, =either (if sb.) trappings (cf. *Ant.* 4. 4. 22, where it=armour), or (if adj.) fine (*v.* BELONGING); 1. 9. 62

TRITON, a sea-god, Neptune's trumpeter; 3. 1. 89

TROOP, group of men, crowd (not of soldiers); 1. 1. 203

TROPHY, symbolic monument (gen. associated in Sh. with funerals; cf. *Ham.* 4. 5. 213); 1. 3. 41

TROTH, truth; 4. 5. 192; 'in troth', truly; 1. 3. 107; 2. 1. 135

TRUE (sb.), truth (O.E.D. sb.2); 5. 2. 32

TRY, test; 2. 3. 191; 3. 1. 224

TUMBLE (intr.), 'roll about on the ground' (O.E.D. 2); 5. 2. 21

TUNE, (*a*) humour, (*b*) tone; 2. 3. 85

TURN, bring (to a certain condition); 3. 1. 282; (ii) make to change, alter; 4. 6. 60

TWIN (vb.), be like twins (cf. *Per.* 5 Pr. 8); 4. 4. 15

TWIST, plaited thread (O.E.D.); 5. 6. 96

TYRANNY, cruelty, ruthlessness; 5. 3. 43

UNACTIVE, inactive; 1. 1. 98

UNAPT, not readily disposed; 5. 1. 52

UNBARBED, unarmed; 3. 2. 99

UNBUCKLE, tear off (in fight); 4. 5. 128

UNCLOG, disencumber, relieve of a load; 4. 2. 47

UNDERCREST, wear as a family crest; 1. 9. 72

UNDO, ruin; 1. 1. 62, 63

UNGRAVELY, in an undignified manner, unbecoming one's dignity; 2. 3. 224

UNHEART, dishearten; 5. 1. 49

UNKNIT, fig. untie; 4. 2. 31

UNLIKE, unlikely; 3. 1. 48

UNPROPERLY, unfittingly, contrary to propriety; 5. 3. 54

UNSCANNED, unconsidered, inconsiderate; 3. 1. 311

UNVULNERABLE, invulnerable; 5. 3. 73

UP, in a position of influence or power; 3. 1. 109

UPHOLD, assist, support; 1. 9. 40

UPON, (i) on the ground of; 2. 1. 225; (ii) for the purpose of, about; 2. 3. 143

USE, treat; 2. 2. 153; 2. 3. 161; 5. 2. 51

USED, wont, customary to be done; 3. 1. 114

USHER, 'a male attendant on a lady' (O.E.D. 2*b*); 1. 3. 48 S.D.

VAIL, lower (in reverence); 3. 1. 98

VALUE (sb.), estimate; 2. 2. 57

VANTAGE, (i) advantage, profit; 1. 1. 159; 2. 3. 259; 3. 2. 31; (ii) opportunity, advantageous moment; 5. 6. 54

VARIABLE, diverse, varying; 2. 1. 209

*VARNISH, lit. put a fresh gloss upon, fig. (of persons) represent in the most favourable light, lay it on thick with (cf. *Ham.* 4. 7. 131); 5. 2. 17

VASSAL, slave; 3. 2. 9

VAWARD, vanguard; 1. 6. 53

VENGEANCE (adv.), mod. slang, 'mortally', 'with a vengeance'; 2. 2. 5

VENT (sb.). Meaning doubtful; 'full of vent' either = full of sport or excitement (<vent = the scent of an animal in the chase) or = bursting with life, providing plenty of outlet for activity of all kinds (<vent = discharge or outlet, e.g. from a cask, in contrast to 'mulled'); 4. 5. 229

VENT (vb.), (i) void, get rid of; 1. 1. 224; (ii) utter; 3. 1. 257

VEXATION, mortification, torment (of mind); 3. 3. 140

VIAND, food; 1. 1. 99

VIPEROUS, venomous, poisonous (fig.); 3. 1. 285

VIRGIN, 'virgin it', remain chaste; 5. 3. 48

VIRGINAL, maidenly; 5. 2. 43

VIRTUE, (i) valour; 1. 1. 39; (ii) power, efficacy; 5. 2. 12

VOICE (sb.), (i) vote; 2. 2. 138; 2. 3. 1, 35, 44, etc.; (ii) voter; 2. 3. 124, 210; 3. 3. 9; 4. 6. 147

VOICE (vb.), nominate, elect; 2. 3. 233

VOUCH (sb.), attestation, formal confirmation; 2. 3. 116

VOUCH (vb.), affirm, guarantee

(a statement); 1. 9. 24; 5. 6. 5

VULGAR, (i) of the common people, plebeian; 1. 1. 214; 4. 7. 21; (ii) among the plebeians; 2. 1. 212

WAGE, hire (as a mercenary); 5. 6. 40

WANTON, (*a*) unrestrained, (*b*) lascivious (fig.); 2. 1. 214

WATCH, lie awake, keep watch (as a soldier); 2. 3. 126

WAVE, waver (O.E.D. 3); 2. 2. 16

WAY, scope, freedom of action (cf. GIVE); 4. 4. 25; 5. 6. 32

WEALSMAN, 'one devoted to the public weal; commonwealth's man' (O.E.D.); 2. 1. 53

WEED, sing. and pl., clothes, apparel; 2. 3. 152, 220

WEIGH, 'be of (much or little) value or account' (O.E.D.); 'as they weigh' = according to their worth; 2. 2. 72

WELL-FOUND, 'commendable, well-approved' (O.E.D., citing also *All's*, 2. 1. 102); poss. = welcome (cf. O.E.D. 1); 2. 2. 42

WHAT, why; 3. 1. 315

WHERE, whereas; 1. 10. 13

WHIP, fig. scourge; 1. 8. 12

WHOLESOME, (i) not mouldy; 1. 1. 18; (ii) salutary; 1. 1. 81; (iii) profitable; 2. 1. 68; (iv) seasonable (+a quibble on (ii)); 2. 3. 59

WHOOP OUT, drive out with derisive cries; 4. 5. 81

WIN UPON, get the better of (or) encroach upon (O.E.D. 10); 1. 1. 219

WIND (vb.), refl., insinuate oneself (into); 3. 3. 64

WITH, 'be with them'=get round them with, play this little trick on them (cf. *Wint.* 4. 3. 116); 3. 2. 74

WOOLVISH=? like a wolf. Doubtful relevance; poss.= simply 'rough, shaggy' (E.K.C.); or simply 'woollen' (q.v.) 2. 3. 114

WOOLLEN, clad in woollen clothing, a 'mark of lowly status' (O.E.D.); 3. 2. 9

WORD, 'at a word'=in short; 1. 3. 110

WORN, enfeebled, exhausted; 3. 1. 6

WORSHIP, dignity, authority, sovereignty; 3. 1. 142

WORSHIPFUL, most honourable; 1. 1. 249

WORTH, 'full quota, due proportion' (Mal.); 3. 3. 26

WORTHY, deserving praise, heroic; 2. 2. 121; 'make worthy'=make a hero of; 1. 1. 174

WREAK (sb.), revenge (again *Tit.* 4. 3. 33); 4. 5. 88

WRENCH, twist forcibly; 1. 8. 11

YIELD, grant; 2. 2. 52

YOKE (with), be coupled (with), associated (with); 3. 1. 57

YOU MAY, =you may have your little joke; 2. 3. 34

YOUNGLY, in youth; 'how youngly'=in what extreme youth; 2. 3. 235